SOUTHERN 100
1955 - 2005
GOLDEN JUBILEE

Fifty Years of the Friendly Races

the story of the Southern 100 motorcycle road races

by Phil Edge

Published in 2006 by Duke Marketing Ltd.

Champion House, PO Box 46, Douglas, Isle of Man, IM99 1DD

www.dukevideo.com

ISBN: 0-9529325-2-0

All text and scans by Phil Edge
Book design by Tabitha Elworthy
Cover design by Ruth Sutherland
Cover photographs by David Collister, G V Kneale and Dave Purves
Production by Pip Kirby

Printed and bound by J H Haynes & Co Ltd, Sparkford, Nr Yeovil, Somerset, BA22 7JJ.

Great care has been taken throughout this book to ensure that all details are accurate. However the publishers and author cannot accept responsibility for any errors that may have occurred.

Acknowledgements

I would like to offer my sincerest thanks to the following people :

Eddy Clague, Geoff Cannell, John Watterson, John Savage, Roy Adams, Tony Breese, Alan Brunning, Derek Clague, Ron Clarke, David Collister, Stephen Davison, Dave Purves, Richard Radcliffe, Eddy Richardson, Bill Snelling, Dr. David Stevens MBE, Peter Duke, Ruth Sutherland, Tabitha Elworthy, Jill Barker, Emily Goren and members of the Committee of the Southern 100 Club.

Without them, this book would not have been possible.

Photography Acknowledgements

Roy Adams
Tony Breese   Racing Photos - Isle of Man
Alan Brunning
Derek Clague
Ron Clarke   Manx Racing Photography
David Collister
Stephen Davison   Pacemaker Press International
Dave Purves
Richard Radcliffe   Road Racing Images
Eddy Richardson
Bill Snelling   FoTToFinders
David Stevens MBE
John Watterson
Geoff Cannell
Island Photographics

Dedication

Fifty Years of the Friendly Races' is dedicated to all riders, past and present that have pitted their skills over the 4.25-mile Billown Course providing countless enthusiasts with so many memorable sights and sounds over the past fifty years.

Foreword

Welcome to Fifty Years of the Friendly Races – the story of the Southern 100 motorcycle road races.

I would like to dedicate this history to all those people who have made the Southern 100 what it is today.

Particular mention must go to the committee and members of the Southern Motorcycle Club, who decided after the success of local riders, George Costain, Derek Ennett and Sid Mizen in the 1954 Manx Grand Prix, to stage a race to enable more 'locals' to qualify for those races on the Mountain Course.

Through the years, the best of British riders have ridden at Billown and it is still the same today.

May it continue to attract the best road racers and long may the Southern 100 bring entertainment to all true road race enthusiasts.

I hope you enjoy this short history.

Phil Taubman
Chairman

Contents

1955 Terry Shepherd	1956 Terry Shepherd	1957 Alastair King	1958 Terry Shepherd	1959 Bill Smith	1960 Ron Langston
1961 Phil Read	1962 Phil Read	1963 Chris Conn	1964 Dave Williams	1965 Dave Williams	1966 Selwyn Griffiths
1967 Bill Smith	1968 Steve Jolly	1969 Brian Steenson	1970 Billy Guthrie	1971 Bill Smith	1972 Charlie Williams
1973 Tom Herron	1974 Steve Tonkin	1975 Ray McCullough	1976 Joey Dunlop	1977 Joey Dunlop	1978 Joey Dunlop
1979 George Fogarty	1980 Dave Dean	1981 David Ashton	1982 Con Law	1983 Brian Reid	1984 Dave Pither
1985 Kenny Harrison	1986 Kenny Harrison	1987 Ian Bell	1989 Dave Leach	1990 Dave Leach	1991 Joey Dunlop
1992 Phillip McCallen	1993 Joey Dunlop	1994 Jason Griffiths	1995 Bob Jackson	1996 Jason Griffiths	1997 Jason Griffiths
1998 Bob Jackson	1999 Joey Dunlop	2000 Blair Degerholm	2002 Ian Lougher	2003 Ryan Farquhar	2004 Ian Lougher

2005 Solo Champion - Ian Lougher

Introduction

Fifty Years of the Friendly Races

Welcome to "Fifty Years of the Friendly Races", the real story of the Southern 100 Road Races, nicknamed "The Friendly Races" by those who know and love this beloved road racing festival.

First run on Thursday 14th July 1955, the Southern 100 Road Races are now an established meeting in the annual calendar of major road races in the British Isles and beyond.

Over the intervening years the 4.25-mile Billown Course has become as familiar as the back of a hand to the riders who have graced the ribbon of road that makes up the Southern 100 Course. Future British and indeed World Champions have raced around the undulating and technical course as they have headed for the chequered flag.

This volume has been created using a wide and illuminating collection of contemporary racing reports, original photographs, interviews and anecdotes from fans, organisers and racers.

While "Fifty Years of the Friendly Races" is a record of the Southern 100 and more latterly the Pre-TT Classic Road Races and the Steam Packet National Road Races, it is also a tribute to, and a record of, the riders - famous, infamous and not so well known - who have entertained and thrilled us over the years providing all with a long-running love affair with the sport of motorcycle road racing.

This book tells a story close to my heart and the hearts of everyone involved, and for this reason I sincerely hope I have been successful in bringing their achievements and disappointments back to life.

If readers derive the same degree of enjoyment from turning the pages, as I did from compiling the book, my aim and that of the Southern 100 Motorcycle Racing Club will have been entirely fulfilled.

Southern 100 Course map

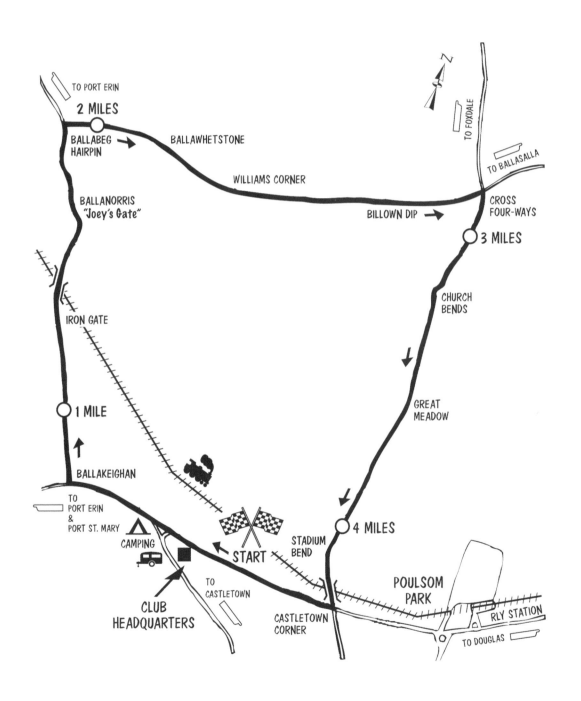

TO PORT ERIN

2 MILES

BALLABEG HAIRPIN

BALLAWHETSTONE

WILLIAMS CORNER

BALLANORRIS "Joey's Gate"

BILLOWN DIP

CROSS FOUR-WAYS

TO FOXDALE

TO BALLASALLA

3 MILES

IRON GATE

CHURCH BENDS

1 MILE

BALLAKEIGHAN

GREAT MEADOW

TO PORT ERIN & PORT ST. MARY

CAMPING

4 MILES

STADIUM BEND

START

CLUB HEADQUARTERS

TO CASTLETOWN

CASTLETOWN CORNER

POULSOM PARK

RLY STATION

TO DOUGLAS

How the Southern started

Prior to the 1954 Manx Grand Prix success of Derek Ennett, George Costain and Sid Mizen, the Southern Motorcycle Club held their race meetings at Andreas Airfield.

As a result of a double win at the Manx, the Southern Club decided there should be a race in the south of the Island and to hold a meeting on what was to become known as the Billown circuit.

In the early 1950s, the Isle of Man Government decided to build a by-pass to avoid the town centre of Castletown, and whilst traffic was minimal compared to today's motorised Island, the by-pass provided an integral part of the new course.

The first meetings to set up the organisation were held in the Station Hotel, now the Viking, in Castletown, which is where the Ennett family lived. This band of gentlemen with foresight also used to meet on a Sunday morning in the Control Tower at Ronaldsway Airport, with Theo Watterson. In between landing planes, the time was taken up planning the Southern 100!

Amongst the first committee were George Costain and Joe Mylchreest, who officially measured the circuit using the official 'chain' measure (22 yards) and walked around the course measuring down the centre line of the road. The total official distance was, and still is, 4.25-miles.

(1) Southern 100 - The Reason it Started - 1954

Tynwald and the Southern 100

The organisers of the proposed new event approached Tynwald, the Island's Government, for assistance in running this first venture in the south of the Island. The reply, after consideration by the Tynwald Race Committee, was surprising to say the least. The report is shown below.

The Tynwald Race Committee Report on the 1954 major sporting events was presented to the April sitting of Tynwald on 19th April 1955.

The TT accounts for 1954 were approved and the sum of £10,000 was recommended to be given to the ACU to run the 1955 TT Races.

Similarly the Manx Grand Prix accounts were submitted and approved. Tynwald was pleased that the organisers had not requested an increase in their Grant for 1955 and approved the same amount as the previous year - £450.

The Southern Motor Cycling Club had also approached the Committee for financial support for a motorcycle race to be held in the south of the Island on 14th July 1955. The Committee however, was not prepared to recommend Government financial assistance to the race for the following reasons:

(a) We consider the TT Races and the Manx Grand Prix to be established events of universal appeal to motorcycle enthusiasts in Great Britain. We do not think that motorcycle racing should be further extended during the visiting season.

(b) We do not think that, at the date suggested, the season requires "build-up" by staging an event of this character.

(c) We regard the event as a local enterprise – possibly justifying support as such from local commissioners in order to attract visitors into

their area from other parts of the Island – but not as an insular event warranting Government support.

Despite this setback, the club persevered with organising the first Southern 100 and local businessman T H Colebourn stepped in and put up £100 to secure the races on 14th July 1955.

Happily, since that initial rebuff, the Isle of Man Government, via the Department of Tourism, have given their full approval of the Southern 100, along with tremendous support over the years and continue to do so.

STEAM PACKET COMPANY

Steam Packet

Southern 100 and the first 50 years

The Isle of Man Steam Packet and the Southern 100 Racing Club have been inseparable for all of the 50 years that the 'friendly' races have been run on the Billown Circuit.

The shipment of motorcycles, cars, motor homes and vans together with the families that support this most popular event have been and continue to be a responsibility of The Steam Packet who remain avid supporters of the Southern 100 Motor Cycle Club and their contribution to motorcycle sport in the Island. Competitors arrive on the Island on Company vessels either by conventional ferry from Heysham, or by fastcraft crossings from Liverpool, Belfast or Dublin often with special timings of sailings being provided to accommodate visitors and riders to the event.

There is no doubt that the popularity of the 'Southern' is not waning but it continues to attract riders and supporters from around the British Isles and further afield joining with the many talented and distinguished local competitors. To aid and continue that success The Steam Packet applies special travel rates for visiting competitors. They enjoy a 'hands-on' relationship with the Southern 100 Committee in organising travel for many riders who are sometimes on tight schedules either travelling from or to a race meeting happening around the Southern 100 event. So much so that there have been many occasions where a combined effort has contrived time for a trophy presentation and the sailing of a vessel! Such support given to the Southern 100 by the riders is testament to the good running and friendliness of the event.

The Steam Packet has provided longtime sponsorship to the meetings at Billown acknowledging the huge costs attached to staging such a successful event as this for amateur riders and also the organisation and time given by a highly motivated and responsible committee of enthusiasts who rely upon sponsorship to promote and continue its undoubted success.

It was in 1991 that The Steam Packet spawned an initiative to include the Billown Circuit and the Southern 100 committee in an extra attraction to the motorcycling fraternity gathered in the Isle of Man. It was a plan to further the thrills and demands of motorcycling enthusiasts and riders who were on the Island for the world famous TT races held in June each year. An 'extension' to the TT is now held on the Saturday following the races on the Billown Circuit catering for the many thousands of fans remaining on the Island. 'The Steam Packet Races' have now become a major attraction for TT visitors and residents of the Island and a most popular event for motorcycle racers both local and visiting to compete on a superb course in a most friendly and sporting atmosphere.

In this very special year of celebration, The Steam Packet are adding extra support by donating special fares to past winners of Southern 100 races to travel to the Island to share in the festivities and the undoubted special atmosphere that will be in abundance and will look forward to welcoming them on their vessels as they make their way from all over the UK.

Hamish Ross, the Managing Director of The Steam Packet Company, says, ' The Southern 100 has become a major event in the road racing calendar and should be proud of its reputation in the motorcycling arena. The Isle of Man boasts that it is the road racing capital of the world and surely it remains so. We at The Steam Packet continue to wholeheartedly support road racing on our Island. We admire the professionalism shown in the planning, promotion and operation of the Southern 100 and acknowledge that such success is due to hard work and sheer devotion to road racing. We congratulate the hard working committee and supporters of the Southern 100 in their and our own special year where we celebrate our 175th anniversary and pledge our continuing support to them and the riders who make the event the success that it surely is'.

(2) 1955 - Start of the first ever race at Billown - 350cc 14th July 1955

Chapter One

Fifty Years of the Friendly Races 1955 - 1964

1955: A race is born

Summer frocks and shirtsleeves were the order of the day as thousands of spectators crowded the vantage points around the course to witness what was described as an ambitious three-race programme for a first ever meeting!

Manxman Derek Ennett took the honours of winning the first ever race, the 350cc over 12 laps of the 4.25-mile course, after a race-long tussle with Manchester's Dave Chadwick. Despite grabbing a 20-yard lead from the starting grid, Manxman Ennett was continually challenged by Chadwick throughout the 12-lap race and only just managed to pip Chadwick by four lengths at the flag. (2)

The six-lap 250cc race was a benefit for Dave Chadwick on Reg Dearden's Special, leading from start to finish. A five second advantage at the end of lap one increased to 39 by the end of the six laps, over runner-up John Patrick, (Velocette). The remarkable 56-year-old Frank Cope finished third on his Norton, only 11 seconds behind Patrick, despite overshooting Alexandra Bridge on the opening lap.

Castletown man Ennett made a great but vain attempt to achieve the "double" in the Senior race over 24 laps of the rectangular circuit, a distance of 100 miles, from where the meeting takes its name. His bid failed on the final lap when a piston on the twin cylinder Matchless collapsed. At the time he was 100 yards behind the ultimate winner, Norton mounted Terry Shepherd who had taken the lead on lap eight. (3)

Second was Alastair King whilst Derek 'toured' in to take third place. Liverpudlian Shepherd's race time was 1 hour 18 minutes 11.8 seconds; an average speed of 78.26 miles per hour, whilst on his ninth lap he set the fastest lap of the race taking 3 minutes 9 seconds to lap the course, which equates to 80.95 mph.

A further ding-dong contest between locals George Costain, (Norton), and Jackie Wood, (BSA), lasted ten laps until Costain missed a gear and was forced to retire with a protesting engine.

1956: 80mph lap by a 350

The sun shone again for the second running of the Southern 100 in 1956 with Terry Shepherd again winning the Senior event, but only after Bob McIntyre was forced to slow due to a painful wrist injured in a race in England some weeks earlier. With prize money totalling £305 and a number of handsome trophies at stake, another impressive field assembled for the three races.

Bob did however take victory earlier in the day in the Junior race, leading from start to finish. Although he had a 'no punches pulled' dice throughout the race with Dave Chadwick, who, in the process of trying to catch McIntyre, sped round in 3 minutes 10 seconds at a speed of 80.26 mph. This was the first time the 80 barrier had been broken by a 350 machine.

Chester's Bill Smith, a newcomer to the course, gained his first victory in the Lightweight Race with a safe ride on his Excelsior after Manxman George Costain R.D.S. initially set the pace before a partial seizure forced him to slow and eventually finish third behind John F Patrick, (Velocette). Meanwhile Frank Cope rode consistently to finish fourth!

1957: Almost a washout!

In stark contrast to the two preceding years of glorious sunshine, rain, pouring lashing rain all but washed out the 1957 Southern 100 programme. It started gently before lunchtime, but by midway through the Senior event, the final race of the day, it had increased to a driving downpour.

For the first time the races had been granted National status allowing a maximum of 45 riders per race. 1957 was also to see the introduction of finishers' plaques. A hardy band of spectators witnessed Dave Chadwick, who had been runner-up in both previous Junior events, make it third time lucky, leading throughout, with Glasgow ace Alistair King in close attendance finishing second. Fron Purslow and George Costain hotly disputed third place in the early stages, Purslow winning that contest but finishing well behind the Scotsman. Denis Christian, (AJS), and Colin Broughton, (BSA), struggled to resolve a private argument for fifth place – Christian snatching victory.

In the following 250cc race, Costain fought a race long duel with the previous year's winner Bill Smith, the Chester ace only managing to confirm a repeat victory on the ninth and

(4) 1959 - The unmistakable style of Bob McIntyre - (Norton) Castletown Corner

final lap. The race undoubtedly suffered from the early departure of Junior winner Dave Chadwick, and Fron Purslow on a much-fancied NSU, who dropped back after a promising start. Purslow at least had the satisfaction of recording the fastest lap of the race: 3 minutes 43 seconds. Remarkably, despite the conditions, only one rider required attention of the doctor; R Gilchrist of Onchan dropped his Excelsior at Iron Gate sustaining an arm injury.

The Senior proved rather a procession. Alastair King lead for each of the 24 laps and finished three minutes ahead of 1956 runner-up Don Chapman. Chapman never gave up the fruitless chase, but such was King's command that during five laps in the middle of the race the lead increased by a minute. George Costain rode steadily throughout to complete his third race of the day in fourth place behind Ginger Payne and ahead of Fron Purslow, the first six all rode Nortons.

1958: McIntyre and Shepherd the heroes

Bob McIntyre and Terry Shepherd provided most of the excitement at the 1958 'Southern', which for the first time was spread over two days. Such was the pace of the leading pair in the concluding Senior event that the existing lap record was bettered no fewer than 17 times!

McIntyre opened the 24 lap Senior with a time of 3 minutes 3.5 seconds and held a slight advantage until lap four when Shepherd, from Liverpool, took the lead. The lead however was to change consistently with neither rider able to confirm his superiority. The crowd were on their toes as the pair began their final circuit. McIntyre lead at Ballakaighan, Shepherd at Ballabeg, McIntyre again at Cross Four Ways, then Shepherd at Church Bends and on to the finish where a mere four-fifths of a second saw Terry Shepherd home to collect the Derek Ennett Memorial Trophy.

Fron Purslow, Norton, finished a lap adrift in third, finding the pace of the leaders far too hot. He was clear however of an intense domestic scrap for fourth between George Costain and Jackie Wood. Costain had held a good lead over Wood in the early stages, but an inspired ride closed the gap with each successive lap. However, Wood failed by just two seconds.

The Junior race held on the Wednesday evening was another McIntyre/Shepherd benefit. Once again the pair

were inseparable throughout, until the final lap when Shepherd, who had held the advantage out of Church Bends, braked at Stadium Corner upon seeing a rider touring home with a silent engine. This allowed McIntyre the chance to shoot past and win by the closest of margins. Tenth at the end of the first lap, George Costain delighted the home fans as he fought his way to third place.

The race was marred when 27-year-old Maurice Bowdery came off at Castletown Corner during the Junior race and suffered serious head injuries, which proved to be fatal.

Thursday's opening 250 race provided regular competitor Fron Purslow with his first success as he sped to a record shattering victory, breaking the lap record eight times. Riding the late Hans Baltisberger's NSU, the motorcycle dealer from Shrewsbury beat runner-up Ginger Payne, (Triumph), by nearly two minutes.

1959: Mac denied again

The 1959 Southern 100 races left flying Scotsman Bob McIntyre with one of his main ambitions – to win the main race – still unrealised.

McIntyre had taken the lead from the start of the Senior race and steadily increased his advantage, on lap eleven he completed the course in 3 minutes flat, to become the first man to lap the circuit at 85 mph. Then amazingly on lap 21, while still in complete command, McIntyre turned into the paddock to retire: a broken valve spring denying the Scotsman the double he unquestionably deserved. Behind the leader there was plenty to keep the crowd interested. John Holder, (Norton), from Beckenham led the early pursuers with Bill Smith, (Matchless), third and Norman Storer, (Norton) in fourth place; he was finding great difficulty in staying ahead of Don Chapman, Norton, twice runner-up in the event. After half the distance Smith moved ahead of Holder, but when McIntyre retired Holder made Smith work really hard for his second Southern 100 race victory. Don Chapman claimed third spot and Bill Tomlinson fourth, but only after the timekeepers had sorted out the confusion caused by giving Tomlinson the flag a lap early. (4)

The afternoon's sunshine had been in vivid contrast to Wednesday evening's blinding rain for the running of the opening Junior event. Favourite McIntyre was soon on his way, continuing to improve his lead while in his wake an intriguing duel developed for second place between Bill Smith and George Costain. For 15 laps excitement raged with the home crowd willing Costain on, but it was not to be, as Smith pulled clear in the closing stages to claim runner-up spot. The weather conditions put paid to many, including the much-fancied John Holder who came off at Ballabeg.

Jack Murgatroyd, from Nelson in Lancashire, led an NSU domination of the Lightweight class, beating last year's winner Fron Purslow by over 20 seconds. In third place Bill Smith provided last lap drama, he had been reported to be losing oil and on the last lap his motor died. Not to be denied third place, Smith pushed home from Castletown Bridge, crossed the line and collapsed, exhausted. He thus became the first rider to finish in the first three in all three races, collecting a first, second and third place.

(4a) 1961 - Gary Dickinson 125cc Race

1960: Mac excluded

Sensation hit the Southern 100 when in 1960 after putting up a brilliant riding display to win the Senior, Bob McIntyre was excluded from the result.

From the outset of the race McIntyre and Ron Langston were locked in an absorbing struggle for the lead, which was to last until lap six when McIntyre began to pull away. By the end of the 22nd lap McIntyre, who had lapped in 2 minutes 59.6 seconds to become the first rider to break the 3-minute barrier, held a commanding lead. Then, remarkably, he pulled in at the end of the paddock and refuelled. Clerk of the Course Bobby Moore and his assistant Joe Mylchreest, naturally puzzled, confirmed that regulations did not permit refuelling during the progress of any race. After the race the Scot could do no more than admit he had forgotten to read the rules, and agree the Clerk of the Course was correct, adding that he had enjoyed the race.

McIntyre's exclusion promoted Langston to the winner's place on the rostrum, making him the first rider to achieve what up to then had become an elusive double.

It was Langston's first appearance in the Southern 100, with his first race on the Wednesday evening being dramatic too. For 18 thrill-packed laps Langston and McIntyre battled it out in the Junior. McIntyre led out of the final corner, but with a tremendous effort Langston pipped him to the flag by three-fifths of a second. In the early stages Bill Smith and Peter Middleton were hot on the heels of the leaders and as the roads dried the speeds and the excitement increased. As the leading pair extended their advantage, Middleton concentrated on consolidating third place. Smith, on the other hand, now joined Raymond Kelly and Robin Dawson had to call on his experience to maintain fourth place, Kelly beating Dawson in an exciting finish for fourth.

After many near misses, John Patrick riding a tried and trusted Velocette, to the obvious delight of the spectators, won the Lightweight race. Norton mounted Robin Dawson finished second, well down on the winner with Northants' Dougie Rose third. Misfortune hit Bill Smith who, having taken the lead, was forced to stop at the end of the first lap with a loose number plate. After making adjustments, which cost him a minute, skilful riding brought him up to a creditable fourth place.

1961: Four races on the programme

1961 saw the introduction of a fourth race to the programme for 125cc machines. This race was to introduce diminutive Gary Dickinson, the smallest man in road racing, to the Southern 100 spectators who naturally took him to their hearts. (4a)

During that first 125cc race, try as he might, Dickinson could not catch winner Dan Shorey from Banbury, on a Bultaco. Dickinson led a host of pursuing Ducatis to take second place ahead of Fron Purslow, Alan Dugdale and Arthur Wheeler.

The year had much to commend it, Luton ace Phil Read became the second rider to do the double and there was the one and only appearance of another legendary rider – John Hartle.

The Junior race provided its own bit of history as Alan Shepherd and Phil Read crossed the finishing line together. The pair had kept close company throughout, Shepherd breaking Chadwick's long standing class record sixth time round, only to see Read reduce the time still further on the final lap. By mistake no official was on the

(5) 1961 - Alan Shepherd and Phil Read approaching the finishing line in the 350cc race

line to see the riders finish and a judge's decision declared a dead heat verdict, which proved to be slightly unpopular with spectators on the grandstand, many of whom had their own opinion as to who had won.

The previous year's victor Ron Langston was first away and led until lap three when Read and Shepherd took over and he had to content himself with third ahead of Dennis Pratt and Fred Stevens on Nortons. (5) & (6)

(6) 1961 - Alan Shepherd (5) and Phil Read (4) Dead Heat in 350cc race

(7) 1961 - Start of 500cc Race Bill Fulton (19), Phil Read (3), Alan Shepherd (2) Cannon E H Stenning

Once again the Island's Governor set the 45 riders off at the start of the Senior race, with Alan Shepherd leading Langston and Read clear of the field. (7)

By the end of lap three Shepherd had put some space between himself and Read, who had displaced Langston for second. Shepherd smashed the lap record with a time of 2 minutes 55.8 seconds, 2 mph inside the old time, but failed to appear at the end of lap four. As Read confirmed his lead, news came through that Shepherd had braked too hard at Cross Four Ways, locked the rear wheel and been thrown off. Read maintained his advantage to the end, Langston too finishing well clear of Fred Stevens and Norman Storer. (8)

(8) 1961 - John Hartle on the 250cc 'works' Honda 4-cylinder machine, looking where the opposition is!

A devastating display of high-speed riding gave John Hartle and his Honda-4 a predictable victory in the 250 race. His ride, however, was not without incident as 30 riders had got away

(9) 1961 - John Hartle on the 250cc 'works' Honda 4-cylinder machine, 'at speed!'

before the red and silver machine burst into life. At the end of lap one Hartle was third behind Arthur Wheeler and Brian Clark. On lap three, the former TT winner was ahead and on lap four he smashed the lap record by 14 seconds. When on lap six the Honda began firing on three cylinders his lead was such that Wheeler on his Italian Guzzi and Dan Shorey, now third on his NSU, could not overhaul him. (9)

Ron Langston

It's July 1961 and we are off to the Southern 100 Races on the Isle of Man, and once again we are staying with my old friend Ralph Varden at Ballaquson Farm at Church Bends, opposite Malew Church.

My first visit to the Isle of Man was to see the Senior TT in 1950 on a day trip; soon afterwards I met Ralph Varden who ran Matthews & Co, who were motorcycle dealers in Stratford-on-Avon.
We became great friends, and he was a great help to me, he was instantly recognisable dressed in his plus four suit and a beret – usually red.

There was no garage at the farmhouse so Ralph rolled back the carpet in the lounge, and we worked on the bike there with the comfort of a log fire. If Ralph ran short of wood he would sacrifice a chair or old table to keep the fire stoked up.

One early morning practice we all overslept, Ralph came rushing in to wake us up, dressed in his long night shirt, shouting "Come on lads, they're going by". Practice had started. I quickly put on my leathers and joined in the practice from Ballaquson Farm, while Ken, my mechanic rode the other bike down to the start. Needless to say it was raining!

Enjoyable Days.

1962: Sidecars enter the Southern

Phil Read was to repeat his success of the previous year in 1962 by winning both the Junior race, which opened the programme and the Senior – cut to 18 laps to accommodate the first ever Sidecar race.

A field of 38 riders lined up for the Senior race, a notable exception being previous victor Ron Langston who proved to be a non-starter. Read soon made the running followed by Sid Mizen, Bill Smith, Robin Buxton and Derek Woodman. By the end of lap five the Luton ace was well clear of a shuffled pack in which Fred Stevens had worked his way to second, ahead of Woodman, Dave Williams, Buxton and Chris Conn. This was to be the order in which they were to finish, Conn passing Buxton on lap eight to lose the place to him near the end of the race.

Read was once again quickest off the mark in the Junior race, pulling clear and unaware of the intense battle raging behind him for second place between Woodman, Williams and Stevens. As Read increased the lead Stevens put in a record breaking lap, taking Williams in the process and tucking in behind Woodman. On lap 13 Stevens was second and a lap later Williams relegated Woodman to fourth. For the remaining seven laps Stevens set his sights on Read and spurred on by the crowd failed by less than a second to snatch a victory in a truly remarkable race.

To the delight of the spectators, 42-year-old Arthur Wheeler riding a 10-year-old Moto Guzzi won the Lightweight race with a new nine-lap race record. Unluckiest man of the evening was Alan Dugdale who was forced to retire on lap six when his Benelli developed ignition trouble while leading by a comfortable margin. John Patrick too was unfortunate, having to retire with a gashed leg, received from the footrest of another competitor at the start. After Dugdale had stopped, Wheeler inherited a winning advantage with B Osbourne, (NSU), beating Terry Grotefeld, (Aermacchi), in a photo finish.

Second finisher in the previous 125 race Gary Dickinson, (Ducati), went one better to win the 1962 race. Taking the lead at the halfway stage he stole the six-lap race from the Bultaco pairing of A Whiteside and W Walwork.

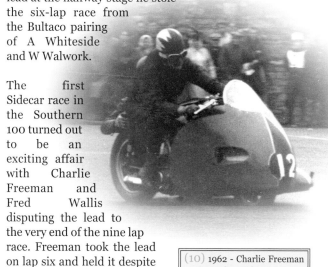

The first Sidecar race in the Southern 100 turned out to be an exciting affair with Charlie Freeman and Fred Wallis disputing the lead to the very end of the nine lap race. Freeman took the lead on lap six and held it despite a neck-and-neck bid from Wallis to regain it. E Peacock finished third, two-and-a-half minutes in arrears, having taken over the position from Stan Nightingale who had crashed without injury. (10)

(10) 1962 - Charlie Freeman - Winner first Sidecar race

(11) 1963 - Sidecar winner Chris Vincent & Keith Scott

(12) 1963 - Start of 125cc Race - J F Carr (22), Derek Woodman (26), J W Wheldon (31), Brian Ball (33)

1963: TT winners take Sidecar class

RAF man Chris Conn, from Bristol, led from start to finish to capture the 1963 Senior race on a sun drenched Thursday afternoon. Grand Prix star Dave Williams, from Leighton Buzzard, had threatened to challenge Conn but engine trouble sidelined him on lap 13; this left the leader with an unassailable advantage. Billy Nelson, Charlie Freeman's sidecar passenger, finished nearly a minute behind in second place with Alan Hunter, from Essex, third.

Conn and Hunter spent most of the 12 lap Junior race disputing the lead until up popped Derek Woodman to take over and do just enough to win. Robin Buxton, Hunter, Conn and Dave Williams were all in close company at the end of lap one with Woodman well out of the picture. On lap two Williams took a slip road and retired, but Woodman was cleverly working his way through the field and caught the leading pair on the last lap. Buxton too was finishing well and caught Hunter to take third, only seconds behind Conn. Hunter had a further surprise to come, as Peter Darvill robbed him of fourth place before the finish.

TT Sidecar ace Chris Vincent flew back from Belgium to contest the Sidecar race and lead from start to finish. He and passenger Keith Scott were never seriously challenged after 1962 winner Charlie Freeman retired on lap one at Ballabeg with a broken primary chain. With John Crick taking a comfortable second place, the main battle of the race was for third where a dramatic bid by Fred Hanks to displace Fred Wallis ended disastrously as he crashed, fortunately without injury. (11)

Londoner Terry Grotefeld, (Aermacchi), had it very much his own way after early leaders Bill Smith and Stan Wright retired in the Lightweight race. Jim Curry brought a second Aermacchi home in second place with Dave Williams on a Parvel in third. (12)

The Ultra-Lightweight class was always an exciting race with no more than 10 seconds separating the first three throughout. Bill Smith took the lead on the first lap and kept his nose in front despite the efforts of the last year's winner Gary Dickinson. Dickinson smashed the lap record on the final circuit in an attempt to retain his title but it was not enough to win. Alvanley's Alan Dugdale brought his Honda home in third place.

1964: Dave Williams does the double

It was only during the closing stages of the 1964 500cc race that Dave Williams was to confirm a victory which made him only the fourth rider to record a Southern 100 double.

Williams contested a battle royale with the previous year's Junior victor Derek Woodman on a day of showers and blustery wind. Billie Nelson grabbed the lead on lap one, shadowed by Williams, Woodman, Peter Darvill and Alan Dugdale. Williams took the lead on lap two with Woodman second and Nelson relegated to third. Third time round Woodman was in front, but on lap six the lead was back with Williams, both of whom were pulling away from Nelson. The following lap saw Woodman ahead, but lap nine signalled Williams' chance to take over yet again. Slowly, Williams began to confirm his advantage, which grew to nine seconds by the end. Nelson in a safe third place and with the retirement of Dugdale and Brian Proctor, Darvill moved into a clear fourth place. Manxman Randall Cowell worked his way through the field after trouble in the early stages to a creditable sixth place.

In contrast, the Junior race had been a much more pedestrian affair, Williams winning very much as he pleased after taking over on lap two from surprise early leader John Evans. Woodman's second place was another lonely ride after he too had disposed of the Evans threat. Peter Darvill made a spectacular bid from the rear of the field, working his way up to third on lap nine, that, however, was to be as far as his challenge was to extend as he could make no impression on the leading pair. Evans continued to lose ground and was forced to retire on the penultimate lap while holding fourth, allowing Keith Heckles to claim the place after getting the better of Billie Nelson.

The Lightweight race, which had opened the 1964 series, certainly held the spectators' interest with little more than 15 seconds separating the first five throughout. From the start Alan Dugdale maintained an early advantage but when he was forced to retire at the halfway stage it was Bill Smith who inherited the winning lead. Runner-up was the fast finishing Terry Grotefeld, who cut Smith's advantage to half by the finish, with Brian Warburton third, giving Yamaha their first leader board placing.

The conditions did not help the 125cc riders in the race, which saw Bill Smith become the first man to achieve a Lightweight double. Smith and Gary Dickinson provided a thrilling duel as they continually exchanged first and second place. When Smith got his nose in front at the end of lap five Dickinson could not pass him, but the difference at the end of the race was no more than feet. The race was certainly a Honda benefit with the first six all mounted on the Japanese machines, John Evans third, followed by Jim Curry, Ron Pladdys and Ernie Johnson.

Charlie Freeman with Billie Nelson as passenger, regained the Sidecar crown with relative ease, beating Wakefield's Peter Kielty by over 20 seconds. Kielty had worked his way up the leader board from fifth on lap one to grab second spot from Maurice Toombs. It had been an eventful race for Toombs who had slipped down the order after a good start only to regain third place with a fine display of riding.

BILL SMITH 125cc Double

Perhaps the funniest victory I had at the Southern came in the 125cc class where I won in the 60s for 2 years on the trot on my CR93 Honda. Now, I am a big lad and even when I was racing I was always around 14 stone. This was a hell of a disadvantage on a 125, so you can imagine my feelings when I found my main opposition also on a CR93 Honda was the diminutive Gary Dickinson, 4' 10" tall and 7 stone 3 lb in weight! The first two years I managed to win the 125s fairly easily, with Jim Curry, Terry Grotefeld and Gary all on CR93 Hondas behind me, but for the third year I knew Gary meant business – he was two seconds faster than anyone else in practice and looked determined to stop my run. Having got alongside him in practice I knew it was going to be difficult, but then I had a stroke of luck. Gary pushed on the right-hand side of his bike and always had trouble because of his size pushing a 125, so when the Governor of the Isle of Man dropped the flag to start the race, I connived to hook my foot under Gary's feet, alongside me, and on looking back was pleasantly surprised to see poor Gary had not only dropped his bike but was sprawled over the top of it unceremoniously. Cracked it, I thought, and got my head down. For 5 laps I had a good lead but on the 6th lap I glanced over my shoulder going down Ballakaighan Straight and there was this motorbike with no rider coming on to me at a much faster speed than I was doing. Sure enough on the main straight Gary flew past me at about 20 mph more than I could extract from my machine, glancing at me and giving me a frosty glare. How the hell was I going to beat him now? I thought desperately, as I struggled to keep him in sight. Throwing caution to the wind I managed to scratch up behind him at Ballabeg Hairpin and slipstream him down the Black Hole and then I brought plan B into effect. I got right close on the inside of Gary and I knew he would not back off in his mood, so I took him side by side into Cross Four Ways knowing full well that we would both finish up on the slip road. I, of course, was prepared for this and after some demon braking, spun the bike round and left poor Gary with his little legs trying to paddle his bike around. Off I went confident that that was it but looking back after Castletown Corner on the final straight I was alarmed to see Gary only 75 yards behind me. He passed me 10 yards after the chequered flag – what a race. I shall always remember Gary in an absolutely filthy mood trying to plant a punch on me on the rostrum after the race.

Chapter Two

Fifty Years of the Friendly Races 1965 - 1974

1965: First Yamaha success

Having made his TT debut Dave Williams provided an effortless performance to capture the top event in the 1965 Southern 100. Williams left runner-up Billie Nelson trailing 28 seconds behind, and to the obvious delight of the majority of spectators, Manxman Sid Mizen recovering from a bad start finished third, less than a second down.

It was Nelson who had led the Senior first time round but by lap three Williams, who had started at the rear of the grid, took command. The lower places settled into a pattern with Selwyn Griffiths third followed by Mizen, Keith Heckles and Jimmy Guthrie. Then on lap 11 the pattern changed as Mizen passed Griffiths and set about closing the gap on Nelson with the obvious approval of the crowd. Try as he might though, Mizen just failed to claim second spot. Griffiths left the race in the closing stages, a victim of a sick motor, which let in Heckles to fourth, ahead of Guthrie and Vin Duckett.

The Junior race proved a comfortable victory for Bill Nelson who led from start to finish. Both Dave Williams and Selwyn Griffiths stopped at Ballabeg early in the race, which made Nelson's job even easier. Most of the interest centred round a duel between Rob Fitton and Alan Dugdale, as for most of the race they contested second place. Then with three laps to go Brian Davis crept up and took them both and Dugdale beat Fitton to third.

Having finished third the previous year Brian Warburton gave Yamaha their first Southern 100 success in the 1965 250cc race. Ron Pladdys' Honda streaked away from the start with Neil Kelly on a Royal Enfield second and Warburton third. As the race progressed Warburton took Kelly, then overhauled Pladdys before becoming the first 250 rider to lap at over 80 mph. Warburton naturally drew clear to win comfortably from Pladdys who held a much smaller advantage over Kelly in third place with Dave Williams who had got the better of Terry Grotefeld in fourth.

For the second year the 125 class provided Honda with a 1-2-3. Jim Curry leading the six lap race from the outset to win by 28 seconds ahead of Terry Grotefeld. Bill Smith finished six seconds adrift in third place in what was to prove the last 125 race of the meeting – at least for the moment.

The Sidecars saw a change in the format. As there were 30 competitors it was decided to set off each outfit at five-second intervals. Charlie Freeman once again showed his mastery of both circuit and opposition with a 35 second victory over another Southern regular, Fred Wallis. The first appearance of the Scitsu, driven by John Worthington, created a great deal of interest; unfortunately the unconventional outfit never really got going. John Wilkinson's outfit did, only to be the subject of a spectacular crash at Castletown Corner, demolishing some railings after the passenger had fallen out.

1966: Brian Davis the star

Former Manx Grand Prix winner and Southern 100 regular Selwyn Griffiths, from Pontypool, won the main event at the 1966 meeting but star of the show was Farncombe builder Brian Davis, runner-up in the Senior and winner of the Junior.

Davis was the initial leader of the 500 race, followed by Dave Williams looking for the third successive victory in the premier class, plus Keith Heckles, Bill Smith and Griffiths. Second time round Heckles was in front with Williams on his shoulder, but all was not well with Williams' bike and he slipped down to fifth on lap four before calling it a day. Lap five saw Griffiths in front pursued by Heckles, Davis and Nigel Warren who had worked his way steadily through the field. Davis took Heckles on lap 12 and from then on the order remained unchanged with Griffiths the winner, then Davis, Heckles and Warren who had held off a determined bid to oust him from fourth by Howard Chandler in the closing stages.

Dave Williams started the Junior race really meaning business with Bill Smith, Selwyn Griffiths, Len Ireland and English short circuit specialist Rolly Capper in hot pursuit. On lap two Brian Davis shot through the field to second with Smith third, Griffiths fourth and Ireland fifth. The fourth lap saw Griffiths sidelined with engine trouble and two laps later Williams too was out with a broken spring. This meant Davis was now the leader with Smith and Ireland in disagreement as to who should be second and third. The dice lasted only three more laps as out went Smith, another victim of mechanical trouble. A further exciting duel had developed down the field between Mike

Jackson and Alan Lawton, which caught the spectators' attention and took on considerable significance with the retirement of Capper on lap 14. Jackson looked set for third until the final circuit when he was caught by a delighted Lawton.

From the moment Neil Kelly stopped his Royal Enfield to make adjustments only yards from the start, newcomer Peter Inchley and his Villiers Starmaker dominated the 250cc race. Inchley increased his lead to 38 seconds by the end of the 12-lap race over runner-up Derek Chatterton, Yamaha. Third place went to Brian Duffy who had come from nowhere on the opening lap to steadily work his way to fourth on lap 10 and pip Alan Dickinson on the final circuit.

Charlie Freeman made it a hat trick of Sidecar wins as he clinched the main race but only at the expense of the unfortunate Nigel Mead. Taking the lead on lap two, Mead gradually built up a one second advantage and looked set for victory until engine trouble intervened. Freeman then closed on Mead who was forced to retire on the final lap giving Freeman victory and the evergreen John Patrick, a former solo winner, second place.

The final race, a Sidecar Handicap provided Ray Weller with the taste of victory after he had caught early pacesetter Stan Nightingale. Freeman and Mead found their handicaps a little too formidable, both retiring on the penultimate lap while outside the first three. N Farrant rode a particularly fine race working his way to second, from 13th on lap one.

Bill Smith

In 1966-1967, Bill Hannah, a well-known Liverpool motorcycle dealer entered Allen Dickinson and myself in the 125cc race on two beautiful Honda CR93 machines. Practice had not gone well for me; I had melted a hole in one of the pistons of the little twin on the day before the race. This now required a top end strip down, and with no spares available I went to look for someone who could help weld up the hole in the piston.

An elderly gentleman was found in Castletown and volunteered to gas-weld the little piston for me.
The welding was done quite quickly but repairing the ring grooves and fitting the rings took a very long time. The next day we were still working on the bike when the time came to take the bike to scrutineering, then out to race. I got clear of the scrutineers and out of the paddock on to the road, by which time everyone including my team-mate Allan was on the grid and awaiting the starter's flag.

Looking to the right about 200-yards up the road, a full grid of bikes was assembled, panic set in – I knew I would have to go round for a full lap of the circuit, some 4.25-miles before I could take my place on the grid.

I set off at full speed in the hope of getting to the start line before the flag dropped. Half way round the circuit I passed a travelling marshal at the bottom of the Black Hole on full noise – it must have given him quite a shock. After rounding Castletown Corner, I was relieved to see the lads were still on the starting grid.

Taking my place on the front row and all the engines had stopped, I was able to speak to the next rider and say how lucky I was that the race hadn't started without me. He said, "we all knew you were coming – everyone could hear you all the way round the circuit and where you were by the gear changes!"

Bill Hannah had come over from Liverpool to see the event, in the hope of a race win for one of his bikes, but it was not to be, my bike expired on lap two and I think Allan's bike also stopped.

That's racing as they say.

1967: Seventh victory for Smith

Production 250 TT winner Bill Smith scored his seventh success in the Southern 100 by winning the 1967 Senior on a Matchless. Smith's cause was aided by the early departure of three fancied men: Brian Ball and Keith Heckles both on the opening lap and Howard Chandler on lap two, all whilst holding second place.

Smith established a lead early in the race despite an excursion at Ballabeg, only to be caught on lap six by up and coming short circuit ace Steve Jolly, (Matchless). On lap nine Smith was back in front, Jolly being another casualty of engine troubles. From then on the Chester ace had it all his own way. Manxman Neil Kelly gave the locals something to cheer with a gutsy performance defending second spot from the persistent Vin Duckett. The battle for fourth place proved very exciting – a young Irish rider named Brian Steenson with only a handful of races to his credit getting the better of the experienced old campaigner and fellow countryman Len Ireland.

Ireland had in fact earlier captured the programme opening 18 lap Junior race, and once again it was Steenson who had given him most of his problems. Taking the lead on lap four from Vin Duckett the Irish pair gradually pulled clear of the field. Behind the leaders, Steve Jolly and Derek Chatterton were trying to resolve their own disagreement, which was now taking them from Duckett who had been relegated to fifth. For a moment halfway through the race, Ireland's bike faltered and Steenson saw his opportunity to take the lead. The fault, however, proved only temporary and back came Ireland to win by a respectable margin. Jolly had got the better of Chatterton for third, and early leader Duckett retained fifth place.

The 250cc race provided Derek Chatterton with sweet revenge over the previous year's winner Peter Inchley who this time rode a works AJS. It was very much a follow my leader race as Chatterton, who was in front from the start, smashed both Inchley's lap and race records. Third placed Mick Chatterton and fourth Terry Grotefeld also maintained their positions throughout.

With the absence of four times winner Charlie Freeman, the Sidecar appeared to be a very open event. Clear favourites with the crowd, John Worthington and John Sanders on the unconventional Scitsu led the race for a couple of laps until a slipping clutch let them down. This left the door open for John Patrick to nip past and win. Patrick thus became the first rider to win both solo and sidecar races at the Southern 100.

Len Ireland

Happy Memories of the Southern 100

In 1965 I took part in the Southern 100 for the first time. Having done the two practice sessions I enjoyed the circuit very much, but it was not a place to make a mistake, as there are farm buildings, stone walls and pillars with which to make contact. In those days the races were long, having to complete 18 laps of the Billown circuit. On the last lap at Castletown Corner I was in third place in the 350cc race, but unknown to me, as I accelerated to the finish, Robin Fitton was on my tail and he slipstreamed me to near the line where he passed me, beating me by a machine's length. This meant I dropped to fourth place in the race.

The following year I did a little better by finishing second to my good friend Brian Davies. I finished tenth the next day in the 250cc race on a Greeves.
During the early morning practice in 1966 I noticed Bill Smith sitting on the wall on the approach to Ballabeg, having had machine trouble.
When practice was over I continued round for another lap and brought Bill back to the pits on the rear of my 350 Manx. Having had to sit on the hump of the seat it must have been most uncomfortable.

I thought if I went back in 1967 it may be third time lucky, and so it was. I led from the start of the race with Brian Steenson quite close behind riding Ronnie Conn's Aermacchi.
On the tenth lap Brian passed me down the start and finish straight where he took over the lead, but I passed him again going out of William's Corner. From then on I had to ride really hard to try and get away from him, this I did and won the race by 11 seconds and had the fastest lap.

Billown is a great circuit and one of the few I haven't fallen off on. I made a lot of friends at the Southern 100, both riders and officials, that adds to the enjoyment of taking part in the parade laps today.

1968: Championship introduced

1968 saw the introduction of what is now the premier race of the meeting, the Solo Championship, for which, at the

(14) 1968 - Kenny Allen - Morris Tri-car

time, the first 15 riders from the three races held on the Wednesday evening qualified.

Large crowds in brilliant sunshine witnessed Steve Jolly in his first full year as a professional road racer carry off the Championship title. Jolly beat second place finisher, TT star Selwyn Griffiths, also on a Matchless, by nearly half a minute, with the ever-popular Keith Heckles third. Rising star Stan Woods brought a 250 Yamaha into a highly creditable fourth spot ahead of Brian Steenson on a 350 Aermacchi. (13)

The Lightweight race had got the meeting off to a blistering start with a pulsating dice between Terry Grotefeld, Stan Woods, Derek Chatterton and Brian Steenson all on Yamahas and Jim Curry on an Aermacchi. Such was the intensity of the contest that both lap and race records were shattered. Grotefeld, who won by a fraction ahead of Woods, became the first 250 rider to lap in under three minutes. Chatterton finished third with Curry fourth and Steenson fifth.

Jim Curry led an Aermacchi 1-2 in the Junior race holding a slender advantage over Brian Steenson at the finish. Woods, (Yamaha), finished a lonely third with Martin Carney on a Kawasaki fourth, well clear of the Greeves mounted Neil Kelly.

Alan Shepherd's long-standing lap record never looked in danger as Selwyn Griffiths, who had played a waiting game, snatched victory during the final lap of the Senior race. Brian Steenson, Aermacchi, held a steady third place for most of the race, finishing ahead of the Norton pairing of Keith Heckles and Alan Lawton. (14) & (15)

(13) 1968 - Steve Jolly - First Solo Championship winner

(15) 1968 - John Worthington - Scitsu

Newcomer Ken Allen aboard the controversial Mini engined tri-car took all the honours in the Sidecar race. 1967 winner John Patrick had to be content with second. Manx pairing of Ernie Leece and John Molyneux were forced to retire whilst holding third place.

1969: British Championship comes to Billown

Three riders scored double successes during an incident packed 1969 series with top honours going to Queen's University, Belfast graduate, Brian Steenson. Derek Chatterton and Charlie Freeman were the other winners in a meeting, which for the first time was raised to British Championship status.

(16) 1969 - Charlie Freeman

Charlie Freeman gave notice of his intention to win back the Sidecar Championship after a two-year absence by capturing the opening six-lap race. Freeman, a great respecter and admirer of the course, had little to spare at the finish over Bill Currie, (Triumph), second and Peter Williams, (BSA), third. (16)

In the Championship race Freeman grabbed the lead before the first corner followed by John Patrick, (Triumph), Williams, Currie, Robin Williamson, (Triumph), and Roy Hanks, (BSA). For two laps Williams and Currie hotly disputed second but neither could threaten the supremacy of Freeman. A slipping clutch ousted Williams' chances and at the halfway stage a bent valve relegated Currie to a final fifth spot. Hanks moved up to second but was nearly a minute down on Freeman at the end, with Williams third and John Worthington, who bravely pushed the Scitsu the last quarter mile, fourth. (17)

During the all-important 350 British Championship round a lap scoring error saw the chequered flag shown a lap early to race leader Derek Chatterton and second placed Bill Smith, both on Yamahas.

(17) 1969 - Poetry in motion!

Martin Carney, Padgett Yamaha, Selwyn Griffiths, George Fogarty and John Graham however all raced on to complete the 12 laps. Chatterton though was able to breathe a sigh of relief after a meeting of the ACU stewards decided to base the results on 11 laps. The performance of the race had come from Ian Richards, who had taken over Terry Grotefeld's Padgett Yamaha after a practice spill had left him with rib and shoulder injuries. Richards led for the first five laps, setting a new lap record in the process and building up a considerable advantage. His tenacity was to be ill-fated as he slid off at Ballabeg, leaving Chatterton half a minute clear.

(18) 1969 - Bill Smith leads Selwyn Griffiths during Solo Championship race

Bill Smith's Matchless led the pack away in the Senior race with Griffiths, Cowles, (Matchless), Steenson, (Seeley) and George Fogarty, (Matchless), in close attendance. Second time round Steenson swept into the lead with Griffiths clinging on to his slipstream. Try as he did, however, the Welshman could not prevent Steenson taking the maximum 15 points. Smith finished third, ahead of Keith Heckles and Championship chasers Robin Duffty and Graham Fish, (Nortons). Fogarty had fallen on melting tar on lap three, picked himself up and remounted to finish a game eighth.

The Solo Championship produced the expected Steenson/Chatterton duel with the Irishman taking the title by just four seconds after 12 intriguing laps of racing. Behind the leading pair a fantastic crowd-delighting struggle raged for third with Smith, Griffiths and Duffty swapping places like musical chairs. Smith eventually claimed third with Griffiths holding fourth and Duffty fifth. (18)

The non-Championship counting 250 race provided Chatterton with the easiest victory of the meeting. The Lincolnshire rider held a 50 second advantage at the end over a spirited battle for second between eventual claimant, newcomer Steve Machin, and third placed Mick Chatterton, all, naturally, Yamaha mounted.

1970: Guthrie takes Championship

For the second year the main prize, the Solo Championship race in 1970 went to a Northern Ireland rider – Billie Guthrie on the 350 Dugdale Yamaha. (19)

Gaining the lead on lap two Guthrie was never again headed and went on to break lap and race records. Lap one leader Brian Adams had to be content with second in front of Terry Grotefeld, (350 Yamaha), holding the positions from lap three. Selwyn Griffiths and Vin Duckett kept the crowd on their toes with a neck and neck tussle for fourth place. Duckett claiming the honour on the last lap.

Wednesday evening began with the usual 250; Mick Chatterton showing a clean pair of heels to the rest of the field. By lap three, however, Chatterton had been caught by Ray McCullough and lap five saw both Ian Richards and

(19) 1970 - A resident gets a close up of Solo Champion Billy Guthrie as he rounds Ballakaighan

Terry Grotefeld relegate him to fourth. This was the order in which they were to finish with Dudley Robinson securing fifth spot after a bad start.

After taking the lead on lap five Bill Smith won the Junior with something to spare, Steve Machin being forced out with engine trouble. Terry Grotefeld had to settle for runner-up spot, 40 seconds adrift but well ahead of Mick Chatterton who finished third after a pulsating dice with Jim Graham. Guthrie finished down in fifth after working his way through and catching Don Padgett on the final circuit.

The evening's final race, the 750, was a dramatic affair. Bill Smith had taken the lead on the 500 Kawasaki only to be forced out on lap three with engine trouble. The Nortons of Brian Adams and Keith Heckles then disputed the lead for six laps until Heckles too was forced to stop, giving Adams a simple victory run-in. Vin Duckett finished second after getting the better of Selwyn Griffiths on lap three. Chester ace John Hughes on a Matchless provided all the lower order excitement pulling up from 15th on lap one to clinch fourth place with the retirement of Heckles and Graham Fish, (Norton).

The programme-opening six lap Sidecar went to Cheshire's Bill Currie and passenger Ken Arthur. They took the lead on lap two from Roy Hanks and John Gladstonebury who finished second, well down on the winner.

The final race, the Sidecar Championship, provided Bill Currie with a double. Currie led from the start and for 10 laps was chased by Roy Hanks who was forced to retire allowing Ernie Leece and John Molyneux second place. John Patrick looked set for third until his motor died, leaving Dave Bradley and Ann Jelbert to claim the place. (20)

1971: Programme settle down

By 1971 the races had fallen into a predictable pattern, which was to operate for several years to come. Two Sidecar races, one to open the programme on the Tuesday evening, followed by three solo races on the Wednesday evening acting as qualifiers for the Thursday afternoon Solo Championship, and then the second Sidecar Championship race.
The 250cc race lost most of its sting on the fourth lap when

Charlie Williams, who had been shadowing race leader Ray McCullough, was forced to retire. McCullough then rode at his own pace ahead of Liverpool's Manx Grand Prix ace Ian Richards, who had nipped into second with Terry Grotefeld, (Padgett Yamaha), third. This was the way they finished, but behind them Dudley Robinson, who had settled for fourth, was to be unpleasantly surprised with two laps to go as both John Stanley and Ken Daniels demoted him to sixth.

Short circuit ace Daniels set the fans talking in an exciting 350cc race by equalling Alan Shepherd's long-standing absolute course record. The race was certainly eventful with Graham Fish grabbing an early lead. However, second time round, Terry Grotefeld had passed him and George Fogarty, Billie Guthrie and Daniels were hot on his tail. As the race progressed more surprises were in store; Selwyn Griffiths now on a competitive Cowles Yamaha after a bad start began picking up the places, one by one. By lap eight Griffiths was ahead and on his way to a 10 second victory. Despite Daniels' memorable lap halfway through the race he could manage no better than fifth behind Grotefeld second, Fogarty third and Gordon Pantall who crept home in fourth.

Two powerful 500cc Kawasakis were the centre of interest in the 750 race. Bill Smith rode one to victory but Gordon Pantall on the other made it far from easy for him until he retired on lap nine. Selwyn Griffiths brought a Cowles Matchless into second spot the best part of a minute down; he had benefited from the last lap retirement of Ray McCullough, (QUB Seeley). Local rider George Short pleased the spectators by claiming third ahead of TT regular John Hughes on another Matchless.

The Championship provided Smith with a second victory; although he was never seriously challenged after getting off to a dream start. Welsh wizard Griffiths could do nothing to halt the rampant Smith and concerned himself with holding onto second ahead of George Fogarty and Gordon Pantall. George Short completed another fine ride in fifth place ahead of Roger Sutcliffe on another Matchless.

An unfortunate accident midway through the Sidecar Championship race resulted in Bill Currie and passenger Ken Arthur, (Weslake), being taken to hospital with serious injuries. They had been lying second at the time behind the KGB of Peter Williams and Mike Casey who were forced to retire near the end with victory a near certainty. Dave French and Neil Thompson, (BSA), took advantage of the leaders' misfortune to beat Gordon Nottingham and H Hundey by a whisker to claim the title. Locals Keith Griffin and Malcolm Sharrocks, (Triumph), pipped Ernie Leece and John Molyneux for third.

(20) 1970 - A close up of Sidecar Champions Bill Currie and Kenny Arthur

Williams had earlier won the six lap opening Sidecar event leading from the start with Bill Currie second, seven seconds down and Dave French third.

1972: Charlie is the darling!

Without a doubt, man of the 1972 meeting was young Cheshire Manx Grand Prix star Charlie Williams. On Dugdale Yamahas Williams swept to a 250/350 double on Wednesday evening, before rounding off a highly successful series by clinching the main Championship race with something to spare.

After his main challengers Bill Smith, (750 Honda), and Stan Woods, (500 Crooks Suzuki), had been seen off, Smith

(21) 1972 - Charlie Williams - triple winner, including Solo Championship

retiring early in the race, the task was that much simpler for the champion Williams. Don Padgett on his own Yamaha beat Woods for third with the surprise of the meeting Roger Winterborn, (500 Seeley), claiming fourth ahead of Tom Herron, (250 Yamsel) and Selwyn Griffiths, (350 Cowles Yamaha).

The opening 250cc race had provided Williams with his first ever Southern 100 success as he beat the Irish pairing of Ray McCullough and Tom Herron, both on Yamsels, by over a minute with Don Padgett seconds down in fourth. (21)

Williams' margin of victory in the Junior was by no means as great and in the early stages he had to play second fiddle to Bill Smith's Honda, which set a record-breaking pace. Once the Honda faltered the way was left open for a relatively comfortable victory. Selwyn Griffiths finished second, half a minute down, but the same distance ahead of third finisher Don Padgett.

The 750cc race afforded Bill Smith and his bigger Honda compensation but only after he had fought off the persistent Stan Woods who was credited with the fastest lap. Selwyn Griffiths brought his Cowles Matchless into third spot ahead of a crowd-intriguing dice between locals George Short, (Seeley), and Roger Sutcliffe, (Suzuki), who were beginning to make it an annual event. Short was able to pull away in the closing stages to confirm his fourth place.

John Watson and his passenger John Wright from Leeds captured the Sidecar Championship on their 750 Windrick outfit having earlier won the six-lap opening race by another impressive margin. Dave French and John Teal,

(750 BSA), who had given Watson all kinds of trouble in the six-lap race before retiring, finished second in the main race.

1973: First 90 lap

The 1973 series brought the first 90 mph lap even closer as firstly Charlie Williams in the Junior race lapped in 2 minutes 52 seconds, 88.95 mph, and then in the extraordinary Championship race, Tom Herron on a 350 Yamaha equalled it.

The Championship was truly a remarkable race with red-hot favourite Williams falling off twice on the opening lap. His first accident was at Cross Four Ways whilst in the lead. After checking the bike he remounted only to fall again at Castletown Corner, where he called it a day. Roger Sutcliffe took over the lead and for 11 of the 12 laps looked set for victory. Tom Herron, however, had things planned differently and pipped Sutcliffe to the post in an incredible finish. A battle for third place was equally as exciting with John Newbold on a Lightweight Yamaha getting the better of Phil Haslam, (Commando). Bill Guthrie finished fifth ahead of another close finish involving George Short, (Seeley) and Derek Huxley, (250 Yamaha). In the end they were both credited with sixth place.

From the outset Charlie Williams had dominated the 250cc race, which left the main spectator interest surrounding a tremendous duel for second place between Ray McCullough, (Yamsel) and Steve Machin, (Sondel Yamaha). At the finish it was McCullough home ahead of the Lincolnshire Imp, but only with three seconds to spare. John Newbold took the Newcomers award with a steady ride in fourth place.

The 350cc race provided Williams with an even more comprehensive victory to become the first rider to score a 250/350 double. (22) Drama struck early on in the race as on the first corner, Ballakaighan, both Bill Smith and newcomer Bill Rae crashed out in spectacular fashion, Smith receiving a sprained wrist, Rae being unhurt. Machin looked set for a deserved second place until misfortune struck on the final circuit when he was forced to stop with a flat tyre. Peter McKinley, (Padgett Yamaha), took advantage of Machin's departure to claim runner-up spot after steadily working through the field from eighth place on lap one. Third finisher Phil Haslam had certainly found it an eventful race dropping down the field before producing a fine piece of riding to climb back to finish two seconds in front of Tom Herron.

Roger Sutcliffe brushed the opposition aside to score a runaway win in the 750 race leading all the way as Williams had done earlier. Bill Smith, 750 Honda, retired on lap two leaving Phil Haslam, (Commando), and Mick Broom, (750 Rickman Metisse), to contest second. On lap seven Broom hit engine trouble and slowed leaving Haslam 10 seconds clear of Bill Guthrie, (Yamaha), who was third. Gordon Pantall finished next after recovering from a desperate start, which had seen him 15th on the second lap. Local runner George Short had to be content with fifth having been caught by Pantall three laps from home.

Newcomers Pete and Ron Hardy won the Sidecar Championship race on their BPF 900 Imp outfit but only by two seconds from Dennis Keen and Pete Saunders, (500 Konig). 1972 winners John Watson and John Wright, (750 Windrick), had to settle for third, two minutes behind the leading pair.

The opening six-lap Sidecar race had been held in torrential rain, which kept spectators to a minimum. Once again the Hardy brothers were victorious but again the winning margin was only seconds with Malcolm White and P Oliver, (BSA), second. The race had been hotly contested with White grabbing second spot on lap four, whilst Watson and Wright were third again, catching Edwin Wright and Melvyn Beanland, (BSA), near the end of the race.

1974: Tonkin cracks it

The 1974 meeting began badly with a fatal accident during practice. In 1973, experienced regular competitor, Mike Pepper had died after losing control following a high-speed wobble at Great Meadow bend. Just a year later Belfast newcomer Jim Farlow died from injuries received in a crash at Church Bends.

During the racing, the Championship limelight was stolen by Carnforth's Steve Tonkin who scored an impressive victory taking half a minute off Tom Herron's race record. The race was dominated by 350 Yamahas whose riders filled the first five places.

From the start Pete McKinley, (Padgett Yamaha), led the race with Malcolm Moffatt second and Roger Nott third. Strangely the Wednesday evening's three solo race winners were nowhere. McKinley disappeared on lap two and Nott took over the lead with Tonkin jumping up to second from fifth. For the next eight laps there was little between the two out front, Nott keeping his nose ahead until he struck trouble, which left Tonkin in the clear. Meanwhile, the battle for second was heating up with Moffatt, who had been holding steady in third, being caught by Selwyn Griffiths' Cowles Yamaha. Griffiths called upon his experience to confirm a final second place with Moffatt a late retirement. Derek Huxley produced a special

performance pulling up from 21st on lap one, to finish a mere three seconds down on Griffiths.

Huxley won the Junior, taking the lead at half distance from eventual runner-up Peter McKinley. Roger Nott took third spot with the unfortunate John Taylor, who suffered machine problems, hanging on to pip Moffatt for fourth. The first 18 all rode Yamahas.

The 250cc race was also a Yamaha benefit, Ray McCullough providing a record-shattering start to finish victory. Ian Richards captured second place taking over on lap two after the unlucky McKinley was forced to retire. Once again the third place went to Roger Nott, a position he held throughout.

The 750 race, in contrast, had three different leaders and five different makes of machine in the top six at the finish. McKinley got off to another super start but was once again dogged by engine trouble. George Fogarty then led for two laps until he too was forced to quit on lap eight and John Taylor, (Seeley Suzuki), inherited a winning advantage. Eddie Roberts then brought his Maxton Yamaha into second, ahead of Alan Jones' Norton and Les Trotter's Crooks Suzuki. Billie Guthrie brought a second Yamaha into fifth with Selwyn Griffiths' Cowles Matchless beating team-mate Dave Williams by half a second, the distance the pair had stayed throughout.

Dave Lawrence and James Bromham, (998cc Grangeside Imp), from Colwyn Bay, smashed the 80 mph lap barrier for the first time by Sidecars. Their margin of victory, however, was only six seconds over newcomers Steve Rowe and Alan Jones, (850 RJS Saab). Edwin Wright and Colin Derbyshire, (749 Windle Weslake), were only five seconds down well clear of fourth finisher Graham Hilditch and Vince Biggs on another 998 Grangeside Imp.

Rowe and Jones showed how quickly they had learnt the circuit by taking the Championship. Initial leaders Malcolm White and Phil Oliver, (741 Tri Fly Weslake), caused most of the winners' problems but they finished 16 seconds down in second place. Hilditch and Biggs held third spot for half the race, but their retirement let in Dave Houghton and Norman Ferr, (750 Woodhouse Honda).

(22) 1973 - Start of 350cc race - Bill Smith (64) Tom Herron (59) Charlie Williams (66)

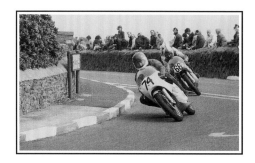

Chapter Three

Fifty Years of the Friendly Races 1975 - 1984

1975: McCullough goes into the 90s

It was to be one of the Southern 100s favourite visitors, Ray McCullough, who in 1975 was to become the first man to lap the Billown Course at over 90 mph.

McCullough created his bit of history in the 350 race, an event he won after taking the lead at half distance from fellow Irishman Mervyn Robinson, (Yamaha). Gradually pulling clear, McCullough increased his advantage to 22 seconds over Robinson who in turn led home a procession of riders, the first six remaining unchallenged from the half way stage. Newcomer Neil Tuxworth from Louth finished third with Welsh Manx Grand Prix regular Dave Williams fourth. (23)

Tuxworth had earlier begun the programme in sensational style by taking the 250cc race on his course debut. The fact that he led from the start only served to make his success all the more remarkable. John Holmes, (Rea Yamaha), held second place for the opening two thirds of the race but was forced to settle for fourth after being caught by Trevor Steele, (Yamaha), and on the final lap Liverpool's Roger Nott on another Yamaha.

The 750cc race provided Bill Smith with yet another victory, leading on every lap. Les Trotter and Roger Sutcliffe brought a pair of Crooks Suzukis into second and third during another race, which became another procession after the early departure of well-placed Frank Kennedy.

It was, however, to be McCullough's year as no one was to deny him his Championship crown. Taking the lead on lap two he dictated the race from the front, fractionally bettering the lap record that he had set up in the Junior race. Leading on the opening lap Mervyn Robinson finished a clear second ahead of Bill Smith who had a lonely ride, holding third spot throughout. The lower places were far from clear cut, Dave Williams' Cowles Yamaha holding a mere five seconds advantage over Gordon Pantall, (Sparton), and James Scott, (Yamaha), who finished so close they could not be separated and were jointly credited with fifth place.

The programme-opening Sidecar race was increased to nine laps and brought victory to the Didcot pairing of Dave Houghton and Roger Page, (760 Konig). Once again Graham Hilditch and Ray Littlemore got off to a cracking start only to go out on lap six with a broken primary chain at Ballabeg,

having built up a minute lead. Houghton was 17 seconds clear of Brian Hall and Pete Minion, (Williams Norton), who had worked their way up from eighth on lap one. Third finisher was Les Walker, and Paul Saunders made even more progress: having been left at the start they shot through from 21st on the opening lap.

Misfortune followed Hilditch and Littlemore into the Sidecar Championship, after leading for eight laps they were again sidelined, this time by a burnt-out clutch. During the early stages Mick White and Philip Oliver, (850 Westlake), pressed the leaders hard but an argument with a pavement coming out of Church Bends on lap four curtailed their progress and they didn't seem the same again, finishing down in seventh spot. Hall and Minion took over the lead vacated by Hilditch to beat R Philpott and M Buxton, (Weslake), by 18 seconds, they also pipped third finisher Mick Worltey and Ralph Crellin, (956 HDW), on the final lap. A domestic scrap for fourth place between Keith Griffin and Malcolm Sharrocks, (850 Weslake), from George Oates and John Molyneux, (680 Konig), ended with the former pair gaining a split second advantage.

The organisers added a 1000cc race to the programme, which unfortunately didn't attract the same quality field as the other solo races. Victory went to local Grand Prix ace, Danny Shimmin, (750 Yamaha), who led the 12-lap race from the start followed home by Malcolm Moffatt on a 351 Yamaha. Snuffy Davies, (250 Yamaha), finished third taking advantage of the retirement of Mike Laverty, Gordon Pantall and Robert Hirst, all of whom had held the position.

HALF A WHEEL by Tony Dawson.

And so the background to this story goes: -

It was at Cadwell Park early in 1975 that I was surveying a badly bent TZ250 Yamaha belonging to that infamous character and great friend Mal Carter (Pharaoh Racing). The bike had been buried head first into the muddy bank at 'Charlies' bend by Ron Haslam.
The front wheel was caressing the crankcases and the petrol tank reflected the shape of the frame's top tubes.
Up strode the rotund figure of 'Big Mal', whereupon a conversation ensued, which went something like this: -
" That thing is just a pile of scrap!" said Mal, to which I replied, " Do you really think so Mal? – I think it could be

straightened and I'm looking to borrow a bike for the Southern 100". " Well if you can straighten the thing you can borrow it!" mumbled he.

Some weeks and a lot of toil later I had a gleaming red and white TZ250 ready to leave for the 'Southern' (one of the very few meetings I would make the effort to contest in my last couple of seasons of competitive racing).

Now the fun begins: -

On arrival on the Island and taking part in that wonderful ritual of 'signing on' in the 'George Hotel' I bumped into my old pal, who was about to become my friendly rival, Rickie Burrows. He was being plied with drink by mechanic Syd Cousins (surely the funniest man ever to wield a spanner). Syd could do a running somersault between the door and the bar after 8 pints of Guinness!

It was not long before Rickie and I were teasing each other about who was to win our private battle. I proclaimed (very tongue in cheek – as Rickie was of MGP leader board calibre) I would beat him by just "half a wheel" to which he retorted, "No! I will beat you by half a lap". I can't remember if money changed hands (nor much else of that evening for that matter!!!).

During the next 'lazy days' and practice that make the 'Southern' such an enjoyable event, Syd (Rickie's mechanic remember!) would mischievously remind me that I would have to ' get my finger out' if I was to have the slightest chance of winning the wager. This only served to arouse the competitive spirit within me and I set about in practice to' blow away the cobwebs' that form from the dearth of events since my previous year at the 'Southern'. Practice went without a hitch and my confidence in the straightened TZ was as high as Snaefell itself.

At the line-up for the start of the 250cc race I was on the second row of the grid just behind the likes of Joey Dunlop, Ray McCullough, Trevor Steele and Neil Tuxworth, all of whom I considered 'Kings of the Road'.

The race started and I found myself being dragged along by the leading bunch of 6 or 7 into Ballakaighan. I remember wishing I was nearer the back as I struggled to concentrate on my own line and braking point into the corner. By Ballabeg I was beginning to feel more confident and my adrenalin was on the ascending. Even more so after a few laps when ahead of me I could just make out the rear profile of Trevor Steele (an Irish ROAD racer of merit) who was lying in about 4th place. I set about trying to reel him in but after several laps of making what seemed little progress I was out-braked at Cross Four Ways by Rickie Burrows – Oh! I suddenly thought, was I actually in front of him till now? - Can I hang on to him? Can I beat him by 'half-a- wheel' as I had jokingly intimated? The scene was now set for the titanic battle of my will and his skill. I re-took Rickie coming out of Great Meadow and pulled 100 yards on him before he came scorching past me on the brakes into Alexander Bridge (Castletown Corner). Every lap we would pass and re-pass with Rickie almost locking both wheels into Cross Four Ways and Castletown Corner as he consistently out-braked me. All I could think of was the wager and the fun of the challenge over the next couple of laps to the chequered flag. The thoughts of keeping up with Trevor Steele, or whatever position I was in, took second place to the task in hand, to keep just ahead of Rickie. On the last lap as I pulled along the inside of Rickie coming out of Great Meadow I looked across to him only to see the veins in his neck standing out like rivers on

an ordnance survey map. He was in no mood for my sense of humour which made me laugh uncontrollably, so much so, that he easily out-braked me into Castletown Corner where I couldn't see my braking point nor the apex of the corner due to the tears of laughter flooding my eyes. I was convinced I could out-sprint him to the finish line even though as my vision cleared I had to mount the pavement onto the by-pass and change up two gears before leaping back onto the road and 'slipstream' him before pulling out and passing him just after the finish line. He had beaten me by about 'half a wheel'.

I leave you to imagine the conversation at 'The George' that night and the 'ribbing' I got from Syd, but nothing can dull the sense of fun and later the realisation that if only I could have concentrated harder on the rear end of Trevor Steele who knows what might have been – but that's what the Southern is all about!

Tony Dawson.

1976: Joey winning debut

(24) 1976 - Joey Dunlop - Ballabeg - on his way to the Solo Championship

Diminutive Ulsterman Joey Dunlop, on his first visit, proved the sensation of the 1976 series with two second places and a third in Wednesday's qualifying race, then most important of all, a magnificent victory in the Championship race, shattering both lap and race records. (24)

Chester veteran Bill Smith got off to a cracking start in the Championship on his 750 Yamaha with Dunlop, (350 Yamsel), and Ray McCullough, (350 Yamaha), tucked in behind. Dunlop slipped past Smith on lap three and by lap five McCullough too was past the Chester ace who was having problems with his front brake. Try as he might McCullough could make no impression on his fellow countryman as they gobbled up the miles. The six-second gap remained to the finish, Neil Tuxworth on another 750 Yamaha struggled to get the better of Trevor Steele, (350 Yamaha), in the early stages, but at the end had 10 seconds to spare. (25)

(25) 1976 - Bill Smith - 750cc race winner - first rider to average 90mph for a race

The 250cc race had also been a lap and race record smasher in what turned out to be an Irish jig. Ian McGregor kept eventual winner McCullough at bay for the opening four laps but once he was ahead he was unstoppable. The previous year's winner 'Tuxworth' held third place until two laps from home when Dunlop slipped past him for an Irish 1-2-3. (28)

The 350 brought a similar result this time; however, McCullough had a much cosier time leading from flag to flag. Dunlop did himself no good with a desperate start but provided most of the interest as he battled his way through the field taking second spot on lap seven. In third place Steele was quite a distance adrift at the finish. Roger Sutcliffe delighted the locals by pipping former champion Billie Guthrie on the final lap to claim fourth place.

Bill Smith became the first man to average 90 mph for a race when he took the honours in the 750 race. From the outset Smith was locked in an enthralling dice with Gordon Pantall, both riding 750 Yamahas. Unfortunately Pantall, who was on Smith's tail, crashed heavily on lap three at Ballawhetstone but this proved to be far from the end of the leader's problems. Dunlop, on a 350cc machine, harried Smith for several laps and seventh time round actually took the lead. With three laps to go, however, Smith was back in command and extending his advantage to 10 seconds by the chequered flag. It was another disappointing race for Billie Guthrie, (Danfay Yamaha), he had held third place for some time when in the closing stages Neil Tuxworth, (Yamaha), and Frank Kennedy, (Sparton), relegated him to an eventual fifth.

1976 saw the introduction of Production bike racing with two classes. Class A was for machines from 175-500cc, Class B for machines from 501-1000cc. (26) & (27)

(26) 1976 - Dave Williams - Winner Class A First Production Race

The riders in Class A set off first with Roger Sutcliffe and Colin Bevan on Kawasakis leading Les Trotter, (Crooks Suzuki). Class B riders had soon caught the earlier starters, Andy Dubost, (900 Kawasaki), ahead of Geoff Kelly, (750 Norton). By lap three Dave Williams on a 750 Cowles Triumph was the overall leader with Sutcliffe second.

(27) 1976 - Roger Sutcliffe - Winner Class B First Production Race.

Leading Class B, Williams gradually pulled clear as the bigger bikes began overhauling Sutcliffe who was, nevertheless, increasing his lead in the smaller class. Geoff Ryding, (903 Kawasaki), was made to work hard before clinching second place, beating Malcolm Moffatt, (886 Ducati), by two seconds with Kelly and Dubost slipping to fourth and fifth. In Class A Trotter and Mike Kneen, (347 Yamaha), were over a minute behind Sutcliffe at the end.

John Watson with new passenger Brian Hoyle on their Italian 981 Laverda completely outclassed the rest of the field in both Sidecar races, rewriting the lap and race records. They had a minute to spare in the opening non-Championship nine lap race over Graham Hilditch and Kevin Littlemore, (700 Yamaha), who for once managed to stay the distance. Steve Grainger and Graham Pettison, (900 Windle Honda), were much closer in third place. The first three places may have stayed virtually unchanged throughout but the contest for fourth was much more appealing with B Philpott and M Buxton, (Kawasaki), taking David Houghton and Chas Birks on the last lap after a race-long dice.

Hilditch and Littlemore had looked set to take runner-up spot again in the Championship but all was not right with them and they were caught on lap nine by Grainger and Pettison and on the final circuit by Philpott and Buxton and had to be content with fourth.

(28) 1976 - Joey Dunlop - Collecting his first Southern 100 Silverware at the Prize Presentation

1977: Ron Haslam rides – briefly!

Joey Dunlop returned to conquer in 1977 during a year which may be longer remembered for events which happened even before the racing began.

Long time Southern 100 campaigner Bill Smith arrived too late for practice and appealed to ride without doing so. The Clerk of the Course had no alternative but to reject the appeal, a decision upheld by the stewards of the meeting. Mal Carter, sponsor of British short circuit star Ron Haslam, a newcomer, threatened to pull his runner out if Smith was not allowed to ride and as this failed to sway the organisers they all packed up and went home. (29)

(29) 1977 - Ron Haslam ahead of George Fogarty in practice

As soon as racing got underway controversy was forgotten, and once again the programme opening non-Championship Sidecar spelt misfortune for Graham Hilditch with Vince

Biggs now in the chair. They had kept their Grangemouth Yamaha ahead for five laps at which point Brian Webb and Colin Booker, (750 Yamaha), took over to win. Newcomers Allen Steele and Tony Barrow, (738 Suzuki), worked their way into a creditable second slot ahead of Brian Hargreaves and Geoff Castlehow, (980 Kawasaki), who had equally been lowly-positioned on lap one. Hilditch had the consolation of sharing the fastest lap with Bill Hall and Peter Minion, (Kawasaki), who retired whilst second.

(30) 1977 - George Oates and John Molyneux

The Manx pairing of George Oates and John Molyneux, (30) (LMS Kawasaki), looked set for a Sidecar victory until a faulty fuel pump intervened two laps from home. Hilditch and Biggs the early leaders struck engine trouble and from the third lap Oates and Molyneux drew clear. Their machine problems relegated them to eventual fourth place with Steele and substitute passenger Pete Minion left to claim a two-minute victory. Artie Oates and Dave Skelly, (Kawasaki), took second place with Peter Dunn and Graham Savage, (Windle Honda) completing a steady ride in third spot. (31)

The first solo race, the 250, gave Joey Dunlop, (Yamaha), a runaway victory leaving the battle for second to provide spectator interest. New man, Clive Padgett eventually took the place but only after he got the better of a race-long struggle involving Neil Tuxworth, Danny Shimmin and, in the latter stages, Ivor Greenwood. Ray McCullough had also been involved early on but had set the fastest lap and retired before the third lap was over. The race had a sting in its tail with Greenwood passing Tuxworth, who retired, and Shimmin, fourth on the penultimate circuit, before coming within an ace of catching Padgett.

Bob Jackson, from Kendal, on the Lambert Yamaha raised a few eyebrows by clinching the 350 in record time.

(31) 1977 - Sidecar Championship winners Allan Steele and Pete Minion

Taking the lead on lap three from McCullough (engine trouble) who was having a wretched meeting, Jackson came home 24 seconds ahead of Neil Tuxworth. The Louth rider had struggled for half the race to get the better

of Grand Prix winner Kevin Riley who was making his course debut. At the end of the race Tuxworth had secured runner-up spot with 12 seconds to spare, but Riley on the other hand had less than a second's advantage over fourth finisher James Scott, (Anderson Yamaha).

The final Championship solo qualifying race, the 1300cc, provided Dunlop with his second victory of the evening. Blackburn's George Fogarty, (Suzuki), in determined mood made the Ulsterman fight all the way and at the chequered

(32) 1977 - Joey leads the Championship pack at Ballakaighan

flag the difference between the pair was less than two seconds. The lower placings were allocated by half distance with Tuxworth, (Yamaha), leading Les Newman, (Yamaha), and fifth finisher Marty Ames, (Lockyam).

The Championship race proved almost a carbon copy of the 1300 race. Dunlop took the lead on the opening lap and maintained a four second advantage over Fogarty – once again runner-up. It took Tuxworth six laps to catch Newman who was only two seconds adrift at the end. Ames once again finished fifth but had been subjected to the continual presence of Jackson before he retired leaving Kevin Riley to claim sixth spot. (32)

The Production races attracted a poor response, non-starters reducing Class B to just six. Class A (up to 500cc) proved the more popular, with newcomer Jamie Garrett from Ramsey, (492 Suzuki), dominating the class from the outset. Suzukis in fact took the first three places – Steve Jopson taking second place ahead of ever-popular Tom Loughridge. The lack of entries did not deny the larger class of a keenly contested battle for the lead. Malcolm Moffatt, (900 Ducati), eventually finished well clear of George Fogarty, (750 Crooks Suzuki), but was aided by the retirement of sixth lap leader Colin Bevan, (1000 Kawasaki). Manxman Geoff Kelly, (830 Laverda), led fellow countryman Alan Phillips, (750 Norton) – the only other finisher.

Bill Hall – Pete Minion

Just before the start of the 1974 race our exhaust split. Officials held up the start to allow us to change the exhaust on the grid. We finished the race in 6th position.

In the first 1977 race our engine blew itself to bits; having no spares left we were out of the Championship Race.
Alan Steele's passenger Tony Barlow dislocated his knee in the same race, unable to compete any further.
Bill's passenger Pete Minion stepped in to passenger Alan, and with the promise of a few beer vouchers if he did well, they went out and duly won the Championship Race.

1978: Dunlop champion again

(33) 1978 - Joey Dunlop - Castletown Corner - The view the rest of the field saw!

It was very much the year of the Irish as far as the solo classes went at the 1978 meeting, with Joe Dunlop collecting three wins and rival Ray McCullough two. (33)

The Sidecar programme had been reshaped, opening with two qualifying races, each allowing 25 competitors. The first 12 in each race were invited to take part in the Sidecar Championship race, and the remainder in a Sidecar Consolation race.

Allen Steele and Tony Barrow, (700 Yamaha), led the opening qualifier from start to finish with runner-up spot going to Mick Harvey and Simon Birchall, (Looke Imp). Brian Houghton and G Jacques, (Kawasaki), finished third, less than two seconds down on Harvey.

John Watson and Brian Hoyle, (750 Yamaha), won the second heat in similar style to Steele and Barrow – but considerably quicker. Bryan Hargreaves and Norman Burgess, (980 Kawasaki), in second place were also well inside the opening race winners' time, as were George Middleton and Paul Howe, (750 Yamaha), third.

In the Sidecar Championship, however, there was no holding 1977 champions Steele and Barrow. The Chester pairing were never headed and finished over half a minute clear of Watson and Hoyle. Newcomers Mike Burcombe and B Dudley, (Yamaha), took and held third spot after the retirement of fellow newcomers Philip Spencer and D Richards, (Honda), early on. Artie and Edda Oates, (Kawasaki), beat John Philips and Andrew Mackay, (Kawasaki), in a photo finish for fourth place.

The solo races got off to a cracking start with an exciting dice between Ray McCullough and Bob Jackson in the 250cc race. The pair had both caught initial leader Graham Young, (Yamaha), by lap three and a piece of inspired riding by Jackson saw him ahead on lap eight. A lap later, however, McCullough regained the lead and increased it to five seconds by the flag. Dunlop took over third place after Young retired only to lose it on lap seven to fellow Irishman Trevor Steele. Con Law brought another Yamaha into fifth place. (34) & (35)

1977 350-race winner Jackson was again to the fore in the 1978 race, he led on the opening lap with Steele, Young, Dunlop and McCullough screaming after him. Steele led second time around with McCullough ominously jumping

up to third. On lap four McCullough was ahead but Steele was in no mood to let him have it all his own way and re-took the lead on the sixth circuit. With two laps to go McCullough made his bid and nipped back in front for a two second victory. Dunlop had been consolidating third place until engine trouble struck, allowing Burgess to beat Jackson who had only five seconds to spare over Conor McGinn who collected the Newcomers' Award.

The 1300cc race turned out to be the most dramatic event of the evening. Marty Ames on the 750 Lock Yamaha got off to a cracking start and, to the surprise of many, began pulling away from Joey Dunlop, on another 750 Yamaha. Dunlop could make little impression on the Leeds flyer, then on lap eight victory was in sight as disaster overtook the leader. At Cross Four Ways Ames and Mick Dunn (who was about to be lapped) collided and down they went. While Ames was picking himself up both Dunlop and George Fogarty, (750 Yamaha), passed him and he had to settle for third. Conor McGinn, (Yamaha), led a pack of Irishmen into fourth place, ahead of Frank Kennedy, (Suzuki), and the Yamahas of Con Law and James Scott.

After the previous excitement the Solo Championship was a rather pedestrian affair, Dunlop retaining his titles pretty much as he pleased, equalling his own lap record. He finished the 12 laps less than a second slower than he had 12 months before – a piece of remarkable riding.

Misfortune again hit the exciting Ames after grimly pursuing the leader for 10 laps. Engine trouble denied him runner-up spot and he slipped down to finish 12th. McCullough, who had settled for third, gratefully took second, albeit over a minute down on Dunlop. Trevor Steele had made rapid progress from a lowly 13th on lap one and passed both Jackson and Burrows to take third. McGinn produced another fine ride in sixth place.

Joey Dunlop had earlier beaten Graham Young, to win the Solo Supporting race with Jim Norbury and Bernie Wright, (Windle Lock Yamaha), leading the six-lap Sidecar Consolation all the way.

(34) 1978 - Ray McCullough 250cc Yamaha

(35) 1978 - Ray McCullough 350cc QUB Yamaha

1979: Millennium year

Despite being forced to relinquish the Solo Championship title Joey Dunlop was once again the centre of most of the conversation during 1979.

Three wins and a second were his final tally but his astonishing escape from injury when a steering damper broke at Ballanorris will perhaps be his most remembered feat.

Dunlop got off to a cracking start in a 250 event that became rather a procession after the opening lap. A collision on the starting line put paid to Graham Young's chances – Lee Heeson, the other rider involved, remounted and finished 11th. As the race progressed Bob Jackson, Clucas Yamaha, edged his way nearer the Irishman, but Dunlop was having none of it and in the second part of the race pulled clear again to win. Ray McCullough resolved an early argument with Con Law in his favour to confirm third. Banbridge's Brian Reid further demoted Law to fifth on lap nine with Trevor Steele sixth.

The 350 provided Dunlop with victory number two. His advantage this time was even more comfortable, once again Jackson being his main adversary. Conor McGinn, seventh in the 250, began in much more determined mood, holding third place until engine trouble struck on lap four. Trevor Steele looked set to take third spot until engine trouble intervened three laps from home, finally dropping him to 15th. Naturally, an intriguing struggle down the field began to take on more significance – Con Law concluding a fine ride by clinching his best result at the Southern. Mike Kneen, who had been hot on the heels of Graham Young, cleverly claimed fourth spot on the final circuit. Sixth place could hardly have been tighter – Ernie Coates, who had an extremely eventful ride, pipping Kenny Harrison by a whisker.

After two start-to-finish wins, the 1300 race was quite a contrast with three different leaders. No one could deny Marty Ames, on the Lock Yamaha, deserved a win after his previous year's misfortune, but the race sensation was newcomer Ian Bell, from Bedlington.

The race was eventful to say the least for Joey Dunlop. After stopping at Castletown Corner to remove some tape from a boiling radiator the initial leader found himself in fifth place. A new lap record of 2 minutes 36.8 seconds soon promoted him back into contention until a near disaster befell him at Ballanorris on lap three. A steering damper broke and jammed leaving Dunlop with no alternative but to head for an open gateway into the field where he jumped off the bike, escaping serious injury. Little known Ian Bell certainly got the spectators buzzing, holding the lead for eight of the 12 laps before regular Marty Ames, on another 750 Yamaha, took over on the penultimate lap to win by half a second. George Fogarty claimed third after Mike Kneen had produced a fine piece of riding challenging him closely before falling off twice and retiring. Neil Tuxworth took fourth, with Rob Brew and Mike Dunn delighting the local fans with fifth and sixth.

The Solo Championship was possibly the race of the week; Ian Bell once again led for most of the race but had to settle for third at the end. This time it was long-time

Championship aspirant George Fogarty that took the title, nipping past Bell at Great Meadow on the final circuit. Joey Dunlop took the runner-up position after Bell's clutch went on the final bend. The Ulsterman had been looking for his fourth successive Championship and despite the restriction of a 350 Yamaha, brought about by his spill in the 1300cc race, he certainly made a race of it. An inspired ride by Graham Young, also on a 350, took him past Dunlop on lap five, and he eventually finished fourth, clear of Marty Ames and Rob Brew. (36)

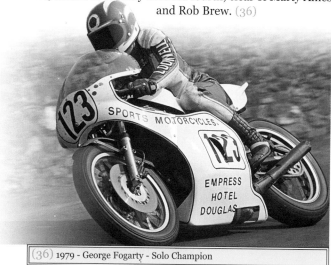

(36) 1979 - George Fogarty - Solo Champion

Three outfits were locked in a tremendous battle for five of the nine lap Sidecar Championship. Heat winner Lowry Burton and Martin Murphy, (Yamaha), led from the start, hotly pursued by eventual winner Malcolm Burcombe and Derek Rumble, (Yamaha), with Wally and Ernie Coates in close attendance. Once Burcombe took over in front he steadily pulled clear, his advantage at the finish being 16 seconds. Burton finished second, with first heat winner and former champion Allen Steele and Tony Barrow taking advantage of the Coates retirement on lap five to take third place.

The six lap Sidecar Consolation race went to Dave Saville and Hugh Sanderson, Yamaha. They had struck trouble in their heat but sliced 12.2 seconds off the Sidecar lap record to win at a canter. Local aces Eric Bregazzi and Jimmy Creer, (Kawasaki), pinched second place by less than a second from George Burton and Les Taylor, (Lock Yamaha).

Dunlop completed a hat trick of wins by taking the 10-lap Solo Millennium race on a 500 Suzuki. Tony Dickenson, from Blackburn, on a 750 Yamaha finished second ahead of George Fogarty, Dave Pither and Dave Dean, all on 500 Suzukis.

1980: Silver Jubilee year

Joey Dunlop was denied a hat trick on the Wednesday evening of the 1980 Southern 100, when the engine of his 750 Yamaha seized on the second lap of the final race of the night.

Dunlop had scored an impressive double, winning the 250 and 350 races, but from the start of the 1300cc race he looked in trouble, having had difficulties during practice with the larger of the Yamaha machines.

Dunlop was well down the field on the first circuit and was even further behind on the second lap, when the Yamaha gave up the ghost between Ballakaighan and Ballanorris in a cloud of blue smoke.

Dunlop had started the evening with victory in the 250 race but it wasn't easy. He had to fight every inch of the way for his win and until late in the race was second best to the super-fast works Cotton ridden by Steve Cull. The Cotton looked a certain winner until it developed clutch trouble and Cull toured in to retire, leaving Dunlop to battle it out with fellow Irishman Conor McGinn for the final few laps. (37)

(37) 1980 - Steve Cull and Joey Dunlop 250cc race

McGinn reduced the gap on Dunlop and managed to overtake him before Ballakaighan corner on the last lap, but Dunlop re-passed and the dice ended with 0.2 of a second advantage for Joey at the chequered flag. Riding steadily Neil Tuxworth held third place until the last lap when his engine seized at Castletown Corner and pushed in to finish tenth. Gary Padgett moved up to third spot followed by Bob Jackson, Paul Cranston and Pete Wild. (38)

The 350 race saw Dunlop lead from start to finish, gradually pulling away from Bob Jackson, who was well ahead of Neil Tuxworth, Pete Wild and Paul Cranston, the latter having a real scrap for fourth place.

With Dunlop's hat trick chances ending early in the 1300 race, it was Geordie Ian Bell, (750 Yamaha), who shot into the lead and he was visibly pulling away from his rivals. By the seventh lap, he was seven seconds clear of Steve Cull, (500 Suzuki), with Dave Dean, (750 Yamaha), not far behind and last year's champion George Fogarty, (750 Yamaha), fourth. But trouble struck for Bell on lap eight

(38) 1980 - Close action between Con Law, Conor McGinn and Paul Cranston

(39) 1980 - Sidecar action at Ballabeg hairpin - Mike Murcombe heads the field

when his Yamaha seized at Billown, leaving Cull in the lead. This gave Cull added incentive and by lap ten he was ten seconds up on Dean and Fogarty, who were scrapping for second place. Dean eventually overhauled Fogarty and by the chequered flag managed to secure the runner-up position. Doug Randall, (Suzuki), Rob McElnea, (Yamaha) and John Robinson, (Spondon Zeger) completed the top six.

Londoner Dave Dean lead from start to finish to win the Solo Championship, riding a 750cc Yamaha, he had a comfortable win over Steve Cull on his 500 Suzuki, with fellow Irishman Conor McGinn, 351 Yamaha, taking third spot.

Lowry Burton and Martin Murphy aboard their Yamaha won the Sidecar Championship. They led from start to finish, setting new lap and race records. John Evans and Tony Smith on a Yamaha took second place with Arthur Baker and John Tindell, also Yamaha mounted, third. (39)

The sidecar consolation race for non-qualifiers for the Championship was won by Des Founds and Jim Craig, (Rumble Yamaha), from Steve and Mervyn Noble, (Kawasaki), with Warwick Newman and Alan Warner, (Kawasaki), filling the final podium place.

Ian Bell, (Yamaha), won the Solo Support race, increasing both race and lap records in the process. Conor McGinn took second ahead of championship winner Dave Dean.

1981: Ashton's honour

1981 saw a change of name regarding the organising club. Southern 100 Motor Cycle Racing Ltd came into existence. It was, however, the same 'team' that organised and ran the popular event.

Stockport rider Dave Ashton came through to win the Solo Championship in 1981 but left his effort to the very end of the exciting 12-lap race. He had trailed Rob McElnea from Brigg, Lincolnshire, for seven laps before finally swooping past on the run to the finish. In the end only three-fifths of a second separated them. Third was Ian Bell from Bedlington.

A downpour marred the race just before the flag dropped, Steve Moynihan from Ballasalla was challenging Peel rider Rob Brew in a race for fourth place. Steve was on a 350

(40) 1981- Lowry Burton & Marty Murphy on the way to their second successive Sidecar Championship

Yamaha on treaded tyres, while Rob was on a 750 with slicks, but just as the battle was to be seriously joined, Steve's clutch gave way and he had to throttle back to make sure of finishing. He was passed by Andy Cooper and Castletown rider Richard Coates, who rode extremely well to finish sixth, eight seconds ahead of Moynihan.

The Sidecar Championship was also a victim of the downpour, even more severe than during the Solo Championship, with outfits skating all over the place on the final two laps when the roads were akin to rivers. Lowry Burton and Marty Murphy repeated their success of the previous year with George and William Middleton runners-up, as Jim Norbury and Norman Elcock settled for third place. (40)

Two six-lap Sidecar 'odds and evens' heats opened the programme on Tuesday evening. Local crew Eric Bregazzi and Jimmy Creer took their 750 Yamaha to victory by ten seconds, with Mick Burcombe and Derek Rumble unable to get near.

It was a fine effort, Tony Baker and Alan Jackson led at the end of the first lap, but second time round they had disappeared and the Union Mills driver had the Yamaha well in front of Eric Cornes and Robert Holmes. They pulled away to hold 20 seconds advantage going into the last lap. The local boys then knocked off the power and cruised home, preserving the motor.

In the earlier odd numbers race, Tom and John White from Doncaster led all the way when the expected challenges from 1980 champions Lowry Burton and Marty Murphy took some time to materialise. However, when it did, it came in a big way, with the first over 90 mph lap by a three-wheeler. This came on the fourth lap as Burton and Murphy hurtled round Billown to come from seventh on lap one to third at the end. They knocked 3.2 seconds off their existing record to set it at 2 minutes 47.6 seconds, a speed of 91.28 mph.

Wednesday evening opened with the 'traditional' 250cc race, with considerable interest in the continued challenge of the Rotax powered machines to the established Yamahas.

Stewart Cole from Haddington took an early lead, but on the second lap, Bob Jackson from Kendal took over and stayed there. He built up a lead of ten seconds before relaxing and being caught by Brian Reid. Jackson turned on the taps

again to win by nearly three seconds. Bill Ingham presented a challenge for second place before his clutch started to wail and he eventually pulled off. Meanwhile, Cole and Paul Cranston were at it hammer and tongs until Cole also packed up. That let in Neil Tuxworth, but on the very last lap Graham Cannell from Ballaugh took Harry Reeves' Cotton Rotax past to claim fourth place and claim the newcomers' award after a fine ride from ninth on the first lap.

There was drama at the start of the 350cc race, when Kevin Wilson and Allan Hannay collided and fell at the start line, with Hannay being unable to continue.

Neil Tuxworth took an early lead, only to be passed on lap three by Bill Ingham and Kenny Harrison. The latter pair then had a furious scrap, which lasted until lap six when Ingham dropped it at Cross Four Ways. Coming through the field was Ian Bell, who soon picked off Tuxworth to take the chequered flag, with Dave Ashton third. Andy Cooper took fourth from Steve Moynihan, who was rammed at the start in the Wilson-Hannay melee, with Stewart Cole filling sixth spot.

Rob McElnea fought a lone stand in the 750 race, with a start to finish victory doing exactly as he pleased. He extended his lead to 20 seconds by lap nine before settling for an 18 seconds advantage at the end. George Fogarty was the early second placeman, but was overtaken by Dave Ashton, and that's the way it stayed. Bob Jackson, Danny Shimmin and Rob Brew completed the top six. (41)

The solo support race was won by Ian Bell on his Padgett Yamaha, breaking the class lap record in the process. He was followed some 20 seconds later by Paul Cranston, (Starplan Yamaha), and Rob Brew, (Yamaha), a further 40 seconds adrift.

In the Sidecar consolation race, Tony Baker and Alan Jackson took the chequered flag from Stuart Applegate and John Gibbard, and Stewart Rich and John Jackson.

1982: Reid's double as Law takes title

The first six-lap Sidecar race saw an easy victory for Lowry Burton and Marty Murphy, in what was not a particularly exciting affair. Such was their superiority that they had no need to come near their own sidecar lap record of 2 minutes 47.6 seconds set last year in the equivalent race. In fact, the fastest laps became a joint achievement by Jim Norbury/Norman Elcock and Pete Whiteley/John Armitage, setting it in 2 minutes 55.8 seconds in a furious dispute for third place eventually taken by a yard by the former crew.

(41) 1981- Rob McElnea Winner of the 750cc race

On the opening lap, Eric Cornes and Robert Holmes lay second to Burton and Murphy, but they slipped right back on lap two, before storming back through to an eventual sixth. Ray Towse and Alan Fisher then took over second, and were nicely ahead of the big scrap behind. John Evans and Dave Hall piled on the pressure for fifth place, forging ahead of Cornes and Holmes.

The second sidecar race proved a lot more exciting, and the Burton lap record was broken by two crews who waged a great contest all the way. But first there was drama on the start line, when three outfits shunted and only two were able to get away.

For the first three laps, Tony Baker and Peter Harper led, on their Yamaha carefully assembled in their Penrith workshop. But leaving no stone unturned in the desire to get past newcomers Steve Webster and Tony Hewitt, they squeezed by on lap four, only to be retaken the following time round. But the Baker and Harper model faltered with petrol starvation and that was sufficient to let the new boys back in to win. They shared the new record in 2 minutes 47.2 seconds (91.50 mph) which was two-fifths of a second faster than the Burton 1981 time. Mick Harvey and Steve Taylor were third, Stewart Rich and John Jackson fourth, Barry Brindley and Chris Jones fifth with George and William Middleton taking sixth place.

The 250cc race of Wednesday evening's programme was the only one to escape the wet weather, and then only just. Overhead, skies were grey and even as the starting grid was assembled there were a few spots of rain, but it held off for the 12-lap, 50-mile race.

Senior TT winner Norman Brown got a flyer at the start and led at the end of the first lap, with Brian Reid and Dave Ashton in hot pursuit. At the end of the second lap, Reid had displaced Brown and was never again headed. Con Law had an awful start, but got cracking to improve from 15th on lap one to 11th on lap two. It was to be the start of a rare fighting comeback that was to yield second place at the chequered flag. Graham Cannell was in trouble with his clutch even on his warming-up lap, so it was little surprise when he went out on the second lap.

At the half distance mark, Reid enjoyed an 11-second lead from Brown, with Ashton third. But the best scrap was for fourth, where Bob Jackson was involved in a clash with Law, as Richard Cotes and Dave Pither were hard at it for sixth.

On the eighth lap, Brown became the last of Law's victims, the Waddon rider wisely settled for second as Reid was too much of a distance away to be seriously considered. Brown then came under pressure from Jackson and Ashton, while Coates and Pither were side by side.

(42) 1982 - Start of 1300cc race - Con Law (120) Dave Ashton (121) Rob Brew (122) Ian Bell (124)

Reid roared home to win by just over 20 seconds, with Law runner-up. In an exciting sprint home, Jackson displaced Brown, who in turn just held off Ashton. With equal determination, Coates squeezed past Pither on the last lap to claim sixth.

The rain started to fall in the middle of the 350cc race making conditions tricky, although it didn't appear to unduly affect Brian Reid who knocked out his second win of the evening. However, he was given a much harder task before victory was conceded by the opposition. Con Law was forced to withdraw from the 12-lap race on the line, when mystery ignition trouble set in.

(43) 1982 - Norman Brown RG500 Suzuki

Dave Ashton led at the end of the first lap, but Reid soon altered that to lead on laps two, three and four. Ashton was displaced by Norman Brown and the three were in close company up to the halfway stage. Graham Cannell was going well in fourth in a battle with Ian Bell when he was forced to retire with mechanical problems. That let in Andy Cooper, with Trevor Steele and Dave Pither making up the top six at the six-lap point, as the rain began to look really menacing and the roads started to get greasy. Ashton took over at the front, but on lap seven Reid made his big effort and whizzed through. With him went Norman Brown and that was the pattern until lap 11, as up to third came Gary Radcliffe, who had moved from seventh in the early stages. Neil Fowler took advantage of one or two retirements right at the end and grabbed fifth, with John Brindley finishing sixth.

There was wholesale action just prior to the start of the unlimited race. The rain had started in earnest, and wheels were rapidly removed to fit intermediate tyres. In fact, the way things worked out, the competitors would have been better to have put on full wet tyres, but there wasn't time. One or two optimists even started on slicks, but were hopelessly outclassed and were extremely fortunate to stay on board. Ian Bell shot away from the start and was never seriously challenged. Such was his rate of progress it was as if it wasn't raining directly under his wheels! (42)

Norman Brown was initially second, but was soon overtaken by Dave Ashton as conditions worsened. Brian Reid's hopes of a hat trick disappeared when his chain snapped at Church Bends. Riders were absolutely on a knife-edge as they diced around the Billown Course with machines struggling to lay their power down. Bell ran out the winner, backing-off the pace to a comfortable half-minute win, with Ashton second and Brown third. Con Law was a cautious fourth, Jeff Jones fifth and Danny Shimmin sixth. (43)

There were some brilliant races on 'Championship Day'. New lap records were set in both the Solo Championship and Sidecar Championship and in the latter there was a new race record.

In almost perfect conditions racing got underway with the Solo support race for those competitors who just failed to qualify for the championship. Irishman Paul Cranston on a Yamaha won the race at a speed of 93.31 mph, and had the fastest lap of 95.15 mph.

It was in the Sidecar consolation that the Isle of Man appeared to be heading for its first win of the week. Eric Bregazzi and Jimmy Creer had been leading most of the way, when they were forced to retire late-on leaving victory to go to Michael Burcombe and Dave Gray. Bregazzi and Creer however had the consolation of the fastest lap at 87.95 mph.

(44) 1982 - Steve Webster and Tony Hewitt await the start of the Championship race in which they finished second on their debut

Junior TT winner, Con Law took his Yamaha to first place in the Solo Championship and on the way set up a new lap record at 96.83 mph. Last year's winner Dave Ashton came second and Jeff Jones from South Wales was third. Brian Reid took fourth, the best of the locals, Rob Brew taking fifth and fellow countryman Gary Radcliffe sixth.

In the final race of the 1982 Southern 100, the Sidecar Championship victory went finally to Tony Baker and Peter Harper after an exciting duel with Steve Webster and Tony Hewitt who was racing for the first time on the Island. Only two-tenths of a second separated the crews at the end, with Baker setting up a new race record at 91.43 mph and Webster setting up a new lap record at 94.79 mph. Third came winners of the last two years, Lowry Burton and Marty Murphy. (44)

1983: Ton barrier broken!

Twenty-eight years after Terry Shepherd won the first Southern 100 and set the first-ever fastest lap at 80 miles per hour, Brian Reid, from Banbridge, Northern Ireland, finally broke the 100 mark on the last lap of his winning ride in the Unlimited race. (45)

In a final dash for victory after a race-long battle with countryman Con Law, Reid lapped the 4.25 mile Billown Course in 2 minutes 33 seconds – precisely 100 mph, carving 3.8 seconds off Joey Dunlop's existing 97.57 mph record from 1979.

The race was a fantastic dispute between two evenly matched Suzuki 500cc machines in the capable hands of the two Ulstermen. They were never more than a second or two apart as each strove to win. It was clear that race and lap records would go, but it was optimistic to expect the 'ton' to go. Nevertheless, it was interesting that the previous outright course record had been set in the unlimited race, rather than the main championship. On lap seven Reid and Law were nose to nose and frightening the pants off spectators as they overtook back markers without shutting off. On lap nine, they were again alongside each other, but drifted apart, until the last lap.

However, Law hit problems in the very last mile and was forced to tour in to belie the closeness of the other 49 miles by trailing 30 seconds at the flag. Had it been an uphill run to the line, Ramsey rider Kenny Harrison might have been second, but he was still six seconds down at the flag after a good ride on Rob Brew's 750cc Yamaha, hampered by broken exhaust brackets. Paul Cranston was fourth, with Steve Moynihan fifth on Des Collins' RG Suzuki, having disposed of an initial challenge by Buddy Yeardsley.

The 1983 Southern 100 started with the two six-lap heats for the sidecars, as they battled it out for places in the sidecar race on Championship Day. The first six-lapper saw 1982 winners Tony Baker and Peter Harper, the favourites, lead from the start, right through to the chequered flag, winning by 42 seconds. Second throughout were Steve Sinnott and Alan Langton, who decided against trying to stay with the flying leaders. They wisely settled for a certain transfer to the main final. Third for the first two laps were Eric Cornes and Robert Holmes, but it was plain that they were under severe pressure from Geoff Young and Ian Colquhoun. On lap three they were overhauled, then faced a challenge from Eric Bregazzi and Jimmy Creer. On the fifth lap it looked as though the local pair might grab fourth place, but a misfiring motor prevented a last surge and the order remained the same. Three crews had a crack at sixth spot, but at the end it was the position's original occupiers, Robert and John Chapman, who took it.

It was somewhat surprising that the second sidecar qualifier proved slower in race and lap speeds. Nevertheless, it mattered little, as the qualifying was not just the top half of each race, but the fastest crews from the two. This meant that the top 15 in the first race went into the main final, whereas only 10 from the second race could maintain the same pace.

The race was led all the way by the 1983 favourites, Lowry Burton and Pat Cushnahan. They completed the six laps 17 seconds ahead of local crew, Artie and Edda Oates. However, for the first two laps, Dennis Keen and Colin Hardman were second, but slipped back to third on lap three, then to fourth a lap later. Artie and Edda pressed hard throughout, and passed Keen and Hardman, then Graham Hilditch and Tony Dalton. Keen and Hardman made a late revival towards the end, and began to catch Hilditch and Dalton. But they weren't quite able to get back past and shot over the line half-a-second in arrears. Sixth place went to Pete Whiteley and John Armitage.

(45) 1983 - Brian Reid on his way to becoming the first rider to lap the Billown Course at 100mph

(46) 1983 - Neil Tuxworth rounds Ballabeg Hairpin on the 250cc British Wicks machine

Louth rider, Neil Tuxworth gave a great boost to the British Wicks project by taking the development machine to an easy victory in the Smirnoff Vodka sponsored 250cc race. He took the lead on the first dash from the line and was never headed. He set a new record race speed and new record lap at 93.17 mph. However, the race was not entirely without its problems for Neil. Trouble with sticking throttle slides gave him more than one hairy moment, and he admitted later he was relieved to have completed the fifty miles without coming to grief. In the end, it was a win by 67 seconds from Bob Jackson, riding an Armstrong, so it was a great race for British bike enthusiasts. The first Yamaha home was that of Graham Cannell, who finished third, ten seconds behind Jackson. Tuxworth and Jackson occupied first and second places without interruption. But third place came under dispute for a while. Fourth, fifth and sixth were occupied by Andy Cooper, Sean Collister and George Hardwick. (46)

With a record lap of 95.74 mph, Kenny Harrison again proved what a very fine road racer he is, when he took his Yamaha to victory in the 350cc solo race. Carving a full second off Ray McCullough's previous fastest lap, set in 1978, Kenny cashed in on his decided policy of restraint in the early stages. Neil Tuxworth again started like greased lightening, and led for the first four laps, before giving way to Brian Reid. He then led until lap nine, when Harrison roared past, when the Ulsterman's streamlining brackets broke and almost jammed the steering. Andy Cooper rode a steady race in third position, once the highly competitive pack had sorted itself out. Tuxworth's reduced pace saw him settle for fourth, with Chris Fargher fifth, ahead of Nigel Wilson, who pipped Sean Collister to sixth.

Harrison was extremely fortunate to finish the race, as his bike seized on the line, but eight times TT winner Chas Mortimer got no further than Ballanorris on lap four when similar problems halted progress after a poor start.

Championship Day got underway with the Solo

(47) 1983 - Charles Mortimer on a 250 Armstrong exits Ballabeg during the 250cc race

Support race, which proved to be a Yamaha benefit, with Trevor Steele taking the victory from Neil Tuxworth, Gary Radcliffe and Ralph Sutcliffe. Chas Mortimer was first 250 home, in fifth on his Armstrong, and George Fogarty was first four-stroke finisher, bringing his 600 Ducati into sixth place. (47)

The Sidecar consolation proved to be a runaway win for Mick Harvey and Trevor Taylor on their 700 Lockyam, some 50 seconds in front of newcomers Lionel and Amanda Fantom. Pete Tyack and Colin Wright secured the final podium position.

Brian Reid took his Topping Suzuki to victory in the Solo Championship race with a 49-second advantage over Kenny Harrison, with Paul Cranston a further 16 seconds adrift. George Fogarty, Andy Cooper and Bob Jackson completed the top six.

The final race of the 1983 programme, the Sidecar Championship, saw Lowry Burton regain the championship he last won in 1981, this time with Pat Cushnahan in the chair. The pairing from Northern Ireland held off newcomers Steve Sinnott and Alan Langton, who were 16 seconds down at the flag, as Denis Keen, with local passenger Colin Hardman, secured third, a mere 3.2 seconds away from runner-up spot.

'Kipper' thrown out! (48)

The Chief Travelling Marshal for the Southern 100 (and of course the TT and Manx Grand Prix) was shocked to be refused service when he and Southern 100 Club Chairman George Costain went for lunch at the Colby Glen Hotel, adjacent to the course on Championship Day, Thursday 14th July 1983.

He was told there was no service to those wearing leathers even though it was obvious why he was doing so and was, as ever, immaculately turned out!

The irony of it all was that the said 'hotel' had a half page advert in that year's Southern 100 race programme inviting you to visit the fully licensed establishment.

Unperturbed, Kipper and George headed south to the Shore Hotel, where they were received with open arms.

1984: Pither's Championship

Artie and Edda Oates were again in top form as they drove their 700 Yamaha to second place in the even numbers qualifying heat for the Southern 100 Sidecar Championship in 1984. Following their fine TT performance, the Ballamodha pair rocketed away from the line in the six-lap race, with fancied runners Tony Baker and Peter Harper left struggling to get away from the grid. At Cross Four Ways on the first lap, the local duo enjoyed a three-second advantage over veteran Dennis Keen, crewed by Colin Hardman. They pulled well clear by the second lap, but then the LCR-type 'worm' machine of Baker and Harper was through the most severe of the traffic and setting about the front-runners.

At Church Bends on lap five, Baker and Harper were right

(48) 1984 - Kipper refused service in the Colby Glen - Advert in race programme

on the Oates' tail and squeezed by on the flat-out burst from Great Meadow to Stadium. The local boys had a brave go at staying with them, but just as in 1983, had little reply to an outfit with considerably more steam. They romped home second, only 2.8 seconds behind Baker and Harper and over 50 seconds clear of Keen and Hardman.

Lowry Burton and Pat Cushnahan's victory in the odd numbers race was from start to finish. They were ahead halfway round the first lap and stayed there throughout. At the flag they were beginning to be pressed by Mike Burcombe and Steve Parker, but were aware that the gap was reducing, finally settling for an advantage of 2.8 seconds. John Phillips and Malc Hollis brought their 750 Yamaha into third.

The Solo races got underway with the quarter-litre class, over twelve laps. Castletown rider, Richard Coates tried extremely hard all through the 12 laps to catch and pass race winner Johnny Rea. Although he always had him in his sights, it was never quite sufficient to force Rea into an error. Sean Collister was going well to start with, however, the clutch started to slip and he fell back to eventually finish 14th. Coates was really forcing on laps nine and ten, but as the rain pelted down, he wisely settled for second spot, five seconds down on Rea, but a huge 2 minutes 13 seconds clear of third placeman John Stoddart. Newcomer Pat McLaughlin was fourth, with Hans Hart fifth and John Harrison completed the top six.

Kenny Harrison led the 350 race from start to finish. Taking the lead going into Church Bends on lap one, he quickly pulled away as he asserted his authority on the treacherous surface. As the roads dried he continued to pull away, leaving Irishman Trevor Steele to wonder where the Ramsey man had gone. The winning margin was 21 seconds, but it didn't reflect Harrison's superiority. Ian Lougher was third, and Andy Cooper fourth.

Richard Coates had an atrocious start, being forced to leap off and push his bike after the planned paddle-start failed to fire up the motor. He must have been in the last few as the pack got away and was faced with extensive traffic to wade through. He stuck gamely to the task and made use of his skill in dealing with the slippery patches all around the circuit. Gradually, he picked them off one-by-one until he claimed fifth place ahead of Dave Pither.

Only minutes after the end of the 350, most of the leading contenders were out again on their big bikes. Buddy Yeardsley was out for the first time on Des Collins' RG

Suzuki and shot away at the drop of the flag and was never seriously threatened. Gary Radcliffe was revelling in the sheer power of the Steve Williams 500 Yamaha. Again it was the first time he had ridden the four and loved everything about it. He had a good go at catching Yeardsley, but after 12 laps was four seconds short of the target. Harrison, riding only a 375cc Formula One twin-cylinder Yamaha, amazingly stayed in the hunt for a while until the pursuit became a little too demanding and he let the pace fall a bit, taking third place. He was never in danger of being caught by Steve Moynihan, who finished fourth. Fifth and sixth were taken by Dave Pither and Ian Lougher. (49)

Thursday's four-race programme commenced with the ten-lap Solo Support race, which was won by Trevor Steele, with Stephen Bull second and David McIlroy third. Douglas man John Crellin was first local to take the chequered flag in fourth, followed by fellow Manxman Sean Collister, fifth and John Stoddart sixth.

The Sidecar Consolation race was next up, and was led by Steve Sinnott and Alan Langton, who were chased hard throughout by Dave Molyneux and Paul Craine, who were well pleased with their runner-up spot, their previous two Southern 100 experiences being unsuccessful. Third were Alan Brown and Andrew Wadsworth. First and second crews, Sinnott and Molyneux shared the fastest lap at 89.68 mph.

The Solo Championship, looked to be similar to the 1300 solo race – in the early stages it was the same riders heading the field; Gary Radcliffe on the Fowler 500 Yamaha was really flying, but one by one, most of the top riders fell by the wayside with mechanical troubles. Favourite to win, Johnny Rea was also out of luck, the Championship going to Dave Pither on his 750 Yamaha. David McIlroy, (498 Suzuki) was second, with Castletown's Richard Coates third on his 347 Yamaha. Colin Wilson, Andy Cooper and Ian Lougher completed the leader board.

The final race of the 1984 series was the nine lap Sidecar Championship. Third in their heat, John Phillips and Malcolm Hollis from Derby came out the winners, as both heat winners, Lowry Burton and Tony Baker were forced out with machine problems. The Oates brothers were riding well and looked set to win the 'best local crew' award, but again engine problems caused the Yamaha to stop. Dennis Keen and local passenger Colin Hardman finished second, as Mike Burcombe and Steve Parker came third. Robert Corkill and Paul Magee collected the 'best locals' award for fifth place.

(49) 1984 - Buddy Yeardsley and Kenny Harrison at Church Bends

Chapter Four

Fifty Years of the Friendly Races 1985 - 1994

1985: King Kenny

To describe the 1985 Southern 100 meeting as a success for riders from the Isle of Man would be an understatement. Ramsey's Kenny Harrison rode to a brilliant hat trick on his 750cc Yamaha, winning the 1300cc, the Solo Founders 1300cc and the Solo Championship. Castletown's Richard Coates rode his 350cc Yamaha and 250cc Cotton machines to two second places, beating Irish ace, Gene McDonnell. Artie and Edda Oates rode to a heat win to start the meeting with a local victory.

Tuesday evening's Sidecar action all began well with Artie and Edda Oates winning the opening race. Lowry Burton and Alan Langton got the verdict in the second heat, after the race was stopped on lap five due to an incident at Stadium Bend, involving Stuart West and Gary Gibson, who thankfully, were not seriously injured. Twenty-four-year-old Gene McDonnell from Port Glenone, scored a convincing win in the hotly contested 250cc race, when he narrowly out-paced local hero Richard Coates after 12 searing laps of the Billown circuit. Ian Newton took a flier and led for five laps until his machine seized. That left McDonnell and Coates to fight it out, but for the Manxman it was a task he was not quite able to complete. At the end he was eight seconds in arrears, but was ahead of Robert Dunlop, who was making his debut at Billown, by 25 seconds. An Ulster trio of Pat McLaughlin, Courtney Junk and Trevor Steele, completed the top six.

In a repeat of the 250cc result, Gene McDonnell and Richard Coates finished first and second in the 350cc race. But it was a lot closer than the 250. Whereas Ian Newton and McDonnell had fought it out at the front with Coates playing a watching brief, this time it was McDonnell and Coates at it hammer and tongs throughout. They changed places constantly, but McDonnell always appeared to have the whip hand. Coates eventually ran out of brakes and was forced to give way at the last corner and sit it out, as McDonnell accelerated for the line with an advantage of a few yards. Andy Cooper was third, with Trevor Steele fourth and Manx duo, Kenny Harrison and Gary Radcliffe, fifth and sixth. (50)

The 1300cc race was a 'Manx' bonanza. Ramsey's Kenny Harrison enjoyed a comfortable win, riding the ex-Rob Brew 750 Yamaha. Kenny led almost from the word go, and finished the 12-lap race with a comfortable 28 second advantage over Lonan's Buddy Yeardsley riding an RG Suzuki. It was a great race for the locals, with no fewer than five Manx riders finishing in the top six. Gary Radcliffe finished third, Paul Hunt fifth and Peter Eaton sixth. The Manx domination was broken by Derby rider Andy Cooper who took fourth position. Championship Day opened with the Solo Founders race and it turned out to be a repeat win for Kenny Harrison following on from his previous evening's win. Gene McDonnell finished second heading a string of Manx riders: Steve Moynihan, Peter Eaton, Buddy Yeardsley and Gary Radcliffe. The Sidecar consolation race was to provide a second local victory. Robbed of a certain championship race placing by a broken drive chain, Dave Molyneux and Paul Craine made amends with a start to finish victory in the six-lap race.

The Solo Championship race saw Kenny Harrison once again out in front on the big Yamaha – chasing hard once again was Buddy Yeardsley on the Wilson & Collins RG Suzuki. Richard Coates tangled with Yeardsley at Ballabeg and fell off, forcing him to retire. As the race continued Paul Hunt looked to have the measure of Peter Eaton, that was until 'Big "H"' slid off at Ballabeg, also retiring from the action. At the flag behind Harrison and Yeardsley, it was Gene McDonnell, Trevor Steele, Andy Cooper and Peter Eaton completing the top six.

The Sidecar Championship provided a win for Geoff Young and Jimmy Cochrane on their 750 Yamaha. Tony Baker and Peter Harper had a shunt on the start line and forced their way up to second at the flag. The Oates brothers and Lowry Burton were still in the picture mid-race and things looked good for a real battle, but all retired within two laps. Third place was eventually claimed by Geoff Bell and Julian Tailford. (51)

(51) 1985 - Tony Baker and Peter Harper 1985 Sidecar Runners - Up, despite a shunt at the start

1986: Kenny unbeatable!

The local contingent made a flying start to the 1986 Southern 100 with a near clean sweep of the two sidecar heats on the opening evening. Dave Molyneux and Paul Kneale won the second leg race, with Robert Corkill and Paul Magee fourth, while Onchan's Colin Hardman chaired Englishman Mick Burcombe to victory in the first leg ahead of local brothers Artie and Edda Oates. Dave Corlett also lending a hand to Steve Sinnott in the third-placed outfit home.

Twice former championship winner Burcombe of Bristol and 'rent-a-passenger' Hardman, who only decided to ride a week before the meeting, led the opening six-lapper from start to finish, after last year's overall winners Geoff Young and Jimmy Cochrane were sensationally sidelined on the opening circuit after doing a 'Joey Dunlop' at Ballanorris, going through the open gateway into the field and out of the race. Artie and Edda Oates could not repeat their success in last year's second heat when they swept to victory on their 750 Yamaha, but were nevertheless a comfortable second on this occasion, some 13 seconds down on the leading pair, in turn a further 26 seconds in front of TT regular Steve Sinnott, who had Glen Vine's Dave Corlett in the hot seat beside him.

The second leg took off at a cracking pace with no fewer than four outfits jostling for position on the opening laps. Bedlington's Geoff Bell and Julian Tailford made the early running up front, but they were chased hard every inch of the way by the local outfits of Dave Molyneux/Paul Kneale and Robert Corkill/Paul Magee, as well as Yorkshiremen Rod Bellas and Geoff Knight on the big 1135cc four-stroke Suzuki. Molyneux and Kneale glided the Eric Bregazzi 750 Yamaha into the lead, exiting from the Black Hole at Billown on lap three and soon set about opening up a lead at the front. They pushed hard, but were never quite able to pull clear of second-placed Bell and Tailford. Nevertheless, the Manx crew recorded the quickest lap of the night with a circuit in 2 minutes 38.4 seconds, a shade over 90 mph, crossing the line a little under five seconds in front of Bell, with Bellas and Knight third and Onchan men Corkill and Magee fourth.

Runner-up twice last year, Richard Coates finally scored a well-deserved Southern 100 victory on his home circuit on Wednesday evening with a start to finish success in the 250cc solo race. The 27-year-old qualified pilot was in a determined mood on Kenyon Crowe's 250cc Rotax-engined Cotton. He never looked threatened from the word go, and soon had a handsome lead as he reeled off the laps in relentless style. Behind him there was a rare old battle for second spot between Phil Burman, Martin Press, John Wilkinson, Sean Collister and Steve Moynihan, the latter making a dreadful start on the Dave Grigson Yamaha. Wilkinson came a cropper at the feet of Manx Radio's Geoff Cannell when winding on the power too quickly at Cross Four Ways, but was largely unhurt and walked to the ambulance with assistance. Burman looked a safe second place, however Moynihan had other plans and, with just two laps to go he nipped past the Gainsborough man to steal second spot. In

(52) 1986 - Sidecar Consolation winners - Geoff Young and Jimmy Cochrane

fact he had begun to reel in Coates' lead in the last few miles setting the fastest lap of the race, but Coates was well signalled and clearly in a position to speed-up had it been necessary. Sean Collister rode a good race on his Armstrong and despite the 'assistance' of Simon Cowin's signal boards, finished a clear fourth in front of the near inseparable trio of Gavin Lee, Peter Wakefield and Raymond Campbell. Kenny Harrison warmed up for the larger capacity races with a 'tour' out on his R&G Video TZR Proddy bike in eighth place.

Kenny Harrison brought his Southern 100 tally to seven wins with a confident double on his brace of super-quick Yamahas. The Ramsey ace, who was born the same year the first Southern 100 was staged on the Billown Course, proved he is the current master of the tight and extremely challenging closed roads circuit without equal. Course newcomer Dave Leach rode extremely well in the early stages of the 350 race, heading Harrison for the first lap until the Manxman powered his Formula 2 Yamaha past into a never-to-be-relinquished lead. Leach was never too far behind on his 320cc special, but he clearly did not have the course knowledge to stick with the experienced Harrison. Steve Moynihan, riding Ronnie Russell's Yamaha, moved into third place when Richard Coates seized his 250cc race-winning Cotton at Church Bends on lap three. Castletown's Decca Kelly moved his way up nicely through the field to pip fellow local Sean Collister, quite literally, on the line for fourth place. Peter Hounsell, also of Castletown, held off Ramsey's Andy Brew for tenth place with Barry Forth riding well in his first Southern directly behind in twelfth.

Kenny Harrison notched up win number seven, less than 40-minutes later when he rode Peter Dawson's faithful 750cc Yamaha to a runaway victory in the twelve-lap 1300cc Unlimited race. Once again he was led away from the line, this time by Irishman Davy Cowan, on the RG Suzuki. But Cowan proved no real threat and, after being overhauled by Harrison and former winner Ian Bell, dropped out on the fifth lap with a broken drive chain. Sadly the fairies were none too kind to Bell either and, after looking in fine fettle again upon his return to the circuit, where he was twice a victor in the early eighties before badly damaging his right foot in a smash at Snetterton, the North Humberside was also sidelined. The problem, a flat rear tyre on the FZ750. This left Junior Manx Grand Prix winner Gary Radcliffe in a secure second place behind Harrison - Gary riding the F1-tuned Dennis Trollope FZ. Although 'Radish' looked equally quick with Kenny on the slower corners, the two-stroke obviously had more steam out of the corners, and Harrison just continued to extend his lead lap after lap. At the close, he had 34 seconds in hand. Moynihan was at it again, clawing his way up through the field after his traditional slow start on the 500 Suzuki. He battled his way from last off the line to fifth at half distance and third at the chequered cloth. Not bad for a forty-year-old who says he doesn't particularly like the circuit! Ulsterman Raymond Campbell followed Steve home in fourth, but it was a good first attempt by Steve Buxton in fifth place some way in front of Gordon Huxley.

Kenny Harrison continued on Thursday, Championship Day, where he left off the previous evening, taking victory in the Solo Founders Race, 21-seconds ahead of Dave Cowan, with Ian Bell third. Dave Leach, Steve Moynihan and David

Montgomery completed the leader board. The Sidecar Consolation was a runaway win for the Geoff Young and Jimmy Cochrane pairing, (52) followed by Howard Oates and Ian Keggin, with fellow locals Keith Griffin and Peter Cain completing the podium. It was that man Harrison, who completed a fantastic week by clinching the newly named "Ronaldsway Shoe Co" Solo Championship from Dave Leach and Gary Radcliffe. Whilst the Sidecar Championship became a Manx benefit, as Dave Molyneux and Paul Kneale lifted the Championship laurels, brothers Artie and Edda Oates, took second spot with Robert Corkill and Paul Magee claiming third.

1987: Changes in programme

1987 saw a re-vamp of the race programme: firstly the two sidecar heats were dropped and replaced with a two-leg Championship, both over nine laps. The 250cc and 350cc races were run concurrently. Classic machines were introduced to the Billown course, which was to prove very popular. Most important, though, was the introduction of 'Match Races', comprising teams from England, Ireland, the 'Rest of Britain' and of course the Isle of Man. These races, sponsored by the Steam Packet Company, were to be run over two, 12-lap legs. Nine races in all, which included the established 1300cc race, the Solo Founders and the 'blue-riband' event of the meeting the Solo Championship.

The 1987 races commenced with the first of the two Match Races on the Tuesday evening. A 'walk-over' victory for Bedlington's Ian Bell by some 76+ seconds would, one supposes, assist towards a commanding points lead as finishing positions were converted into points. But, with Steve Bateman coming home second for the RoB team, Gary Radcliffe third for the Isle of Man, then Dave Madsen-Mygdal fourth for England, followed by Steve Moynihan, Richard Coates, Paul Hunt and Ralph Sutcliffe for the Manx team, it was the locals that headed the scores with 149 points, second was England with 114, third RoB – 64 and Ireland in fourth with 39 points.

Ian Bell and Gary Radcliffe led the home charge in the second leg of the Steam Packet Seaways sponsored Irish Sea Challenge Match. With Andy Ross and Brent Gladwin also packing into the top four behind lone Manxman Radcliffe, it was indeed a good day for the English, who, with the added assistance of Mike Skidmore in tenth spot, went on to win the concluding part of the contest with 133 points. However, with Richard Cotes seventh, Paul Hunt eighth, Phil Hogg 13th, Barry Forth 14th, and Decca Kelly 16th the Manx team salvaged second place on the day and victory overall with 268 points to England's 251, Rest of Britain on 139 and Ireland on 112.

On current form, anyone who attempts to get the better of Kenny Harrison on the Billown circuit is a brave man! Welshman Ian Lougher had the 'audacity, to try it on during the early stages of Tuesday evening's Solo Founders race, but soon had his tail between his legs again as Harrison turned up the wick on the Peter Dawson 750 Yamaha storming away to a 50-second win, in a race cut to three-quarters the originally scheduled length by rain. Speeds were way down though, with Harrison's best of 86.63 mph, some 10 mph slower than the all-time class record produced by Ian Bell back in 1981. Lougher had, in fact, made a late change from a 250 EMC to a 350 Yamaha - causing a fair bit of confusion for the lap scorers - and his decision demoted local rider Gary Radcliffe to second in the 350 class, whilst promoting Sandbach rider, Peter Wakefield, seventh overall, to first in the quarter-litre category.

Steve Moynihan was another rider who had stuck with a 350 machine, but his 'wise' decision to leave the unwieldy RG500 in the van didn't actually help much as he ended up throwing the Yamaha down the road at Alexandra Bridge anyway – luckily without injury. Another man to test the seat of his leathers was Merseysider John Davies who high-sided his Yamaha twin exiting Cross Four Ways. Newcomer, Steve Bateman took third place overall behind Harrison and Lougher, as fellow newcomer Steve Taylor of Chesterfield rode well to oust David Madsen-Mygdal and Gary Radcliffe for fourth.

Castletown's Richard Coates was the filling in two slices of Welsh bread in the opening event of Wednesday evening, the combined 250/350cc race. Ian Lougher, who the previous night had nibbled at Kenny Harrison's heels in the Solo Founders, took charge from Richard, after the Manxman had led the charge on the early laps on Kenyon Crowe's 350 Yamaha, then went on to win the race by almost 20 seconds. Fellow countryman, Kenny Shepherd, an experienced road racer, but a newcomer to the Southern, was the first 250 home in third spot – zapping past the fallen Steve Moynihan on the sprint to the line. Steve had mounted one of his renowned late charges, sneaking ahead of Shepherd and Coates in the dying stages – only to throw the Yamaha up the road at precisely the same spot he had done 24 hours earlier in the Founders race. The pint-sized jockey was once again unhurt, and quickly remounted to salvage fourth place in front of Henry Januszewski. One of the best results of the race came from local man Barry Forth, who, after an almighty crash at the bottom of Bray Hill in last year's Manx, scored one of his best ever results in sixth spot.

Ramsey's Kenny Harrison, twice a former Solo Champion, rattled up his 11th success on the Billown circuit – his second in two nights, and his seventh aboard Peter Dawson's 750 Yamaha. From the off, Sheffield's Brent Gladwin had grabbed the hole shot at Ballakaighan from Davy Cowan and Ian Bell. Then another Sheffield man made a stab for glory, but, sadly, the brave attempt by newcomer Andy Ross was short-lived. His race coming to an abrupt and painful end at Ballabeg Hairpin on lap three, where he dropped the plot. Bell had a lap at

(53) 1987 - Selwyn Griffiths back racing at Billown after a 12 year break

the front before Harrison took the reins on lap four with the quickest circuit of the race – two minutes 40.8 seconds (95.14 mph). Behind Harrison, Bell rode a good race to finish some 10 seconds in front of the ever-consistent Gary Radcliffe in third. Brent Gladwin hung on to fourth, fending off the usual late charge from Steve

Moynihan in fifth.

Double TT winners Lowry Burton and Pat Cushnahan recorded another victory on Manx soil in Wednesday evening's first leg of the new-style Southern 100 Sidecar Championship. The Ulster duo led from the very early stages of the nine-lap race after local favourites Dave Molyneux and Paul Kneale retired at Ballanorris with gearbox problems on the Bregazzi Yamaha. The Manx boys had suffered gear selection difficulties on the warm-up lap, but there was little they or anyone else could do as the seconds ticked away on the start line – other than cross their fingers!

Another local crew in trouble at the start were the Foxdale flyers – Artie and Edda Oates. They'd had difficulties bump starting their outfit all week, and, when the flag dropped, the popular brothers had to push the reluctant beast halfway to Ballakaighan before it eventually fired into life. They battled through the field behind another slow starting pair – Scots Gordon Shand and Johnny Shedden – to eventually take seventh spot at the flag. Up front, Burton and Cushnahan had no problems at all, and, after another midnight-oil-burning-rebuild, the Ironside Yamaha behaved perfectly. Geoff Young and Jimmy Cochrane had a great dice in the early stages for second place with Ian Bell's brother Geoff and Julian Tailford, until the latter went out with fuel pump problems. Rod Bellas and Geoff Knight took third some 20 seconds adrift.

The first Classic race to be held on the Billown circuit was a great success. Bob Hirst, now fully recovered from his Manx Grand Prix spill, won the event on his 1971 Rob North works replica Triumph Trident leading from lap two onwards after seeing off the 'spirited' efforts of Norton Commando mounted Stan Thomas. Welshman Thomas performed all kinds of heroics on his sit up and beg yellow Commando, but sadly his efforts came to an abrupt end on the tenth lap when he came off on the fast left-hander at Ballawhetstone – miraculously escaping serious injury.

Former Manx Grand Prix winner Selwyn Griffiths enjoyed his first outing for more than 12 years, bringing his Ray Cowles G50 home in second place ahead of John Knowles, Seeley, and local plumbing contractor Roger Sutcliffe, who was also riding a 500cc Matchless in the green and red livery of Ray Cowles, this one in a brand new rolling chassis. "It was a marvellous experience," admitted the 1970 Senior Manx Grand Prix winner, "After a few laps familiarising myself with the old single, it was as if I'd never been off one!" (53)

(54) 1987 - Dennis Christian

Former Island resident, Denis Christian, now based in Manchester, made a comeback to the sport after almost 30 years, and rode his Manx Norton well to take eighth spot just in front of Mike Dunn's 250 Greeves. (54)

Hot tip for three in a row, Kenny Harrison was forced to settle for third place in the main 12-lap Solo Championship race, when a slipping clutch at roughly half distance slowed the former Isle of Man champion considerably. Harrison had, in fact, just taken hold of the lead in the race, after shadowing Bedlington's Ian Bell in the initial stages. Bell, always impressive on the Billown circuit, had opened an early lead over the Manxman, but later admitted that there was no way he would have stayed in front of the Dawson Yamaha rider had the clutch difficulties not slowed his progress. As the said clutch began to slip, then so too did Harrison's two-year hold on the Southern 100 Championship title. By three quarters distance, Bell had pulled out a 12-second advantage, one he extended rapidly to 15, then 20 seconds as Harrison slowed further – enabling Gary Radcliffe to draw closer.

With just over one lap to go, 'Radish' powered past the floundering Harrison though by this time it was far too late to do anything about Bell who was just about home and dry. At the chequered flag, Bell was over half a minute clear of Radcliffe, with Harrison a further nine seconds adrift in third spot. Steve Moynihan broke free of the main pack midway through the 52 mile event to finish a lone fourth on the RG 500, some nine seconds up on similarly-mounted David Madsen-Mygdal. Sixth, claiming the best newcomer's award, was Sheffield's Andy Ross – who recovered well after badly grazing his arm in a spill at Ballabeg hairpin the previous evening.

On an aggregate basis, there was no feasible way that Dave Molyneux and Paul Kneale would retain their sidecar championship after dropping out of the Wednesday evening race with a stripped sixth cog on the 750 Yamaha. But, try as they did, and despite a lack of top-end on the straights, the Manx pair fought well to finish the second leg less than eight seconds down on double TT winners Lowry Burton and Pat Cushnahan. Third were Geoff Bell and Julian Tailford and fourth again were local centre championship leaders Rob Corkill and Paul Magee, and this earned them a well-deserved runner-up spot overall behind runaway winners, Burton and Cushnahan. Third overall were Geoff Young and Jimmy Cochrane.

1988: Hat trick for Leach

Such was the popularity of the newly-introduced Classic Race in 1987, that a second Classic Race was added to the programme in 1988, otherwise the schedule remained similar to the previous year.

Quite literally last man away from the line at the start of the first Isle of Man Steam Packet Seaways Irish Sea Challenge Race, Dave Leach was already up into the top 15 at the completion of the opening lap of the rain-drenched circuit. Fellow Englishmen Brent Gladwin and Steve Taylor were making bow waves out in front. Charging hard, and determined to prove Isle of Man team manager Steve Moynihan wrong at not choosing him for the original home team, was Ramsey's Billy Craine. He was still well placed in third spot for his 'adopted' Rest of Britain team as the riders came round to complete lap two, with top local Richard Coates, and team reserve Sean Collister already sidelined. Chesterfield's Steve Taylor grasped hold of the lead on lap three, and slowly but surely began to pull away from team-mates Gladwin and Dave Woolams. Leach joined the chasing pack of six or seven riders behind, which included best placed Manx duo of Gary Radcliffe and Phil Hogg. Craine was shortly to go out of the hunt with a badly misfiring GSX750 Suzuki motor, and, going like a train, Leach was soon up into third spot and pressing down heavily on Woolams. Blasting the RG500 down the start-finish straight at an incredible 142mph, Leach shot past Woolams, four-stroke 750 on lap five, repeating the treatment a lap and a half later when he similarly outpaced the impressive Taylor at Great Meadow.

It was indeed a tremendous ride by Leach to come from last away on the grid, right through the ranks for victory in such a determined style. With Leach, Taylor and Woolams recording a complete rout of the top three positions for the Sassenachs, and Gladwin a high-scoring seventh, it gave the English an early lead in the two-legged Challenge Match of some 14 points. Packed well into the midfield placings, the six local finishers – led by Radcliffe and Hogg in fifth and sixth – achieved a good result to stay well in touch with the leaders on 199. Ireland finished third, helped by a superb debut performance from Portadown's Phillip McCallen in fourth spot, and a determined Raymond Campbell who rode on a front wheel puncture for the last eight miles. The Rest of Britain had a disaster, meantime, with just two riders making it to the finish – both in the bottom quarter of the list.

Tanking down the Castletown by-pass at an incredible 124 mph in the pouring rain, Staffordshire's Bob Hirst won his second Southern 100 Classic event in two years on the melodic Triumph-three. Trailing the G50s of Selwyn Griffiths and Alan Dugdale for most of the eight-lap Manx Telecom sponsored race, Hirst made a successful all-out bid to overhaul Dugdale on the final circuit, after Welshman Griffiths retired for the fourth time in four races on the Billown Circuit this year. Out of luck in all four Pre-TT races on the Southern 100 course in June, Griffiths was more determined than ever to pull off a victory this time, and led away from Dugdale throughout the early stages. Riding the Team Obsolete Matchless, Dugdale was, however, never far away from the plume of spray gushing from the rear wheel of the Ray Cowles-tuned Seeley, and, when Selwyn went out with a broken primary belt drive on lap six, it looked as though Dugdale was on for the win.

However, with a forlorn Griffiths pushing in yet again, Bob Hirst had other plans, and giving the 750 triple its head in the last few miles, he easily reeled in the Matchless, to win by a margin of just under four seconds. Local rider, Michael Cain rode tremendously well on Robert Dowty's 250cc Suzuki to finish third in front of John Knowles, (G50), John Stone, (BSA-3) and Tony Russell on the Ridgeon G50. In conditions not dissimilar to those which 'greeted' riders to the 1987 Solo Founders Race, it was ironic that Dave Leach covered nine laps of the 4.25-mile Billown circuit in a winning time almost identical to Kenny Harrison's effort 12 months earlier – in fact just 1.8 seconds faster after some 38 miles. Once again, Leach struggled to coax the Suzuki into life at the start, and was sixth at the end of the opening circuit with Welshman Ian Lougher well out on his own in front of Phillip McCallen and Brent Gladwin. Leach picked off a couple of places in the next two laps, but found Gladwin, Lougher and McCallen tougher nuts to crack. It took him until lap four to edge past Gladwin's 1000cc Yamaha four-stroke, but it looked as though he may well struggle to clinch a double.

Nevertheless, the gritty Yorkshireman battled on through the constant rain and, in sensational fashion, the three pacesetters headed down the by-pass road in line abreast at the start of the penultimate lap. Needless to say, Leach had the RG in front on the final circuit, eventually taking the chequered cloth just one bike's length in front of the flying McCallen, with Lougher a further second down, after nosing back in front of Leach at the Billown Dip. Gary Radcliffe rode a steady race on a visibly slow 350 Yamaha to take fifth spot behind Gladwin, with Phil Hogg happy to gain seventh with road tyres fitted back and front on his big 1000cc Genesis Yamaha. Decca Kelly was well and truly soaked by the time he splashed across the line in 11th spot, completing his third race of the night in extremely uncomfortable conditions. "I quite enjoyed it really," admitted Decca later with a masochistic glint in his eye! (55)

Irish newcomers Phillip McCallen and Chris Dowd set the Southern 100 alight with a superb one-two in the 250/350cc Solo race. Riding like seasoned veterans, the two young Ulstermen showed without any shadow of a doubt that they are the men to watch in the future with a superb start to finish result on the 4.25-mile Billown circuit. The two were locked together in the early stages of the 12-lap race, and once local hope Richard Coates had spluttered to a halt with a seized 350 Yamaha engine, it was a two horse race all the way to the flag. McCallen, the reigning Irish 125 and 250 road race champion showed his pedigree though, and slowly but surely edged the NS250 Honda clear of his fellow countryman, who was astride the Joe Millar 350 Yamaha. The gap at the completion of the final circuit was some 20 seconds. Welshman Ian Lougher rode a steady race for third, and once other leading hopes Gary Radcliffe and Buddy Yeardsley also retired, Preston's Dave Montgomery finished a lonely fourth. Ralph Sutcliffe enjoyed one of his best rides of the season to bring his Yamaha twin home a solid fourth, three seconds in front of fellow local Barry Forth with Decca Kelly and Dave Broadhead both going well to get into the top ten.

Local rider Phil Hogg was the surprise winner of one of the closest and most thrilling 1300cc races on the Billown circuit for many years. Breaking free from a bunch of eight riders at mid-distance, the 22-year-old joiner from Douglas came under increased pressure in the latter stages of the 12-

(55) 1988 - Phillip McCallen in his debut ride at Billown

lapper from TT ace Dave Leach, who had made another gallant effort after losing the best part of half-a-minute at the start. The early stages had seen three local riders at the front in a superb, and sometimes heart-stopping battle for the lead. Billy Craine led the charge for the first three laps, hard-chased by Hogg and Paul Hunt – all aboard flying four-stroke production-based bikes from rival Suzuki, Yamaha and Kawasaki camps. Billy "Jug" was eventually displaced by Hogg on lap four of the Total Oil sponsored race, with the ensuing pack swallowing Craine in a fashion not unlike the tactics imposed by frontrunners in the Tour De France. Hogg powered onto the Castletown by-pass to start his fifth lap, with Ulsterman Liam Quinn, (Yamaha), Chesterfield's Steve Taylor, (Suzuki), Manxman Gary Radcliffe, (Yamaha), Middlesborough's Dave Woolams, (Suzuki) and the local trio of Craine, Dave Madsen-Mygdal, (Suzuki) and Paul Hunt, (Kawasaki), all hot on his heels. Meantime, after struggling to fire the Padgett-Suzuki into life at the start, Leach was again scything his way through the field. 31st at the end of the first circuit, he moved to 19th, 12th, 11th, 10th and ninth at the half-way point in the 12-lapper. Could he make it past the leading bunch of eight and through for a third victory in two nights?

His plight was aided by the unfortunate departure of Billy Craine one lap later, when, after trying desperately to cling onto the main bunch, he dropped the GSX-R750 on the right-hander at Ballawhetstone. Miraculously, Bill escaped injury – his Manx Leathers taking the brunt of the punishment as he skidded along the course. "That's what happens when you try too hard on a slow bike," he admitted later. "The only thing that hurts is my pride!" Billy was not so fortunate with his bike, "It's a write-off," he revealed. Leach now moved up into eighth spot in this fascinating race, with Hogg consolidating his advantage in front of Quinn and Taylor. Getting used to the big Yamaha four-stroke again – having not been able to get new parts for the Kingswood RC30 Honda in time – Gary Radcliffe was starting to make an impression and nosed free of the pack into fourth spot. Still going like a train, Leach leap-frogged into fifth place ahead of Hunt, Woolams and Madsen-Mygdal on lap nine, while the latter man retired his Ronaldsway Shoe Company sponsored RG500 with a blown clutch on the very next circuit.

Radcliffe was having problems too, and a holed exhaust, which reduced his top-end speed dramatically, softened his late bid for glory. Leach soon dealt with the lame sheep and Steve Taylor, then with two laps to go set about Quinn and Hogg. Going into the last lap, he was five seconds down on the Ulsterman – second place was on the cards, but victory was out of the question unless Hogg did something stupid. Sure enough, Hogg brought the day-glow orange Smart Tyres Yamaha Genesis home first for an extremely popular victory, with Leach overhauling Quinn for an equally commendable second place in the final sprint for the line - recording the fastest lap at 97.70 in the process. "It's beyond my wildest dreams," admitted the down-to-earth Hogg inspecting the scratches on his crash helmet after a last lap brush with a branch. "I'd have been delighted with a top five result, but to win and beat Dave Leach is something I never contemplated." Just for the record book, all the top six bettered Kenny Harrison's winning time in the same race last year, with Radcliffe hanging on for fourth spot behind Quinn and Big 'H', Paul Hunt, fifth on the ZX10 ahead of Dave Woolams.

Ulsterman Lowry Burton notched-up a textbook start to finish victory in the first leg of the Sidecar Championship. With regular ballast Pat Cushnahan holidaying in America, Burton signed Geoff Bell's sidekick Julian Tailford for the annual Southern 100 jaunt, and despite the threat posed by Dave Molyneux in practice, the Carrickfergus veteran never looked in any danger once the flag dropped on race night. Molyneux too had a new man beside him in the Bregazzi Yamaha, in the shape of the vastly experienced Colin Hardman of Onchan. But, despite all-out attempts on the back part of the course, Burton seemed to have the legs on the long straights, pulling yards out on the Manxman on every lap. The gap was only 0.8 of a second at the end of the first circuit – Hardman later revealing that Burton was in fact holding Moly up on certain parts of the course – but from thereon in, Burton's Ironside Yamaha just stretched away into the distance. After three laps (one-third distance), Burton had 11 seconds lead. That advantage was 16 seconds on lap six, and a comfortable 20 seconds by the completion of the ninth and final lap, with Moly wisely settling for a safe second place. Behind them, Rod Bellas and Geoff Knight were third throughout with Steve Pullan/Tony Darby fourth, Gordon Shand/Johnny Shedden fifth, Robert Fisher/Trevor Crowe sixth, and Eric Cornes/Graham Wellington continuing the procession in seventh.

Local passenger Dave Corlett helped Steve Sinnott into eighth spot, while the ride of the race was surely the last-to-ninth performance of Artie Oates and the relatively inexperienced Stuart Pitts. After changing plugs at the very last minute in the holding area, the pair were still in a fluster on the start line when they were left with a gassed-up motor. Eventually getting into the fray, the pair drove a real stormer to pick-off one outfit every lap. "That's as hard as I've ever ridden around here," admitted Artie between gasps later, "but the true hero was Stuart." Passenger Dicky Gale was lucky to escape with nothing more serious than broken bones in his hand after losing his grip and falling out of the back of Kevin Christian's 750 Yamaha exiting from Iron Gate. "I'm probably the first man to go over the Ballanorris Railway Bridge on the seat of my pants," quipped Dicky later.

With a push start from the rear of the field, Yorkshire flyer Dave Leach made his best getaway of the week in the second and concluding leg of the Isle of Man Seaways Irish Sea Challenge Match Race on Thursday afternoon. Nevertheless Leach was forced to contend with 1300cc class winner Phil Hogg, who was still over-brimming with confidence after his famous victory the previous evening. Leach eventually edged clear to cross the line just 3.6 seconds in front of Hogg, but the pair recorded identical laps of 97.27 mph for the joint fastest times of the race. Irishman Liam Quinn repeated his third place from the 1300cc race, with Gary Radcliffe fourth and Dave Woolams fifth. With Steve Taylor, Dave Madsen-Mygdal and Steve Dowey all making it into the top ten, it gave England another leg victory and overall success by 276 points to the Isle of Man's 215. Ireland were third with 188 points and the Rest of Britain 87 points.

After luckless Selwyn Griffiths suffered an unprecedented fifth successive retirement on the Billown circuit this year, Alan Dugdale and Alan Smith went on to score the closest ever finish to a Southern 100 race to date, in the second Manx Telecom Classic race. Griffiths went out on the third circuit, and with race one winner Bob Hirst already similarly sidelined, the lead was handed over to Cheshire's Dugdale on the Team Obsolete G50 Matchless. However, he was overhauled by John Stone's BSA Rocket-Three on lap six, only for the latter's clutch to start slipping a-lap-and-a-half later. This signalled the start of a great challenge by Alan Smith of Leicester on his three-cylinder Triumph and it was he who came through to 'dead heat' with Dugdale at the finish on Castletown by-pass at the end of the eighth and last lap. Stone coaxed his ailing Beeza home third, with local man Decca Kelly fourth on the sweet sounding Honda four. Mike Cain was fifth with yet another good performance on Bob Dowty's 250 Suzuki twin, while Hull's Trevor Beharrell brought the 7R AJS into sixth spot.

The 1988 Solo Championship race was stopped on the sixth lap, when Derbyshire's Steve Taylor was fatally injured. The Solo Championship race was not restarted at the wishes of Steve Taylor's fellow riders and the result was announced null and void. Dave Molyneux knew only too well before the start of the second and concluding leg of the Southern 100 Sidecar Championship race that, realistically, he was racing for second place. More than a match for Ulster veteran Lowry Burton on the slower twistier stages of the Billown circuit, 'Moly' was equally aware that there was no way he could stay with Lowry on the straights. On what was virtually a re-run of the previous evening's opening leg, Burton and Julian Tailford led Molyneux and Colin Hardman throughout, with Rod Bellas and Geoff Knight again third. As consistent as ever, Burton's winning time for the nine laps was – amazingly – just eight-tenths of a second quicker than on the previous evening. Fourth, after the retirement of Steve Pullan and Tony Derby, were Gordon Shand and Johnny Shedden, with Artie Oates and Stuey Pitts this time enjoying a clean start-to-finish run in fifth spot.

The fatal crash involving Steve Taylor cast a cloud over the final day of racing in the 1988 Southern 100. Up until that point, the meeting had been one of the most exciting for years. And, despite the far from ideal weather for at least one of the evenings, there had been no serious incidents.

Barry Wood

I first saw the Southern 100 in 1971 when one of our neighbours, Henry Faragher, gave us a lift down from Willaston in his brown J4 van. We parked near the airport and walked across a bridge and some fields to Church Bends to watch the 250cc, 350cc and 750cc races.
That was my first taste of the Southern 100 atmosphere and I was hooked! Ray McCullough won the 250cc race and diced for the lead in the 750cc before retiring, this one being won by Bill Smith after he had been hard pressed by Gordon Pantall, both on 500cc Kawasakis.

In those days it was a long journey on the 'red' bus from Douglas Bus Station to Castletown. I say 'red' bus because we only usually travelled on the 'yellow' Corporation buses from town to Willaston, where I lived. A ride on the 'red' Road Services bus was a great treat because it meant going out-of-town, exciting stuff because we had no other mode of transport. In the early 70s, this bus was always crammed with people, locals and holidaymakers alike, heading down to watch the Southern 100. I can remember the excitement of the bus being overtaken by racing bikes

being ridden to scrutineering. Not road-type machines like today, but Nortons Aermacchis, Ducatis and screaming two-stroke Yamahas and Suzukis. You could smell them as they passed!

As we got off the bus opposite the Duck's Nest (now the Sidings), and walked up the road to Castletown Corner, we encountered people selling programmes at the road-side and rushed to buy one to see who was racing: McCullough, Herron, Guthrie, Charlie Williams, Ian Richards, Bill Smith, George Fogarty plus our own Danny Shimmin and Neil Kelly. Magical names to a 7-year-old road race fan!

In those days my mother could only afford to take us to one night's racing owing to the cost of the bus fares, so I had to choose either the Tuesday or Wednesday evening races, and settle for having to stay at home and tuning in to the Manx Radio commentary from the start and Ballabeg for the other races.

In 1973, I opted for the Tuesday night programme of a Sidecar Race and Kart Races – secretly hoping I would somehow be able to go again the following night! Unfortunately it turned out to be one of the vilest, coldest, wettest on record, and we still have a cutting from the Sunday News, a Manx Sunday paper from that period, which has a photo of a rain-soaked grandstand with about half-a-dozen people on it and the caption 'Not even the rain could deter these hardy fans.' That was us! Of course, we didn't get back down the following night either!

I managed to see almost every race at the Southern from the mid 1970s onwards. Seeing as the Thursday Championship race was also the day of the Eastern District Inter-School Sports (which I was never in), it was deemed to be OK for me to stay off school in order to go to Castletown that day!

I remember Joey's debut there, learning his trade following Ray McCullough. Also Ian McGregor and Trevor Steele from the Dromara Destroyers, crossing swords with Mervyn Robinson and Frank Kennedy of the Armoy Armada – just like in Ireland! I got all their autographs in the paddock – Joey, Mervyn, Jim Dunlop, Graham Young etc and still have them.

In 1977 I watched Ron Haslam complete several super-quick practice laps on the Pharaoh Yamaha, with spectacular wheelies out of Castletown Corner, before Bill Smith, following a dispute with the club race committee, pulled him out of the meeting.
I remember the first 100mph laps by Brian Reid in the solos and Steve Webster in the Sidecars.

And so to roll forward a few years...

I first competed myself in the Southern 100 in 1988 on a brand new Yamaha TZR250, which I had purchased for the Newcomers' Manx Grand Prix, which I debuted that year.

I had a strange experience in an early morning practice there, which was amusing looking back but was actually quite scary at the time. The 250/350 was the first session at 5.00am, and I was there very early and got my bike through scrutineering. No other bikes seemed to want to go out, for some reason, which was rather odd as it was a beautiful morning. Anyway, next thing was a marshal opened the gate – it could have been Gordon Clague – and he told me to go. I said to him "What about the others?" to which he replied "Bugger them, just get going!" Now this wasn't a very nice feeling at all, and I reckoned the marshals had it all wrong and the roads were actually still open. I did a lap on the left-hand side of the road, like it was a Sunday afternoon, in case a car or tractor should appear coming towards me on the road. At the end of the first lap there was still no sign of anybody, so I decided to crack on. At the end of a third lonely lap, I was delighted to spot Decca Kelly at the roadside by the paddock, warming up a TZ350.

Next time round the chequered flag was put out – it was quite a relief to get back to the paddock and discover that there were two sessions per class, and most of the riders had opted for an extra hour's kip and go out in the second session. Somebody told a friend of mine at work later that day, that in the first session this morning there were only four bikes out – and three of them were Barry Wood!"

I remember on the first lap of my first ever Southern 100 race on my TZR, and heading flat-out towards Great Meadow, near the back of the pack, when I saw yellow flags being waved furiously, but nobody seemed to be slowing up. Through the right kink and thankfully no big crash as it first suggested. Then I saw the problem – a collie dog was sprinting down the right-hand parapet, chasing the bikes and barking at them. He could have run into the road at any moment with disastrous consequences, but thank God he didn't. There was no sign of him after that, so he must have been 'apprehended'.

I first rode in the Pre-TT Classic in 1990 on Bob Dowty Junior's 250cc and 350cc Suzukis. It was my first ever ride on these machines and I hoped to impress. On my fourth practice lap on the 250, I was over 9 seconds inside the lap record, although I was unaware of this at the time. As I came over the rise before Church Bends and shut off, the bike suddenly seized and locked-up the back wheel. It slid out to the left, then the right and flung me down the road into the wall, which was thankfully well baled. Everyone (including myself) was of the opinion I had been showing off and trying too hard, so in a way, it was a relief to discover that it HAD seized. I could hardly move next day and spent most of it having LUMA baths, while Bob and Selwyn Morgan repaired the considerable damage to the bike.

The next day, Race Day, I was totally clad in bandages to my upper body and was allowed to start at the back of the grid with the aid of a pusher. The weather was atrocious, dark with torrential rain, and I only managed one lap in each race before I had to stop with misfires. I remember it was so wet; the rain soaked through my red leathers and turned all the bandages pink!

Another embarrassing incident occurred at the start of the 125/400cc race in 1992, but it could easily have been much more serious. I lined up on a 250cc Suzuki RGV, and when the flag finally dropped gave it a big handful of throttle. Incredibly, my steering damper broke and somehow jammed the steering slightly to the left. I grabbed the front brake and crashed, mounting the left-hand parapet and into the pig-wire fencing. I only got about 20-yards! I was unhurt, but I can remember seeing people scarper as I got into trouble, and my bike could so easily have gone through the fence into the spectators.

I always dread breaking down at Castletown Corner and having to walk back to the paddock, as I know it's going to take me at least an hour. I used to work for the Highway Board for many years, and lots of the old Southern fellows like to watch the races from down the Straight. The trouble is everybody insists on being told what is wrong with the bike. There could be three (imaginary) fellows, Kelly, Corlett and Kinley all watching together, and Kelly asks what's wrong, while the other two listen in to the story. Then you have to tell Corlett the exact same story while Kelly and Kinley listen too. Then you have to tell Kinley. The dozens of others on the way! Of course I don't mind really – I'd be more upset if they didn't ask me – but it can take ages to reach the paddock. These Manx fellas can't half yap, Yessir!

I had the misfortune a few years back to go down at Stadium Corner during the first session on Monday evening, wrecking a new 250 in the process. The marshals, as always, were wonderful, and kept me there a few minutes before bringing a stretcher and carrying me down the road to an ambulance at Castletown Corner, then off to Nobles. Although very shaken and with both elbows badly ripped open, I wasn't too bad considering where it happened! As I lay in the ambulance, I became aware that someone else behind me was also receiving treatment. But it wasn't another faller. It turned out that one of the marshals had quickly grabbed a lump of broken fairing from the road, and the jagged edge of the fibreglass had sliced his hand open. I felt awful about it!

Last year I went down in my van to the Presentation in the Square on Thursday night. Seeing as I had to be up for work at 4.00 am the next morning, I decided on a nice quiet evening, collect my trophies and head for home. I have a corgi dog called Benji, who occasionally is allowed to go to a motorbike race. So he came with us to the Presentation. He had a wonderful time meeting lots of people, stealing chips, and generally being the centre of attention, which is typical of him. All went perfect until about 10.00 pm, when a surprise firework display erupted from behind the Castle walls.

The bangers and loud music caused Benji to freak out completely, barking and squealing, with a large crowd watching us and laughing. Very embarrassing. So that was the end of my night. He was taken back to the van and home to bed. Must remember to leave him at home this year! Southern 100 memories- hopefully there will be many more yet. Like the time in 1990 when there was a last lap spill at Ballabeg in the Senior Solo Founders Race, and I saw the yellow flags and slowed – only to be confronted by Des Evans, Travelling Marshal, standing right in my path, just out of sight around the corner. I hit him with a wallop, and saw him put both hands out towards me in an attempt to deflect the inevitable contact. I managed to stay on and finish the race, pig-sick that I had knocked Des over. First thing was to find out if he was OK – it was a great relief to see him in the paddock, with a big grin on his face, looking for me to see if I was OK!

I hope everyone reading this has a great time at the Southern 100 this year, and for many more years to come, with many of your own amusing and remarkable experiences.

Barry Wood

(56) 1989 - Start of first Match Race

1989: Five out of five for Leach (56)

Yorkshireman Dave Leach made a blistering start to the 1989 Southern 100 with two runaway victories and a record-equalling 100 mph lap of the 4.25-mile Billown circuit. Clearly in a class of his own, the 26-year-old professional road racer from Halifax wasted little time jostling his way past the quicker starters in the opening race of the meeting – the 12-lap first leg of the Invitation Match Race – powering to victory on the 750 OWO1 Yamaha in front of local men Kenny Harrison and Gary Radcliffe. Both Kenny and Gary rode extremely well in the wake of the double TT winner, but more importantly bagged 53 points between them in the team race contest, with full support from Dick Coates (7th), Brian Venables (8th), Ralph Sutcliffe (10th), Norman Kneen (14th), and Paddy Martin (17th). This gave the Isle of Man the lead going into the second leg, with a tally of 142 points. England, led by Leach and supported strongly by Nigel Barton (4th), Island resident David Madsen-Mygdal (5th), and Colin Wilson (6th), were a clear second on 108 – lacking midfield domination of the Manx. The Rest of Britain squad held onto third spot, but their best-placed man across the line was Kevin Jones in ninth. Ireland were struggling at the bottom of the table after leading hopes Davy Cowan and Davy Johnstone both retired, and TT favourite Sam McClements failed to turn up. Team Result – IoM 142 points, England 108, Rest of Britain 98, Ireland 52.

Londoner, Asa Moyce, a former regular TT man who's making a comeback on the Classic scene at the ripe old age of 34, had played a waiting game before gunning his Triumph-triple past the single cylinder G50 of veteran Alan Dugdale on the final lap, pipping the Cheshire garage owner by a wheel's length. It had been a close race, though, with Moyce virtually in the slipstream of the Matchless throughout. Selwyn Griffiths finally broke his run of bad luck on the course to finish a steady third on the Ray Cowles G50, while Tony Osbourne brought another of the howling Trident triples into fourth place. Moyce's last lap "ace card" gave him a new outright course record for the Classic at a speed of 86.83mph – not bad for a newcomer! (57)

By the time Dave Leach came to the line for the Solo Founders Race he was well fired up, and after getting a considerably better start he was soon out on his own in front of initial second place man Dave Madsen-Mygdal on the ex-Tony Mang HB Suzuki 500. Kenny Harrison soon swept past Madsen-Mygdal who was later also overhauled by Gary Radcliffe, so-producing the same 1-2-3 as in the opening

race. Those three were phenomenally quick through the frightening left-right twist between granite stone walls at Ballanorris Farm, but it was the infamous "Black Hole" at Billown where Leach and Harrison both had hairy moments. Each of them later blamed 'rider error' quite modestly, and relatively nonchalantly – by all accounts Leach had the rear end of the bike stepping out on at least a couple of heart-stopping occasions. Harrison had another hairy moment at Great Meadow on lap six when overtaking a backmarker. "The bike got into a tank-slapper and it was still wobbling at the Castletown Stadium," admitted the Ramsey ace later. But, it did little to slow the pace of either man, and Leach equalled Brian Reid's six-year-old 100mph record on the third lap, when the roads were still relatively clear, without lapped riders. In a considerably quicker race, all three leader board men upped their finishing times quite considerably, with Harrison just 18 seconds down on Leach, and Radcliffe in turn a further 16 seconds behind Harrison on his 1000cc Fowler Yamaha – having ridden the Kingswood RC30 in the team race. Madsen-Mygdal rode well to hang onto fourth, while Ralph Sutcliffe produced one of his best rides for some time with a superb result in sixth place, behind Nigel Barton. Only the elite top six escaped being lapped by the flying Leach.

Richard Coates won his second Southern 100 race in three years when he took his immaculately prepared Kenyon Crowe Yamaha twin to a calculated victory in the 250/350cc race. Out on his own from the very first lap, the Manx Airlines sponsored rider always maintained the gap a safe five to six seconds over Preston's Dave Montgomery with Ulsterman David Johnston nursing his raucous sounding Honda to a class victory in the 250s, some 40 seconds down on Montgomery at the flag. Davy Cowan, Mick Withers and Peter Wakefield enjoyed a great scrap for fourth, eventually falling in Cowan's favour from Withers and fast finishing Ralph Sutcliffe, who, together with fellow local Sean Collister, ousted an ailing Wakefield for sixth and seventh places respectively in the latter stages. Gary Radcliffe went out when holding onto third place at half distance, fearing his LC engined 350 was seizing up.

Win number three for the impregnable Dave Leach came in the Total Oils 1300cc race, as he finally cracked Ulsterman Brian Reid's six-year-old outright Southern 100 lap record when he gunned his 750 Yamaha around the 4.25-mile Billown course in two minutes 34.4 seconds, equal to 100.39 mph. Again out on his own from the very early stages of the race, the Yorkshireman was made to work a good deal harder by the insistent Kenny Harrison – who came agonisingly close to the magic ton-up lap as he pulled out all the stops to stay with his rival. Gary Radcliffe went out of his second race of the evening, when an ignition fault was thought to have caused intermittent cutting out on the big Yamaha – leaving the two virtually untouchable. After wisely settling for second place in the latter half of the race, Harrison was finally denied a finish by a blunder in his own camp, when the Yamaha ran out of fuel entering Church Bends for the 11th time. Always tightly marked for excess weight in the tank, Harrison obviously

(57) 1989 - Classic Master Asa Moyce

never estimated for consistently lapping quicker than he'd ever done before – and he paid dearly for his mistake by losing a certain £100 in prize money! Nigel Barton, who'd sat comfortably some half a lap in arrears of the leading pair, gratefully accepted a hoist-up into the runner-up place, shadowed across the line by similarly RC30 mounted Colin Wilson. Superb rides again from Ralph Sutcliffe and Brian Venables, who kept plugging away steadily to deservedly fill fourth and fifth places respectively, while one or two of the pre-race favourites slipped by the wayside. Sixth home was newcomer Kevin Jones.

Dave Molyneux and Colin Hardman were denied almost certain victory in the first leg of the Sidecar Championship, by a broken gearbox. Molyneux had powered the Bregazzi Yamaha into an early five-second lead over a posse of chasing outfits, then a gearbox failure on the third circuit saw them lose third cog altogether, enabling the hounds to close in. His superior skills on the twistier parts of the circuit enabled the Manxman to keep his nose ahead of a titanic struggle for second between Geoff Bell/Janet Low, Victor Jefford/Peter Hill and Rod Bellas/Geoff Knight. Then, just when it looked as though Moly would hang on for victory, the gearbox finally gave up the ghost at Great Meadow on the penultimate lap, and he and Colin were forced to push in for an eight-lap finish in 12th spot. This left the chasing outfits with a final five-mile scrap for the honours - and it was Bedlington's Geoff Bell (brother of former solo champion, Ian) who finally outwitted his rivals in what was one of the closest ever sidecar finishes on the circuit, with just 1.6 seconds covering the first three across the line. Jefford and Bellas were the men at the helm in those two hard-chasing outfits, but it was the lady sat beside Bell in that winning machine who deservedly was the happiest. Janet Low had stepped in to replace Geoff's regular ballast-man, Julian Tailford, at a late stage, and was surprised, to say the least, at her own piece of history-making, achieving the first ever victory by a woman on the Billown circuit in more than 30 years of racing. The new class for 350cc machines saw Southern first-timers Neville Turner and John McGregor setting a scorching pace to win from Gordon and Julie Jones by some 74 seconds, good enough for ninth place overall.

Dave Leach had one worrying moment during the concluding leg of the Invitation Irish Sea Challenge Race, when, after rolling back the pace at mid-distance due to an overheating problem with the Yamaha, he was very nearly caught napping by twice former champion Kenny Harrison. "I was worried when the temperature gauge went to red, but I thought I was OK when I mistakenly read a +12 board coming out of Ballabeg for the last time. What it really said was +2," admitted the friendly Yorkshireman. "Then coming into Cross Four Ways there was Kenny creeping up the inside to overtake me!" Another squirt from the right-hand saw Leach just out-sprint the Manxman to the line – but it was the nearest anyone came to actually getting the better of the Production TT winner all week. When Dave's father checked the radiator of the OWO1 shortly after, there was no more than a cupful of water present.

Harrison had in fact led Leach on the first lap and a half or so of the race before the Yorkshire star swept past – but quite honestly the 35-year-old Ramsey man was having to stretch himself to the limits to stay in touch – although he was in turn head and shoulders above the rest of the field.

Gary Radcliffe brought the RC30 Kingswood Honda into third place some 43 seconds behind the leading pair at the flag, while local resident David Madsen-Mygdal represented the English team in fourth. On the day, the Manx boys extended their team advantage to a winning margin of 50 points over the English – again thanks to midfield domination provided by Brian Venables, Richard Coates, Ralph Sutcliffe and brothers Norman and Phil Kneen. Overall points: Isle of Man 293; England 243; Rest of Britain 167; and Ireland 75.

Hampered by a cracked cylinder barrel in the first Classic race, Londoner Asa Moyce made no mistakes in the second Manx Telecom sponsored race. He rode his Miles Triumph Trident to a runaway double some five seconds clear of the leading G50 Matchless singles piloted so smoothly by Alan Dugdale and Selwyn Griffiths. Any slim hopes Kenny Harrison had of getting one over on Dave Leach in the main race of the week were very soon dashed when he struggled to fire his 1000cc FZR Yamaha into life at the start of the 12 lap Solo Championship. Leach was off like a rocket, chased hard by Nigel Barton, Dave Madsen-Mygdal and company, while Harrison was as low as 15th or 20th going into Ballakaighan after being accidentally struck a glancing blow by close friend Richard Coates in the start-grid melee.

Leach was already some 80 yards clear of fellow Englishmen Colin Wilson and Nigel Barton at the start of lap two, while Harrison was charging, and already up into the top 10. He was sixth on lap three, fourth soon after – and back up into his traditional second place behind Leach by half distance. So quick was his pace that he, in fact, began to eat away at Leach's comfortable 20 second advantage, but once acknowledged, Dave was not in the mood for charity this time – and he upped his pace once more to cross the line for his first ever Southern 100 Championship victory some 24 seconds in front of the Manxman. Gary Radcliffe got the better of Nigel Barton to grab his fourth third place of the week behind Leach and Harrison, while Madsen-Mygdal also edged Barton out before the flag for fourth. Colin Wilson completed the leader board.

To round off another superb week of road racing on the Billown circuit, all eyes were focused on Dave Molyneux and Colin Hardman to avenge their previous evening's disappointing gearbox failure, which had cost them certain victory in the opening leg of the Sidecar Championship. They got a flyer of a start, and were leading the race comfortably at the start of the second lap when the gremlins struck again. "I was accelerating up through the box onto the start and finish straight, when again third gear went amiss," revealed Moly later. "It's incredible, we changed the entire engine and gearbox unit over after last night's breakage – but the same problem has occurred. It's a tough course on gearboxes." A similar fate was to befall up-and-coming Victor Jefford, later the same lap, while leg one winners Geoff Bell and Janet Low went through the open gate at Ballanorris, and did a quick pirouette in the field before retiring – Janet suffered a painful neck with whiplash.

This series of events – all within a couple of miles of one another – left Rod Bellas and Geoff Knight out in front ahead of Ayrshire's Gordon Shand and Phil Gravel. Bellas and Knight went on to win the race, and take the overall honours after being third in the previous race, while regular top dog Steve Sinnott rode his tuned Yamaha into runner-up spot with local passenger Dave Corlett – following the departure of Shand and Gravel. Following a race-long dice for third between Alan Budge and Bob Munro, Manxmen Artie Oates and Stuart Pitts finally split the pair of battling four-strokes for a superb fourth after struggling away last at the start and scything their way through the field. The Formula Two class went to Gordon and Julie Jones of Shropshire, who grabbed victory in the second leg, when hard-charging Manxmen Paul Kneale and Karl Ellison overshot Cross Four Ways on the last lap. The pair had also fluffed the start, but had come through to lead after pre-race favourites Neville Turner and John McGregor were black-flagged in the early stages after bursting a tyre on a kerb.

1990: Leach dominates!

The new decade saw a revamp of the race programme; the Match Races were no more in the 11-race programme, which now included an additional Sidecar Championship for Formula 2 machines. The 125cc class returned after an absence of 25-years – to this class was added the new 400cc Supersport class, plus the 600cc Supersport category, whilst the Solo Founders race

(58) 1990 - Kenny Harrison

was now split into two races: one for Junior, the 125/400 and 350cc machines; the Senior catering for the 600s and unlimited machines up to 1300cc. The top three names at the 1990 Southern 100 chalked-up a win apiece on the opening night of racing. Welshman Ian Lougher stormed to victory in the Junior Solo Founders; Dave Leach cakewalked the Senior race; and local star Kenny Harrison blitzed the opposition in the Manx Telecom Classic race.

Leach and Harrison both shattered the previous existing lap and race records in their respective races. In spite of his tremendous Junior TT victory, many were still surprised by the way Ian Lougher rode to success in the opening 12-lapper with such consummate ease – particularly when the line-up included Dave Leach. But Lougher's a tremendously underrated competitor, and, whilst Leach did attempt to stay glued to the rear wheel of Ian's machine in the early stages of the race, there was never really any way he was going to get the better of the Cardiff man and the super quick Ray Cowles 250 Yamaha. The bigger surprise, perhaps, was the fine ride of Ulster's Derek Young who caught and passed Dave Leach for second place in the closing stages of the race. Richard Coates was the best of the local brigade in fifth spot on his eight-year-old TZ350 Yamaha, with new resident Andy Bassett, Laxey's Paul Rome, and Ramsey man Greg Broughton in line astern, 9th, 10th and 11th.

More at home on the 750, Dave Leach wasted no time getting to the front of the pack in the following Senior Solo Founders race. He had 50 yards or more in hand on Kenny Harrison and Colin Wilson at the end of the first circuit, and he'd extended that to very nearly 50 seconds by the end of the race. Harrison went out on lap three after the rear tyre on his RC30 deflated, and the runner-up slot was taken over by Ian Lougher – riding well first time out on

Bob Heath's 750 Honda. Gary Radcliffe rode another blemish-free race to secure third place in front of fellow Manx Grand Prix winner Nigel Barton, whilst Peel's Brian Venables came good at the end to finish sixth behind Ulsterman Davy Cowan. There was no living with Leach, though. His race average at 98.667 mph was the second quickest ever, up until then, which was a race record, and his fastest lap on the fourth circuit equalled his own previous outright best at 110.525 mph.

Kenny Harrison's victory in the Manx Telecom sponsored Classic race was equally predictable. The combination of the best rider on the fastest machine was just too much to cope with for the remainder of the 40-strong field. 'Pumped-up' after losing the wind out of his sails in the earlier race, Harrison had gunned the sweet sounding Triumph Trident into an amazing 12-second lead by Cross Four Ways on the opening circuit, just three miles into the race! He upped his speed further to break Asa Moyce's previous 85 mph lap record on lap three, by which time he was already closing down rapidly on back markers, before setting an incredible 89.26 mph circuit next time round. He slackened the pace in the closing stages to cross the finish line some one and a half minutes - half a lap - clear of runner-up Selwyn Griffiths on the G50 Matchless - Selwyn having pipped Dave Storrey at the line by six-tenths of a second. Danny Shimmin brought the Dowd Norton into seventh place, two places in front of Ramsey's Derek Whalley. (58)

Dave Leach rewrote the Southern 100 record books on the second evening's racing when he became the first ever rider to lap the 4.25-mile Billown Circuit at 101 mph. And he did it without any real pressure, suggesting that it's well within his capabilities to raise the outright record even further.

Fellow TT hero Ian Lougher was in good form too, and as well as notching up another win in the combined 250/350 race, he recorded a first ever ton-up lap in the 1300cc class. Leach blasted to the front of the pack in the Total Oil 1300cc Race, and was soon streaking into a comfortable lead. Such was his pace that the new outright record came on the second lap, completing the circuit in a shade over two and a half minutes.

By this time he was already some six seconds clear of Lougher, with Dave Madsen-Mygdal, Colin Wilson, Gary Radcliffe, Paul Hunt and Kenny Harrison vying for third. Harrison had leap-frogged his way into third place on lap five, but was clearly too far behind to challenge

(59) 1990 - Geoff Bell and Jimmy Cochrane approach Ballawhetstone

Lougher for second. The Ramsey man's race eventually came to an end on lap ten when the RC30 spluttered to a halt with fuel surge. Paul Hunt had come to a halt at Cross Four Ways, and he was to be joined there on the very last lap by the unfortunate Brian Venables – after looking certain of another good top ten result. By this time Leach and Lougher were home and dry, with the ultra-steady Gary Radcliffe completing a carbon copy 1-2-3 of the previous evening's Senior Founders Race. Dave Madsen-Mygdal held off a fast finishing Nigel Barton for fourth – the Senior Manx Grand Prix winner having been as low as 20th on the first lap.

Earlier, Lougher had won the 250/350 race at a canter, but the performance again of the Southern 100 debutant Derek Young in finishing second was indeed impressive. Richard Coates rode well again on his museum piece, and very nearly held Dave Leach off for third, until the dying stages of the race. Artie Oates and Stuart Pitts completed two Southern 100 sidecar races in less than an hour on Wednesday evening, and finished in the top seven in each. Their best ride was a second place in the Formula Two race, which rounded off the evening's proceedings, a result matched by fellow locals Mike Masheter and Greg Mahon in the preceding Formula One race over a similar six-lap distance.

The opening race was the better of the two with no fewer than four different crews enjoying a share of the lead before impressive newcomers Jeff Smith and Andrew Jarvis of Goole took the chequered flag. Early leaders Vic Jefford and Pete Hill got no further than Iron Gate, whilst Alan Budge and Dave Mitchell went out a lap or so later after also setting the pace for a short time. This left flying Scotsman Gordon Shand and stand-in passenger Keith Cornbill out in front for the next three laps – only to overshoot on the penultimate circuit and slip to fourth. Mike Staiano and Peter Williams looked like battling it out with Jeff Smith and Andrew Jarvis over the last handful of miles, but a mistake let through the rapid finishing locals Masheter and Mahon for a superb second place, with Mike Salmon and Tony Wilde of Cambridge just one second behind in third.

Tom Bennett recruited internationally known chairman Chris Founds to edge Oates and Pitts out of the top six. "That was only a bit of a practice session," claimed Artie minutes later, as he readied the dual-qualifying 600 'Kwacka' for the F2 race. And it certainly looked that way as Artie and Stuart fired away alongside Geoff Bell and Jimmy Cochrane at the head of the field. Those two crews battled closely for the first half of the race, sharing the fastest lap at 85 mph dead. Slowly but surely, though, the Englishmen extended their advantage into a ten second lead at the flag. It looked as though Oates and Pitts had thrown the towel in as the pair flashed past the paddock to start their final lap – but Stuey was discarding his baseball boot, the lace of which had come undone and was flapping dangerously close to the rear wheel! Dougie Jewell again partnered Ormskirk's Derek Rumble to a good result, the pair finishing fifth, just ahead of Dennis Proudman and Dicky Gale – whilst Alan Warner and Cat Jenkins rode extremely well to pip Steve Sinnott and Dave Corlett for seventh after being left at the start. (59)

Realistically no one predicted anything other than a Dave Leach victory in Thursday's finale to a sizzling Southern 100 week, 1990. But few expected his winning margin to be less than three seconds at the conclusion of the fastest ever race

at that time. Hero of the hour was local man Kenny Harrison, who, after bitter disappointment in the two 1300cc qualifying races earlier in the week, was in sensational form. He pushed the triple TT winner every inch of the way, making him work hard in the late afternoon heatwave for his £600 prize money.

Having checked carefully that both tyres on the RC30 were fully inflated, whilst the machine was also carrying a substantial amount of petrol, it was indeed Harrison who grabbed the holeshot into Ballakaighan on the opening lap. He held off Leach until Church Bends where the Yorkshireman dived up the inside. At that point it looked as though Leach would once again dictate the pace from the front, but a fiercely determined Harrison had other ideas. And, despite giving away almost ten years to the Yamaha man, he continued to stay right with the Ulster based star. Having never gone above the 100 average before, Harrison did just that on the second lap, then joined the exclusive '101 Club' alongside Leach next time round.

Behind these two, Ian Lougher was again the buffer between the pacesetters and the chasing pack which included Nigel Barton, Colin Wilson, Gary Radcliffe and Dave Montgomery. At mid-distance, Harrison was still stuck firmly on the tail of Leach. The latter man admitted that he'd slackened the pace at one point after the temperature gauge on the OWO1 hit boiling point in the scorching heat, only to see Kenny literally breathing down his neck. Needless to say he was forced to forget nursing his bike to the finish, and instead he screwed the twist grip even further to enter the unknown territory with the first ever sub two-and-a-half minute lap – 102.13 mph. It was just enough to fend off Harrison – the pair separated by a marginal 2.6 seconds at the end of one of the closest Solo Championship races. (60)

Ian Lougher was never troubled for third place, as indeed was Cumbria's Nigel Barton for fourth, whilst Gary Radcliffe lowered his race time even further to take another superb top six placing in fifth. Hard luck stories were once again abundant, none more so than from David Madsen-Mygdal, who saw his hopes of a top eight spot disappear when he came off the Motorfair RC30 on lap eight at Cross Four Ways. He'd been engrossed in a tough three-way battle for a top ten spot with fellow local Brian Venables and impressive newcomer Derek Young. Venables eventually went one place better than last year to bring Paul Panter's bike of many colours home seventh. Richard Coates was the best of the 350s finishing a respectable 14th overall at a best-ever average speed.

(60) 1990 - Close up action with Davy Cowan, Ian Lougher and Gary Radcliffe

If you could have omitted just one name from the finishing order in the combined Supersport/125 race, which opened racing on Thursday, then the locals would have had a field day! Unfortunately, the one name necessary for omission was that of Dave Leach - and there was no way he was going to be beaten in a class which he more or less made his own since its introduction nationally. He simply waltzed away to a runaway victory on the 600 Yamaha. In his wake, David Black of Douglas had a fine ride to take second place on the ex-Loctite Yamaha. He'd made the position relatively safe in the early stages, but then almost slackened the pace too much in the closing stages to very nearly enable Castletown's Peter Hounsell to snatch the number two place away from him. Black managed to fend off Hounsell's late charge, although he admitted taking a few extra chances in the dash for the line where he was a mere two tenths of a second in front. Behind these two, Brian Venables was a good fourth, just ahead of a hard-trying Barry Wood.

The second leg of the Formula 2 Sidecar race went to newcomer Alan Warner with Cat Jenkins in the chair. Second were Artie Oates and Stuart Pitts, who were later declared the overall winners of the Formula 2 class, with Derek Rumble and local passenger Doug Jewell completing the podium. Kenny Harrison repeated his victory in the second Manx Telecom Classic Race on the Triumph Trident, as once again Selwyn Griffiths took runner-up place. John Knowles climbed one place higher, to fill the final podium position, with Vin Duckett, Derek Whalley and Charles Wield completing the top six.

Kenny's win brought his tally of victories at the Southern 100 to thirteen, equalling the long-standing record set by Chester's Bill Smith.

Finishing second in the final leg of the Open Sidecar Championship race, which brought the 1990 Southern 100 to a close, Gordon Shand and Keith Cornbill lifted the Championship. Bob Munro and David Samuel headed the three-wheelers across the line, nearly a minute ahead of the field, as local crew, Michael Masheter and Greg Mahon came home third, collecting the Christian Cup as the best local crew.

1991: Six out of six for Joey!

Ulster's favourite son, Joey Dunlop, made a triumphant return to the Southern 100 with two wins in little more than an hour on the opening evening of racing.

The Ballymoney ace had to contend with the Welsh wizard Ian Lougher in the 12-lap Junior Solo Founders race, but had things all his own way in the Senior race, despite a spirited charge through the pack by late-starting Dave Leach. Dunlop and Lougher were rarely more than a couple of bike lengths apart in the first race. Joey grabbing the hole-shot into Ballakaighan corner on lap one, on damp roads, only to relinquish the lead to the Yamaha-mounted Welshman on at least two occasions over the first half of the race. At the flag, Dunlop took the nod by just eight-tenths of a second, with fellow Ulsterman Steve Hazlett a steady third some 20 seconds down on Lougher. The relatively unknown Dave Milling from Cumbria, eventually took fourth place, following the unfortunate retirement of Castletown's own Richard Coates. The Manx Airlines pilot had been holding onto fourth place when first the clutch on the 250 Yamaha

(61) 1991 - Joey Dunlop (RC30) Honda Approaching Ballakaighan

began to slip, further problems occurring in the shape of a broken footrest. Gary Radcliffe upheld the local honours, though, enjoying a race-long scrap with Dave Leach before settling for sixth, behind the Ulster-based Yorkshireman. Leading 125 was the Honda of Bob Heath, narrowly edging out former Southern 100 champion Ray McCullough's nephew Denis.

Pre-race favourite for the Senior honours, Dave Leach was last away from the start at the beginning of the 12-lap race. On the warm-up lap he discovered that the headstock on the OWO1 Yamaha had come loose, and it was whilst Steve Hazlett's mechanic was kindly tightening this on the start line that Dave was delayed. Some ten seconds down on the field at the drop of the flag, Leach came from 45th to 20th on the opening circuit, working his way through the ranks like a hot knife through butter to move up into 13th spot on lap three, tenth on lap four, and sixth at half distance, setting a new lap record for the class along the way at 100.92 mph.

Meanwhile, Joey Dunlop had led from the word go on his RC30 Honda, Steve Hazlett ousting Kenny Harrison from second place on lap two, with Gary Radcliffe, Nigel Barton and Kevin Jones all in close company. Leach continued his incredible fight back, ousting Kevin Jones at the Ballanorris railway bridge on lap seven, Nigel Barton shortly after, and Kenny Harrison on lap eight – the latter man retiring with poor vision. Steve Hazlett was having problems with his RC30 Honda, and Brian Venables was unfortunate to go down on some oil, which had sprayed out from the rear of the Irishman's machine. Luckily Brian did not suffer any injuries in this minor step-off. With two laps to go, and Joey Dunlop well out on his own, Dave Leach completed his amazing ride by nipping through to vacate Gary Radcliffe of second place, crossing the line less than ten seconds behind the five times Formula One world champion. Barton held onto fourth place, whilst another Senior Manx Grand Prix winner, Paul Hunt, rode well to come in fifth ahead of Davy Cowan and Kevin Jones. (61)

Kenny Harrison predictably won the opening Manx Telecom Classic Race, though it wasn't perhaps quite as convincing as many would have expected. He tailed Walsall's Bob Heath for six of the eight laps, apparently under instruction to run the Triumph Trident in properly before turning up the wick. Once past, Kenny simply powered off into the distance crossing the line some 15 seconds in front of Heath's Seeley G50. Selwyn Griffiths rode a considerably more authentic looking Cowles Matchless into third place after a race, long dice with John Knowles. An excellent ride by Willaston's Barry Wood earned him the 350 class honours on Bob Dowty's twin cylinder Suzuki. "It's taken two years to win that one, but it was worth it for Bob's sake," said Barry a little later.

Joey Dunlop, written off by many in recent years, once again socked one in the eye of the pundits when he shattered race and lap records on his way to another double success on the second evening. Hoisting the outright Billown circuit lap record to 103.79 mph in the Unlimited Solo Race, the then 39-year-old "King of the Roads" had earlier come to within 0.8 of a second of the first ever 100 mph lap on a 250. But, whilst Joey, in his own familiar way, made the whole business of winning look deceptively easy, it certainly wasn't a one horse race in either of the two solo qualifiers. On both occasions he was faced with stiff opposition in the shape of the two men who had dominated the same races 12 months earlier: TT favourites Ian Lougher and Dave Leach. Lougher cursed a bad start in the 250 race, which saw him losing valuable ground to Dunlop in the first ten miles as he struggled to get by Steve Hazlett. Once past, Welshman Ian set about hauling in Joey – but it was somewhat of a lost cause as the Ulster ace controlled the race beautifully from the front, never for one moment looking in any doubt as the eventual winner.

In a carbon copy repeat of the previous evening's top five in the Junior Solo Founders race, third placed Hazlett was chased home by Dave Milling, Dave Leach and Gary Radcliffe. Leach held on grimly, only to lose the tow on Dunlop when he was hindered by a back marker. When Dave's Yamaha OWO1 began to overheat he was forced to slacken the pace, the gap growing from three seconds to more than ten in the latter half of the race. Steve Hazlett was another to suffer overheating problems, and he was very nearly caught napping for third place on the final corner when Kenny Harrison made one last-ditch effort at Castletown Corner. Gary Radcliffe had another typically solid ride for fifth place in front of Nigel Barton, while Dave Madsen-Mygdal chased Irishman Davy Cowan home in eighth. Denis McCullough took the 350 award in 15th spot. The race was marred by the horrific accident involving Andy Basset on the exit from the Black Hole.

Joey Dunlop again wasted no time at all stamping his authority on the Total Oils 1000cc race, but once Dave Leach got by local ace Kenny Harrison on lap two he immediately set about challenging the Ulsterman's domination. And, braking into Iron gate for the third time, Leach slipped through on the inside of Dunlop to grab the reins in a determined fashion. Joey stayed with him, though, ousting the Yorkshireman on lap five with a staggering first ever 103 mph lap in a time of two minutes 27.4 seconds. Steve Hazlett was third, Kenny Harrison fourth, Gary Radcliffe fifth and Nigel Barton completed the top six.

Dave Molyneux and Karl Ellison had an easy route to victory in Wednesday evening's first sidecar race of the 1991 Southern 100. Riding the Protech Overseas sponsored outfit, with the grunt of the full 1100 Suzuki power plant

beneath them, the local pair pulverised the opposition from the word go in the six lap Formula One race. Former winners Rod Bellas and Geoff Knight provided limited opposition in

(62) 1991 - Kenny Harrison Master of the Classics

the early stages, but when they retired Eric Cornes and Graham Wellington were left some way in arrears, in turn over half a minute clear of Mike Salmon and Tony Wilde of Cambridge. The only other local pair to go the distance were Artie Oates and Stuart Pitts, aboard a borrowed 750 Kawasaki, finishing tenth.

But Artie and Stuart had a considerably better ride in the following Formula 2 race on their own 600 Kawasaki. This race, which started in rapidly failing light at almost 9 o'clock, was won quite comfortably by Geoff Bell and Keith Cornbill on the Jacobs Yamaha. However Oates and Pitts were involved in a thrilling three way dice for the runner-up spot. At the flag it was Artie Oates and Stuart Pitts in second, with Derek Rumble and Doug Jewell claiming third.

Ramsey's Kenny Harrison came to within eight-tenths of a second of scoring a double success on the final day of the 1991 series. Having made a pig's ear of the start, he quickly scythed his way through the mixed field of machines in the Steam Packet Seaways Supersport race to get on the tail of Scotsman Iain Gibson in the latter part of the eight-lap race. But Gibson out-paced the respected course expert on the final spring to the line, both men aboard similar 600cc Yamahas, with newcomer Ian Scott a good third some ten seconds down. Next of the locals was Castletown's Peter Hounsell in sixth place, while Dave Leach took the 400cc honours in eighth, from Dave Madsen-Mygdal and Rupert Crowe. Joey Dunlop won the 125 class by some half a minute from Andy Godber with Bob Heath, third. (62)

Thursday's two sidecar races, saw a repeat result from the previous evening's first legs. Geoff Bell and Keith Cornbill set an overall greater average speed for the second Formula Two race on their way to beating locals Artie Oates and Stuart Pitts, although their quickest lap was fractionally down on the 88.23 set in race one. A good ride from Oates and Pitts, while newcomers Eric and Ewan McIntosh of Forfar had an impressive ride to grab third spot. Dave Molyneux and Karl Ellison were never headed in the Formula One race for machines up to 1300cc. They hit the front from the drop of the flag, and never once looked under threat on their sweet-sounding 1100 Suzuki – upping their lap and race standards from the previous evening. Gordon Shand and Janet Lowe retired from second place on lap five

(63) 1991 - Joey Dunlop - Out on his own at Church Bends

t o

let Eric Cornes and Graham Wellington back into the runner-up place at the close, with Derek Rumble and local passenger Doug Jewell going well after a sluggish start to take third.

Kenny Harrison narrowly missed out in the Supersport, but he made up with another runaway win in the Manx Telecom Classic, riding Colin Aldridge's 750 BSA Rocket-3. Harrison again came from behind after a poor start to move ahead of early leader Selwyn Griffiths, (G50) on lap three of the eight lap race. Early leader Barry Wood of Willaston seized the motor of Bob Dowty's 350 Suzuki at Cross Four Ways one lap later, whilst another of the leading runners, Bob Heath, retired shortly later when the carb came loose on his Seeley. Dave Storrey worked his way into third place at the close, with Ramsey's Derek Whalley the leading 350 in sixth spot on the Ducati.

By far the most spectacular of Dunlop's six wins came in the main 12-lap Ronaldsway Shoe Company Solo Championship race. Trailing 1990 champion Dave Leach in the early stages, Dunlop simply bided his time before shooting up the right-hand side of his rival on the fast approach to Castletown Corner from Stadium on lap three. Credit to Leach, though, he fought back tenaciously to nail Dunlop on the brakes into Iron Gate, only for Joey to power past for a second time shortly later at Great Meadow. (63)

Dave was then forced to hang on grimly as the five times Formula One World Champion dictated the pace superbly. Odd laps he seemed to tease Leach as he rolled back the throttle to enable the Yorkshireman to close the gap, then Joey was gone again. In short, he 'toyed' with Leach – the latter man's Yamaha no match for Dunlop's crisp sounding RC30, in the same way as Dave himself was not in the same league as the master on absolute peak form.

Just to rub salt into the wounds, Joey gave one final tweak of the twist grip to set a staggering new outright course record on the tenth lap. Circulating the 4.25-mile Billown circuit in a shade under two minutes 26 seconds, Joey's average speed was an amazing 104.93 mph; the previous best from 1990 was only 102, and prior to that the 100 mph had been the standard for seven years! This supersonic victory brought Dunlop's Southern 100 tally to 16 wins, including a record number of four Solo Championships.

In the wake of Dunlop and Leach, local men Kenny Harrison and Gary Radcliffe came through to fill third and

fourth places respectively on their near identical RC30 Hondas, following the retirement on lap nine of Ulster's Steve Hazlett. Nigel Barton and Paul Hunt completed the top six, the latter man recording his first ever ton-up lap at the Southern, while Ian Lougher rode a real stormer of a race to take seventh place on his 250 Yamaha. One final comment from veteran campaigner Selwyn Griffiths summed up the Southern 100 quite adequately. "It was the best run road race in the 1960s," he said, "and it's still the best now in the 90s!"

1992: McCallen stamps his mark on the Southern.

The first evening of racing at the 1992 Southern 100 proved a good night for the lesser lights of road racing - the unsung heroes of the sport who are perhaps not quite so well known as the factory supported superstars that so often hog the limelight.

Harrogate's Lee Pullan won the opening 12-lap Junior Solo Founders after pressurising Brian Reid into an uncharacteristic mistake. Brian Reid had led the race from the very early stages after Ian Lougher seized in the opening 300 yards. Gaining a super start, Lougher was a good 15 yards clear of Pullan and Reid, when the Padgett's Honda nipped at the end of the paddock entrance, luckily the remainder of the field managed to miss the Welshman as he rolled to a halt just before Ballakaighan Corner. Reid and Pullan were neck and neck at the end of the first circuit, and it took the Ulsterman two or three laps to gain a slender advantage over the hard-trying young Yorkshire rider.

Then, when it looked as though the four-times TT winner had the race sewn up, Reid overshot Ballabeg hairpin on lap seven, letting Pullan through into a comfortable lead. Reid's slip enabled third placed Jason Griffiths to close right up with him, but the experienced Banbridge man was not about to make another mistake, and held off the young Welshman's advances. Pullan had his first ever Southern 100 neatly tucked under his belt, however, and he was justifiably delighted with himself after what was a fine ride on the Manton Yamaha. Dave Milling, double Manx Grand Prix winner finished a lone fourth in front of Buckinghamshire's Neil Richardson and leading local Gary Radcliffe.

Jet-setters Derek Young and Johnny Rea made an early morning flight to Ulster worthwhile when they won their respective classes in the Senior Solo Founders Race. They and Phillip McCallen had taken a private plane out of the Island immediately after the culmination of the morning practice session to contest the important latest round of the Regal 600 series at Nutts Corner near Dundrod. Johnny won that race, with McCallen second and Young fourth, returning to the Isle of Man to take another 600 Yamaha to a class win in the Senior Founders race after a close tussle with Bob Jackson. But the main honours went to Derek Young, brother of former Southern 100 star Graham, who led the 50-mile race from the word go on his 750 Morton Honda. He set a new race average speed with the first ever ton plus average for the Senior Founders, finishing some seven seconds in front of similarly RC30 mounted Jason Griffiths.

The young Welsh ace had made a sluggish start, and took ages to get by Ian Lougher (the man he used to be mechanic for!), before setting off in hot pursuit of the race leader. He could just about see him in the distance on the longer straights, but despite a 101.32 mph record lap on the tenth circuit, wasn't quite able to reduce the gap enough. Lougher rode his slower Yamaha into third spot ahead of top local Gary Radcliffe, whilst Shrewsbury's Neil Parker ousted Paul Hunt for fifth spot in the latter stages.

The final race of the first evening's programme was the first Manx Telecom Classic race, over eight laps. Chelmsford's Glen English made a dream debut in the Southern 100, when he rode Colin Aldridge's 750 BSA Rocket-3 to success. Riding second string to local ace Kenny Harrison, he was forced to take over the reins at the front when Harrison's 850 Triumph from the same stable went onto two cylinders midway round the fourth circuit. To that point, the Ramsey man looked to be running away with the race recording a lap record with a 90.96 mph second circuit. But the same problem, which beset the big Triumph in the Classic TT returned, forcing Harrison out and leaving team-mate English to fight it out with Ulster's Billy Keenan. The two young pilots rode the machines with real 'gusto', English eventually pulling clear to win by a margin of nine seconds, with another Irishman, Trevor Reid, third.

Dave Milling and Lee Pullan scored a Manton Yamaha one-two over Ulster ace Brian Reid in Wednesday evening's record breaking 250/350cc solo race.
All three men enjoyed a spell at the front in what was a most thrilling race, but it was double Manx Grand Prix winner Milling, of St Bees in Cumbria, who eventually pipped his Manton team mate Pullan to the post at the completion of the 12th and final circuit. TT hero Reid decided to give up the chase when Pullan turned up the wick to produce a staggering new lap record of 100.26 mph on the tenth circuit. But the same man certainly wasn't popular with local rider David Collister when Pullan came up to lap him at Ballanorris on the last circuit – Collister diving for cover in the field to the right of the stone wall (where Joey Dunlop ended up some years ago), only to emerge minutes later covered from head to foot in cow muck! Jason Griffiths retired from fourth spot on lap eight, leaving Neil Richardson, Denis McCullough, top newcomer Gary Dynes and local man Gary Radcliffe to scrap it out for the minor placings.

Phillip McCallen won his first major race since the unfortunate Ulster Grand Prix crash when he cruised to victory in the Total Oils 1000cc race. Still nursing a painful shoulder, McCallen was clearly cautious in what was his first outing back on the Formula One TT winning Castrol RC30 Honda. He trailed fellow Ulsterman Derek Young for more than half the race, indeed it wasn't until the rejuvenated Young overshot on lap nine that McCallen snatched the opportunity to power through into the lead, finishing the race 3.6 seconds in front of the previous evening's Senior Founders winner. (64)

Newcomer Chris Day of Preston rode superbly to finish third on his Kawasaki ZXR, helped on the penultimate lap when Neil Parker was forced to retire after looking set for that third spot.

Jason Griffiths came off at Castletown Corner at the end of the opening lap, suffering torn ligaments in his shoulder.

(64) 1992 - Phillip McCallen - Close action at Castletown Bridge

Centre champion Dave Black rode another steady race to bring the Martin Bullock/Mannin Collection's Honda home in eighth spot after another race long battle with former top motocrosser Paul Orritt. Ralph Sutcliffe ousted Dave Milling and 350cc class leader Denis McCullough to grab 11th spot.

Gordon Shand and Pete Hill won the opening Sidecar race of the 1992 Southern 100, but they certainly weren't the most popular winners of the week. Many spectators and race officials who were witness to a most appalling-looking crash at Church Bends midway through the six lap Open Class race, felt Shand, in particular, failed to slow down sufficiently under the yellow flag. One ACU steward called for both Shand and race runners-up Geoff Bell and Keith Cornbill to be "banned", whilst others were simply disappointed at what appeared to be a complete lack of consideration for medical personnel and marshals who were risking life and limb to help the two riders hurt in the smash.

John Watterson of the Manx Independent newspaper was marshalling at the scene of the Phelim Owens/Herbie McHenry spill and stated at the time that Shand was well out of order, taking little notice of the waved yellow flags, as he and another marshal tried desperately to slow riders down on the approach to the accident scene, where there were around a dozen people working to assist the injured men. Bell and Cornbill, in Shand's slipstream, did acknowledge the latter two flags, whilst every other crew slowed almost to a standstill as they went past the scene. The race was stopped at the end of the fifth lap – the result declared on the order the riders crossed the line at the completion of the previous lap.

Geoff Bell and Keith Cornbill recorded a start to finish victory in the first leg of the Formula 2 sidecar championship, which drew racing to a close on the second evening. Using the same 600 Jacobs Yamaha, which brought them a TT double in June, the North-East pairing were never in any doubt as to the race winners. Manxmen Dave Molyneux and Karl Ellison were a comfortable second from veteran Steve Sinnott and local passenger Dave Corlett.

A new race in the 1992 Southern 100 was the Regal 600cc Championship Race, part of one of the main championships, which had been running a number of years in the Motor Cycle Union of Ireland (MCUI) events. Phillip McCallen played a 'cat and mouse' game, turning up the wick in the latter stages of the race to ensure victory over rival Johnny Rea in the only round of the 'Regal' Championship outside Ulster, pipping Rea by just under a second at the chequered cloth. Bob Jackson, always a good man on a 600, finished third, with Derek Young a superb fourth after being last in the early stages of the nine lap race, setting a new lap record at 99.73 mph in the process. Cheshire's Tim Poole was fifth and Kenny Harrison sixth, on a one-off 600 ride.

Geoff Bell and Keith Cornbill, who were followed home by Dave Molyneux and Karl Ellison, with Eric and Ewan McIntosh third, won the second leg of the Formula 2 Sidecar Race convincingly.

The combined 125cc/400 Supersport race was stopped after an unfortunate first lap accident involving Keith Rose, who suffered serious head injuries when he crashed his 250 Kawasaki on the approach to Ballakaighan. The race had to be stopped while he was rushed to hospital. The restart saw Denis McCullough leading the way on his 125 Honda ahead of Tim Poole's 400 Honda and Ian Lougher's Honda tiddler, but again it was that man McCallen who came from behind to grab the glory.
Third on lap two, McCallen was out in front of the pack after a record breaking third lap on the RC40. He went on to win the race by a margin of 7.2 seconds from Brian Reid.

There was an exciting climax to the 125 class with McCullough and Lougher split by just two-tenths of a second at the close after setting identical record laps of 94.14 mph on the fifth and final circuit of the shortened race.

Kenny Harrison made up for the disappointment of having to retire in the opening Classic race of the meeting, when he blasted Colin Aldridge's over-bored 850 Triumph to victory on Championship day.
Sidelined when a bent push-rod reduced the big triple to a twin, Harrison suffered no such problems in the second Manx Telecom sponsored Classic, indeed leading home first race winner Glen English in a comfortable one-two for the Aldridge camp, following the demise of lap one leader Billy Keenan.
Barry Wood rode another great race to once again take the 350cc class honours on Bob Dowty's 315cc Suzuki, with fellow local Derek Whalley third. Danny Shimmin, like Harrison robbed of success in the first race, finished runner-up to runaway 500cc winner Dave Storrey. All three race records were broken.

Double TT winner Phillip McCallen added the Southern 100 Solo Championship to his ever-growing list of titles after a calculated ride on the Turkington Windows Castrol Honda. In a carbon copy repeat of the previous evening's Open Solo qualifier, he stalked fellow Ulsterman Derek Young for most of the race before slipping through on the fast run into Iron Gate three laps from home. From the word go there was never anyone else in with a serious shout. Ian Lougher's ITL Yamaha never looked rapid enough to stick with the leading two Hondas, while TT quick men Johnny Rea, Brian Reid and Bob Jackson were all astride 600s. (65)

Young led the way from the change of the lights on his light blue Morton RC30, but was never able to shake off the menacing McCallen who sat in behind ready to pounce. All credit to Young though, he held on superbly to finish 0.4 of a second down on McCallen at the close, notching up the

quickest lap of the race on his 12th and final circuit at 103.79 mph – just 1.2 seconds short of Joey Dunlop's ultimate course record. Lougher finished a lone third almost one minute down on the two Ulstermen, while impressive newcomer Chris Day of Preston

(65) 1992 - Phillip McCallen - Solo Champion

finished a superb fourth on his 750 Kawasaki, with Stuart Jones some 9 seconds adrift in fifth. Former Senior Manx Grand Prix winner Paul Hunt rode an excellent race on his Motek-tuned Yamaha 750 to pip fellow local Gary Radcliffe to sixth place. After a first ever ton-plus lap, "Big H" slowed considerably in the latter stages after picking up a rear wheel puncture. Gary made up ground wholesale in the last half of the race after getting boxed-in in the middle of the 40-strong field on the early laps.

Dave Molyneux and Karl Ellison retained their Open Southern 100 Sidecar Championship title with a sensible ride in the second leg and final race of the 1992 programme. Leaders early on in the eight-lap race, they eventually scored a comfortable victory after their two main rivals went out in the latter stages. Leg one winners Gordon Shand and Pete Hill came to a halt at Ballanorris on lap five when the carbs fell off their big four-stroke after again setting the pace, while TT winners Geoff Bell and Keith Cornbill crashed out in dramatic fashion half a lap later.

In the lead for the first time in the race, Bell was keen to get away from Molyneux when he clipped the back of a slowing outfit, ridden by Ken Tomlinson and Malcolm Preston, on the approach to Cross Four Ways. The glancing blow fired Bell and Cornbill off into the gable end of the cottage on the inside of the course, throwing the passenger off as it rolled over, pinning Bell to the ground. Whilst the crash looked horrific, thankfully Geoff's injuries were largely fractures and cuts. This unfortunate crash handed the lead back to Molyneux and Ellison, the local pair going on to win the race at a canter, from former champions Rod Bellas and Geoff Knight. Tommy Bennett and Dougie Jewell rode the race of their lives to narrowly miss out on a top three position. Elevated to third following the demise of Shand and Bell, they were pipped by 0.2 of a second at the line by Beverley's Simon Christie and Adrian Walduck.

1993: Dunlop hat trick

(66) 1993 - Jason Griffiths on his way to winning the Senior Solo Founders Race

(67) 1993 - Simon Beck

Welshman Jason Griffiths opened up with a double success when racing began at the 1993 meeting.

He made light of the wet conditions to win both the Junior and Senior solo races, winning the opening race at an average speed of 88.69 miles per hour on his Cowles Yamaha and followed this up with victory in the Senior race at a speed of 91.47 mph, beating Joey Dunlop into second place. (66)

The winner had comfortable margins in both races, finishing 26 seconds ahead of his pursuers in the Junior and 27 seconds in the Senior. Second and third in the Junior were Dave Milling and Gary Dynes, the top six being filled by Richard Coates, Joey Dunlop and Gary Radcliffe.

Joey was runner-up in the Senior race, having been battling it out with Simon Beck for most of the race until Beck crashed out, without injury, at Cross Four Ways on lap ten. Tim Poole slotting into third, fourth was Gary Radcliffe, fifth went to Derek Young and the final leader board place was occupied by Dave Madsen-Mygdal. (67)

The evening's third race, the Classic, was won by Trevor Reid of Donaghadee, riding an Oldfield BSA; he averaged 79.89mph for the race. Dave Storry took second on his 498 Seeley Matchless, securing the 500 honours, with Glen English third on the 830 Miles Triumph. Best 250 was Bud Jackson in sixth position.

Wednesday evening's action commenced with the 250/350cc race. Joey Dunlop was in record-breaking form, setting a new race record with a time of 31 minutes 9.7 seconds equal to 98.19 mph.

Lee Pullan was quickest off the line on the Manton Yamaha but at the end of lap two it was Joey Dunlop in the lead. Pullan was closely involved in a battle with team-mate Dave Milling but neither of them had an answer for eventual second place man Jason Griffiths. At the cloth Richard Coates claimed fifth and Bob Jackson slotted into sixth.

The re-match between Beck and Dunlop in the 300/1300cc race saw Joey retire on lap three with gearbox problems. The superior power of Beck's Ducati saw him pull away from Griffiths, equalling the lap

(68) 1993 - Ian King - Regal 600 Race

record at a speed of 103.79 mph on the eighth lap. Chris Day took the final podium position.

The first leg of the Open Sidecar race was won by Rod Bellas and Geoff Knight on their 750 Yamaha, who were followed home by Simon Christie and Adrian Walduck driving their 1000 LC Suzuki, with Nick Hudson and Norm Oxley third on their 700 Baker Yamaha.

The opening leg of the Formula 2 Sidecar race proved to be a comfortable victory for Dave Molyneux with Karl Ellison in the chair of their 600 Yamaha. Second and third were Richard Crossly/Colin Hardman and Steve Sinnott/Dave Corlett.

In the 600 Regal Championship race, the opening race of Championship Day, Joey Dunlop was again to stamp his superiority on the circuit, though he had first to wait an hour and a half because of the weather conditions. The original leadership battle between Derek Young and Johnny Rea was soon challenged by Tim Poole, but there was no stopping Dunlop who came through to win on the last lap. Pool had to settle for second while Ian King beat Rea for third, as Derek Young had to settle for fifth, with Jason Griffiths slipping into sixth to complete the leader board. (68)

(69) 1993 - Second and third in the 125cc race - Denis McCullough and Gary Dynes

Dave Molyneux completed a double in the second leg of the Formula 2 Sidecar race, with the same pairings as the first leg filling second and third places.

In the shortened 125cc/Supersport 400cc race, Bob Jackson snatched victory from Derek Young. Joey Dunlop led home the 125s followed closely by Gary Dynes and Denis McCullough. Third 400 was Dave Madsen-Mygdal who finished eighth overall. (69)

(70) 1993 - Solo Champion again - Joey Dunlop

In the second Manx Telecom Classic Race, Trevor Reid became an unfortunate spectator as he had to pull the Oldfield BSA off the start line after last-minute repairs failed to make the bike race-ready.

Kenny Harrison won by a comfortable margin of nearly 20 seconds over Glen English. Karl Wilkie took third, as Colin Bevan, Stan Thomas and John Knowles completed the top six.

(70) Joey and his Castrol Honda overcame fog and the Sports Motorcycles Ducati assault of newcomer Simon Beck – to notch his fifth Solo Championship win. Beck's expected challenge lasted for four laps before the burly Preston, Lancs., rider ran the Italian V-twin into straw bales at

(71) 1993 - Bill Davie and Neil Miller - Sidecar Champions

Ballabeg Hairpin, he was 14 seconds down at the end of the nine lap race. Ulsterman Derek Young, last year's runner-up, finished third when his RC30 finally came on song after a troubled week.

(71) Bill Davie and Neil Millar took the chequered flag in the final race of the 1993 programme, the Open Sidecar Championship second leg, and in doing so, took the overall victory and the Championship on their second visit to Billown, having finished fourth in the opening leg. They ran away with the second outing ahead of double runner-up crew Mick Hudson and Norman Oxley. Graham and Tony Parkins took third spot.

1994: Griffiths' glory by a whisker (72) & (73)

(72) 1994 - Joey and the Club Committee outside the New HQ

(73) 1994 - Joey Dunlop Officially opens the new Club HQ

Joey Dunlop made a blistering start to the 1994 meeting with a brace of record-breaking wins in Tuesday evening's two Solo Founders Races. In ideal conditions, Dunlop led the 12-lap Junior Solo Founders race from start to finish. Initially shadowed by fellow Ulsterman James Courtney, Joey edged clear of his rival with a record-breaking 100 mph lap on the third tour. Richard Coates overhauled Welshman Jason Griffiths for third place on lap four, and when Courtney's 250 Honda developed problems on the very last lap it enabled both Richard and Jason to move up the pecking order one place – Courtney eventually touring across the line on fourth spot. Gary Radcliffe was a lonely sixth at the close, some 10 seconds behind Craigavon's Gary Dynes.

Bob Jackson and Derek Young had a close scrap for the 400cc Supersport/125cc class honours in the early stages, but once Jackson got ahead Young appeared to lose incentive, dropping a second a lap in the latter part. In contrast, comeback star Dave Leach and 125 Honda

mounted Phelim Owens slugged it out every inch of the way for third place. Swapping and changing positions throughout, Owens eventually took the line judge's nod at the chequered cloth after both riders were granted identical times.

(74) Jason Griffiths made the early bow waves in the Senior Solo Founders race, sponsored by Lloyds Bank. But despite determined efforts to hold off Ulster hero Dunlop, he was eventually forced to settle for second best. Simon Beck had better luck on the big Ducati, finishing a comfortable third, while Tim Poole of Northwich caught local champion Paul Hunt napping on the last lap to take an impressive fourth on his class-winning 600 Honda. Sixth place went to Chris Day.

Favourite from the word go in the Classic Race, Kenny Harrison notched up his 19th course win with consummate ease astride Colin Aldridge's melodic Triumph Trident. With little or no opposition from any serious contender on a similarly powered machine, Harrison was 20 seconds clear of the field in as many miles, having established a new lap record at 91.01 mph on the second circuit. Bob Jackson drew clear of Danny Shimmin to comfortably take

(74) 1994 - Jason Griffiths leads into Ballabeg Hairpin

the 500cc class honours and second overall, while Alan Phillips came from the back row of the grid to take a superb fourth overall on his BSA Rocket-3. Derek Whalley had a steady, if far from quiet, ride on his Honda to take the runner-up spot in the 350cc category behind Mark Baldwin.

Jason Griffiths became the first rider since fellow Welshman Colin Bevan in 1977 to win a Southern 100 solo race astride a Kawasaki on Wednesday evening. Fired up after being left on the line with a flooded Yamaha in the 250 race earlier, the then 23-year-old Griffiths out-braked the old maestro Joey Dunlop as the pair shot into Cross Four Ways for the first time. Joey held onto the back of the Webb Kawasaki for the next lap or so, but the pace proved too hot for the 42-year-old Ballymoney star, who admitted to being tired out after wrestling the RC45 to submission the previous evening. He eventually pulled in to retire at the end of the third lap, leaving Ducati mounted Simon Beck and Douglas fireman Paul Hunt to take up the chase. When Beck also went by the wayside, Hunt was left in a secure second place on the 750 Yamaha, although he was forced to keep a sharp eye behind for local rival Gary Radcliffe, who came through from sixth to third just under three seconds behind Hunt at the finish. Preston's Chris Day and Egremont's Marc Flynn had a race-long dice for fourth, eventually decided in Day's favour on the penultimate lap; Derek Young and Brian Venables had somewhat lonely rides to sixth and seventh places ahead of Paul Orritt. Such was Griffiths' pace, even after slackening off in the latter stages, that he still broke both lap and race records.

Much of Joey's reserves had probably been sapped up in the 250 race, which had opened the evening's programme earlier. Counting as the second round of the new British Isles Road Race Series, it undoubtedly proved more vital to Joey to score maximum points in that event than the unlimited race. Initially, it was local airline pilot Richard Coates who set the pace, holding off Joey and co. until quarter distance. Even when he had slipped through into the driving seat, it wasn't all plain sailing for 'Yer Maun' as he then had to contend with a determined Bob Jackson on the Manton Yamaha. Looking at the pair and the way they were riding, it was hard to believe that the same two men were scrapping it out in a similar race as far back as 1977. But 17 years on, Dunlop was to gain a long awaited revenge by holding on to take the honours by just a fraction over three seconds at the chequered cloth. Coates held on for a well-deserved third spot in front of Gary Dynes, Gavin Lee and Gary Radcliffe. Once again, winner Dunlop established new lap and race records.

A spate of accidents, thankfully none too serious, caused major disruptions to Wednesday evening's two sidecar races. A heavy crash at Ballawhetstone on the second lap of the Formula Two event, involving the father and son duo of Phil and Ian Carr, brought the red flags out and a 25 minute delay before a restart was possible over a shortened four lap distance. The Sheffield crew were taken to Nobles for x-rays to possible fractures. It made little difference to the eventual outcome, however, as hot favourites Dave Molyneux and Pete Hill soon shot straight back into a never-to-be-relinquished lead ahead of star newcomers Kenny Howles and Rob Parker. The winning margin was just over six seconds at the finish. Locals Graham Hayne and Dougie Jewell were cruelly robbed of a probable top three finish when the gear lever snapped off their machine at Cross Four Ways on lap two. But there was joy for another local as a result of their demise: Dickie Gale of Colby partnering Greg Lambert to the number three slot ahead of Bob Munro and another local chairman Paul Fargher. Big Billy Quayle and David Clucas went into the field at Ballanorris on the opening lap of the restarted race without actually crashing.

And there was another scatter at the same point at the start of the Open Sidecar race an hour later when the co-favourites Vic Jefford and Chris Ault went through the same open gate at an even greater rate of knots. Passenger Ault was thrown out of the chair heavily, injuring his chest, and it was again deemed necessary to stop the race at half distance so he could receive immediate medical attention. Within half an hour of the roads opening time at the point the race was stopped, it was not possible to make a restart. At the time of the curtailment, last year's winners Bill Davie and Neil Millar were already nine seconds clear of Rod Bellas and Geoff Knight, with Simon Christie and Adrian Walduck third.

The opening race of Championship Day, the Regal 600cc race was won by Tim Poole, followed some 14 seconds in arrears by Derek Young, who had Marc Flynn in his tyre tracks, just 9/10th of a second behind. Bob Jackson, Simon Trezise and Peter Hounsell completed the top six; all were Honda mounted.

Kenny Howles and Rob Parker continued their memorable debut by going one better in the second leg of the Formula

Two sidecar race and taking the chequered flag, after first leg victors Dave Molyneux and Pete Hill's Yamaha motor went flat after just a couple of laps and they were forced to settle for runner-up place with Greg Lambert and Dickie Gale claiming third for the second time.

(75) 1994 - Bill Davie and Neil Miller - double winners in Open Sidecar races

Having arrived in the Island too late for official practice, Derek Young set lap and race records en route to success in the Supersport 400 race ahead of Bob Jackson. Joey upped the class record in the concurrently run 125cc race, heading home fellow Ulstermen James Courtney and newcomer Owen McNally.

Local man Kenny Harrison won the first classic race, but was forced out of the second leg with a broken gearbox. Welshman Colin Bevan stepped in to win that race, while Bob Jackson, Danny Shimmin, Derek Whalley and Mark Baldwin all tasted success in the smaller capacity classes.

The Scottish duo of Bill Davie and Neil Millar made a hectic 25-hour, non-stop overland journey from the Czechoslovakian European round worthwhile with a double success in the Open Sidecar. (75)

One of the most exciting finishes in the 40-year history of the Southern 100 saw Pontypool's Jason Griffiths pip veteran Ulsterman Joey Dunlop to the line by just a fifth of a second in the main Solo Championship race. Trailing Dunlop's RC45 Honda throughout, 23-year-old Griffiths smashed Phillip McCallen's absolute lap record for the Billown circuit as he forced his way past on the penultimate lap. (76)

But exhausted Dunlop refused to give in and he out-gassed the Webb Kawasaki man down the Castletown by-pass, leaving Griffiths with it all to do again. Griffiths stalked the Ballymoney ace for the next four miles, forcing him into making an uncharacteristic mistake at the right-hander coming onto the start and finish straight. Griffiths was surprised to discover that he had set a new lap record on roads still damp in places from early-afternoon rain. His best of 105.08mph was a 10th of a second quicker than the target McCallen set in the post-TT meeting in June. Marc Flynn just held off a hard-chasing posse of Derek Young, Chris Day and Gary Radcliffe for third place, with Tim Poole going great guns on his 600 Honda for seventh. However, Joey still managed to extend his incredible number of race wins to 29 on the Billown Circuit.

(76) 1994 - Joey leading the Solo Championship race at Ballakaighan with Jason Griffiths tucked in behind the maestro

Chapter Five

Fifty Years of the Friendly Races 1995 - 2004

1995: King Bob!

The fortieth running of the Southern 100 brought many past champions back to the Billown circuit to celebrate the occasion. However, the weather played havoc with the first evening's racing – a complete washout – causing the abandonment of the programme, and leaving the officials the task of re-scheduling the Wednesday races. Conditions were a whole lot better 24-hours later and the 40th anniversary meeting got off to a cracking start.

The opening race of the programme, combining races one and four (for 250 and 125cc and 400cc machines) was an absolute classic, with two of the all-time great names of racing on the 4.25-mile circuit providing a grandstand finish.

Led from the start by Denis McCullough, the 25-year-old nephew of the great Ray McCullough, who won the Southern 100 Solo Championship 20 years ago, the race looked to be in the bag for the Ulsterman at mid-distance with a safe seven seconds in hand on Jason Griffiths. But Griffiths, whose dad Selwyn was a double winner on the course in 1968 and 1971 had other ideas. Third in the early stages behind fellow Welshman Ian Lougher, he set about reeling McCullough in, and with a lap to go the two Yamaha riders were wheel to wheel down the main Castletown by-pass. Still fighting back from his TT injury, Griffiths got the drive out of Alexander Bridge to out-sprint his rival to the chequered cloth, crossing the line one-tenth of a second ahead – half a wheel. Buckinghamshire's Neil Richardson rode well for third place some 26 seconds astern, with Ulsterman Gary Dynes pipping Bob Jackson and Manxman Richard Coates for fourth place. Tony Duncan finished a good ninth, just in front of Dave Leach on the leading 400, while Brian Venables had a race-long scrap with Newcomers MGP prospect Richard Quayle for 11th place, Brian eventually sprinting across the line three-tenths of a second in front of a determined 'Milky'. The leading 125 was ridden by Darran Lindsay of Lisburn in 14th place overall. (77)

Cumbrian veteran Bob Jackson, a 350cc winner on the Billown circuit as long ago as 1977, won his first big bike Southern 100 race after a tremendous battle with local ace Paul Hunt. Jackson led from the lights, powering down the Castletown by-pass ahead of fireman Hunt and pre-race favourites Jason Griffiths and Simon Beck. But the Griffiths challenge lasted no more than a couple of laps when a bent steering damper on the Webb Kawasaki left him lock-to-lock and virtually out of control in the infamous 'Black Hole'. He pulled in at the start and finish line after his close moment, while Beck overshot one of the near-hairpin bends to lose the tow for third. With his Ducati slowing slightly behind former champion Dave Leach, Beck kept his nose in front of local champion Brian Venables and similarly RC30 mounted course newcomer Steve Ward. The battle up front raged on, however, and while Jackson set the pace on his McAdoo Kawasaki, Hunt simply refused to let go. Quicker on the back section of the course, he squeezed in front of Jackson for a brief time on lap five, but Jackson's ZXR was quicker out of corners than Hunt's big Yamaha and the Windermere man soon regained the reins. At the finish of another thrilling race, just over half a second split the leading pair with Dave Leach also averaging more than 100mph for third a further 12 seconds down. (78)

Dave Pither made easy work of the rescheduled first Classic race on Wednesday evening after local favourite Kenny Harrison was forced out on the first lap. Chasing Pither's Commonwealth Racing Triumph out of Ballabeg Hairpin, Harrison's Phil Pick-entered triple skidded to a halt just after Ballawhetstone when the rear brakes jammed on solid! Co-favourite Glen English had to pull Norman Mile's Trident off the start line with a broken fairing bracket, leaving Pither a comfortable victor. He cantered across the finishing line one minute and 23 seconds in front of Millisle's Karl Wilkie a second behind in third spot on his BSA Rocket-3.

The leading 500 was Vin Duckett's Seeley Matchless in fourth, with Alan 'Bud' Jackson the 350 class winner in fifth. Dave Molyneux and Yorkshire passenger Peter Hill totally dominated Wednesday evening's Open Sidecar race on their awesome 500 Krauser outfit. Setting the outfit up for the forthcoming European GP in Czechoslovakia, they grabbed the lead on the second lap, after a sluggish start, from Scotsmen Bill Davie and Neill Millar. Once ahead they were never challenged, eventually crossing the line some 20 seconds clear of the 1100 Suzuki crew at the end of the 8 lap race. Jim Silver and Michael Singer of Aberdeen finished third, with the only all-local crew, that of brothers Brian and Neill Kelly, a fighting sixth after out manoeuvring Paul and Neil Smart of Wakefield on the final lap. (79)

Geoff Bell won the Formula Two race earlier in what was his comeback on the circuit after a major crash in the 1992 Southern 100 Championship race. Breaking both legs in the crash at Cross Four Ways, Bell was out of the sport for nearly a year. But he has since made a good recovery and was a clear winner with passenger Nick Roche. Newcomers Martin Clarke and Lee Farrington had a sensational ride to finish runners-up, half a second in front of experienced campaigners Kenny Howles and Steve Poynter.

(80) 1995 - Dave Leach - Winner of the 40th Anniversary Race

Ian Lougher was the initial leader in the 40th anniversary 250cc-600cc race which got the Thursday afternoon programme underway in glorious sunshine. Leach hit the front midway round lap two at Wheeler's, but it was Bob Jackson on the Clucas Honda who set the race alight with a record-breaking lap of 101.05 mph on the sixth circuit, making up ground wholesale after a sluggish start. He reeled in Leach lap by lap, narrowly failing in a brave attempt to slip through on the inside of the Yorkshireman at Castletown Corner on the final lap. In a week of close finishes, just two-tenths of a second separated the pair at the line, with Jason Griffiths a clear third in front of Steve Ward and the leading 250 ridden by Denis McCullough. (80)

Billown Circuit newcomers Martin Clark and Lee Farrington of Leeds won the Formula Two Sidecar Championship at their first attempt with victory in Thursday's second leg and the runner-up spot behind Geoff Bell and Nick Roche in the opening race the previous evening. It initially looked as though Bell and Roche were going to score a repeat success over Clark and Farrington, the former champions steaming off into an early runaway lead on their 600 Yamaha. But they coasted to a halt at mid-distance leaving the newcomers in the driving seat. Eventual runners-up Rod Bellas and Geoff Knight had a good dice with Greg Lambert and local passenger Dickie Gale until they too went out.

Win number two for Leach followed, when he scythed his way through a field of 125s on his 400 Yamaha from last away, breaking the class lap and race records in the process. Early leader Denis McCullough was the best of the tiddlers, followed by fellow Ulstermen Darran Lindsay and Gary Dynes. Local man Dave Madsen-Mygdal was the second

400-rider home in seventh spot, with Richard Bairstow third 400 and 14th overall.

The second leg of the Eurocars Classic was a classic in every sense of the word. Denied a real tear-up the previous evening when Kenny Harrison and Glen English both went out before the race barely got underway, Dave Pither had his hands full this time. The Moreton-in-the-Marsh man got the start, thundering into Ballakaighan in front of his two rivals, but from thereon in there was rarely more than a few feet between the melodious triples. Pither always appeared to just have the edge on speed down the straights, but English and Harrison tried their darndest to nip through on the tight corners. (81)

It really was an armchair thriller. Going into the final lap it was Pither-English-Harrison nose to tail along the Castletown by-pass, but then Pither got into a bit of a slither at Ballakaighan, pulling up at the Iron Gate with a suspected oil leak onto the rear wheel. Harrison wasn't able to get past English on that final circuit, despite breaking his own lap record with a speed of 93.86mph (his previous best 91.07!), Glen bringing Norman Miles' BSA Rocket-3 home 1.2 seconds in front of the Manxman on the Phil Pick-owned 850 Triumph. Both men were well inside the

(81) 1995 - Glen English (4) Kenny Harrison (1) Dave Pither (2) - Classic action at its best

previous race record. Although some way down on the tremendous scrap for first place, local excavation expert Alan Phillips rode another storming race to get onto the podium in third place for the second time in 24 hours. Veteran Vin Duckett was the leading 500cc rider in fourth place on the Seeley G50, one place off 350-class winner Bud Jackson on the 250 Suzuki. Derek Whalley of Ramsey was runner-up in that class on John Turner's Honda twin, with Ivan Coates of Peel a good third on a similar machine.

Bob Jackson won his first ever-Southern 100 Solo Championship title after 20 years of trying. (82) As old as the race meeting itself, Cumbrian favourite Bob scored his maiden success on the Billown circuit as long ago as 1977 on a 350 Lambert Yamaha in what was his second appearance at the Southern. Faithful to road racing and the Southern ever since, this was surprisingly only the fifth outright victory for the Windermere man and by far his sweetest. After a dress rehearsal win in the previous evening's 1010cc Solo race, Jackson rocketed into the early lead on the McAdoo Kawasaki.

(82) 1995 - Bob Jackson leads Simon Beck and Paul Hunt on the way to winning his first Solo Championship

Manxman Paul Hunt was also in the groove on his 1000cc Yamaha, having finished runner-up to Jackson the night before, and he stuck to the Cumbrian's rear wheel like glue in the early stages of the 12-lapper.
Former champions Dave Leach and Jason Griffiths were on the pace also, and these four slowly pulled away from the thundering pack of nearly 40 riders. Simon Beck, Tim Leech and Steve Ward were the pick of the bunch behind, but there was no luck for Centre Champion Brian Venables who went out on the opening lap at Ballakaighan with a broken gearbox on the Bullock/Mannin Collection's RC30 Honda.

By half distance Jackson had a four second advantage over Hunt with Leach and Griffiths a similar distance behind in third and fourth. With lapped backmarkers becoming a problem, the gap continued to widen with Jackson eventually stretching out to a winning margin of just over 10 seconds on Hunt.

'It was a trouble free ride,' admitted Jackson later, having controlled the race from the front. Hunt was happy too, admitting he had slackened off once he knew he was safe for second place. But the battle for third went right down to the wire with Griffiths nipping through on the inside of Leach at Castletown Corner to snatch the last place on the rostrum. Beck was a lone fifth ahead of Ward and Tim Leech, with Ian Lougher on the 600 Yamaha getting the better of a trio of Yamaha twins ridden by Denis McCullough, Neil Richardson and Gary Dynes for eighth.

Dave Molyneux and Peter Hill smashed former world sidecar champion Steve Webster's outright lap record at the Billown circuit on Thursday afternoon, then promptly retired from the race less than three from home with a broken rear sprocket on the super-quick 500 Krauser. Slow off the line, the Manx driver was no higher than fourth midway around the opening lap. But he picked off the outfits ahead of him one by one, taking over the lead from Scotsmen Bill Davie and Neil Millar at the end of lap two.

Molyneux and Hill's lap record came on the fourth circuit when they were attempting to break free of the chasing 1100 Suzuki. The lap of 96.95mph was substantially quicker than Webster's long standing 1982 standard of 94.79 and better than the majority of solos in the preceding Southern 100 Championship race. But the icing on the cake of a double victory was to be denied, the rear sprocket of the screaming two-stroke breaking under severe strain of acceleration exiting Ballabeg Hairpin for the

last time. Molyneux and Hill's sad demise left Davie and Millar clear to win their third sidecar event in as many years. Newcomers Sean Hegarty and Stuart Cole took second place. Geoff Bell and Nick Roche made up for breaking down in the F2 race by finishing third on the same 600 Windle Yamaha in the open class.

Remembering the Southern 100

The Southern 100 has always been one of my favourite road race meetings. The club is always well organised, very friendly and always runs very good meetings. From my first to last races I have always felt welcome. My first race was one to forget, as I did not finish due to machine failure; that was back in 1975.
My first national road race win was at the Southern 100 in 1977 on a 350 Lambert Yamaha with lap and race records. As I remember it was a very hectic first lap when I was almost knocked off going into 'Cross Four Ways', someone tried to out-brake me and touched my handlebars as he went past. He did not get around the corner! Luckily I stopped on and went on to win.

I also had a win in 1981 on a 250 WLT Yamaha. I stopped going after 1983 as I had opened a motorcycle shop at the start of 1984. I then went back in 1993 for the Steam Packet races after the TT and won the 400 race after a good battle with Derek Young.

The circuit is very demanding: my favourite part is along the Great Meadow and around Stadium Corner, and it is very fast.

(83) 1995 - Past winners help celebrate 40 years of the Southern 100

(85) 1995 - Bill Smith Parade Laps

(86) 1995 - Terry Shepherd Parade laps

(87) 1995 - Steve Cull Parade Laps

(88) 1995 - Bob Dowty Snr Parade Laps

(89) 1995 - George Short Parade Laps

(90) 1995 - George Ridgeon and Frank Fox Parade Laps

1995 was my first 750 race win on Winston McAdoo's Kawasaki. This was the hardest race. I remember I had a real race with Paul Hunt (Big H) for the first half of the race, we kept swapping places for the lead then I slowly pulled away. They always say the first win is the hardest and it was. The championship race seemed easy!

1998 was to be my final race at the Southern. I won the first 125 and 750 races early on in the week. That week on the final day, Thursday, I was second in the 125 race to Robert Dunlop. I had a win in the 600 race, which I thought would be the hardest race. Then the Championship race I led from the start. I remember thinking to myself how fast should I go? So I just set off at a pace I was happy with. I think it was about lap 9 when Jason Griffiths out-braked me going into Iron Gates so I followed him for a lap to see where he might be slower than I was and I might get past him. I knew I could go a bit faster. So I passed him and went for it! It was a fantastic end to the week with a new circuit out-right lap record.

I always enjoyed racing at the Southern 100, I remember it fondly and miss it greatly.

Bob Jackson

40th Anniversary feature
(83; 84; 85; 86; 87; 88; 89; 90; 91; 92; 93; 94; 95; 96;)

(84) 1995 - Club Committee

1996: Jason's week!

Windermere's Bob Jackson got the defence of his Southern 100 Championship title off to a flying start with a clear victory over Ramsey-based Welshman Jason Griffiths in the ten lap Inflight Catering Services Senior Solo Founders Race – the opening race of the 1996 meeting. The McAdoo Kawasaki ace led the race from the word go, and, although Griffiths remained on his tail for much of the way, he eventually slowed to give Jackson an 8.6 second cushion at the close, Griffiths experiencing handling problems with the Morris/Webb Honda UK RC45 in the tricky cross-winds. Helsall's Tim Leech pipped the largely unknown Steve Ellis and the back-from-injury Simon Beck for third in what was a thrilling race-long tussle. Beck slowed in the latter stages after a component broke in the rear suspension of his Peachurst/Reve Kawasaki, forcing the rear end of the bike to jump and knocking both his feet off the rests at the end of the Castletown by-pass.

Best of the 600s was Ulsterman Adrian McFarland on the Schimmel Honda in sixth spot, followed by former TT winners Dave Leach and Ian Lougher. Bob Jackson was denied a double minutes later when the drive belt to the primary chain broke on his G50 Matchless in the eight lap Classic Race. Another early departure was Glen English, who was black-flagged for having a loose exhaust on the Teese Aermacchi at the end of the first lap. Pitched against the larger capacity three-cylinder Triumph Tridents and BSA Rocket-3s, Bob Jackson had just taken the race lead on lap three when the belt broke going through the twists at Ballanorris. His departure left Glamorgan's Jeff Jones in the driving seat ahead of Karl Wilkie and Colin Bevan. Wilkie dropped his Rob North Triumph at Ballabeg hairpin on the penultimate lap, leaving Jones with a 20-second lead going into the final lap. But then he crashed heavily at the Iron Gate breaking a shoulder, promoting fellow Welsh veteran Bevan back into the lead he originally held on the first lap. He crossed the line some 16 seconds in front of Karl Bell, with Alan Phillips a good third on his Rocket-3. John Knowles was the first 500cc rider home in fourth place, followed directly by the leading 250s in the hands of Bud Jackson and local man Barry Wood.

Ian 'Lucky' Lougher celebrated his 31st birthday a few hours prematurely with a narrow victory in the Station Garage sponsored Junior Solo Founders Race. Astride the DTR/Ray Cowles 250 Vee-twin Yamaha, in preference to the 125 Aprilia

(91) 1995 - Eddie Crooks Parade Laps

(92) 1995 - Charlie Williams Parade Laps

(93) 1995 - George Costain Parade Laps

(94) 1995 - George Fogarty Parade Laps

(95) 1995 - Jim Curry Parade Laps

(96) 1995 - John Worthington Parade Laps

he was scheduled to ride, the popular Welshman beat Southampton's Gavin Lee to the line in what was a nip and tuck battle from the word go. The pair were joined in the early laps by Ian's former spanner man, fellow Welshman Jason Griffiths, but when his Morris Honda seized on lap three, Lee and Lougher were left to fight it out between themselves. Lougher led for the first four laps until Lee found a way past, the lead changing hands several times from thereon in, although Lee only led once across the finish line at the end of a record-breaking eighth lap. A winner many times on the Billown circuit, the Southern 100 provided Lee with his first taste of closed-roads racing when he made his debut there in 1983, prior to finishing third behind Robert Dunlop and Steve Hislop in the Junior Newcomers Manx Grand Prix a month or so later. Ulsterman Phil Reid finished third, after a similar race-long duel with Neil Richardson. The leading 125 was the Honda of Ulsterman Nigel McCullough, followed by Bud Jackson and Jimmy Rodgers.

The absolute lap record was cast aside not once, but four times in the Total Oils Senior race, as Bob Jackson and Jason Griffiths continued to do battle as the main championship race approached. McAdoo Kawasaki ace Jackson came out with guns a-blazing in the first open capacity race of the week on Tuesday evening, but Ramsey-based Welshman Griffiths wreaked his revenge 24 hours later with a 1.5 second victory in the next head to head. Jackson took the early lead and looked initially like scoring a repeat success of the previous night's 10-lap encounter. But Griffiths had other ideas, and he powered the Morris Oils/John Webb Honda RC45 through into the lead on lap three with a new lap record at more than 105mph. Veteran campaigner Bob held on for a couple of laps, but then seemed to slow-up, before gaining his second wind and fighting back in determined style in the latter third of the race. He went quicker than Griffiths' lap three effort on lap eight, quicker still on lap nine, cutting Jason's lead from a comfortable five seconds to a decidedly shaky two and a bit, before establishing a new all comers best of 105.59mph on a blistering final lap. But it wasn't quite enough, and Griffiths got his head down out of Castletown Corner to power over the line just 1.5 seconds in front at the end of a thrilling race. Big Tim Leech followed up his previous evening's third position with another rostrum place on his privately entered Kawasaki. He had another close dice in the early stages with fellow Lancastrian Simon Beck, course newcomer Dave Goodley and surprise Welshman Steve Ellis; all three, like Leech, identically mounted on ZXR750 Kawasakis. Beck slipped out of the reckoning when he overshot one of the hairpin turns on lap five, enabling Leech to steal a march on the other two. Tim eventually crossed the line 40 seconds down on the two race leaders, but five seconds clear of Goodley, with Ellis a similar distance behind in fifth. Ulsterman Adrian McFarland was again the leading 600 rider in sixth place.

Manx pilot Richard Coates pushed professional road racer Jason Griffiths every inch of the way in the Mann Auto Services Junior Race. The pair were wheel to wheel for much of the way, but Griffiths turned up the wick of his 250cc Morris Honda in the latter stages equalling his own 250 lap record of 100.72mph on the eighth circuit to fend off the then 37-year-old Manxman's advances. Southampton's Gavin Lee got off to a flying start as the lights turned to green at the commencement of the 42.5-mile race. He was yards clear of the chasing pack two miles into the first lap at Ballabeg where Ian Lougher, the man he had enjoyed such a close dice with the previous night, came to grief after being high-sided from his 250 Yamaha. Early celebrations turned to birthday blues as Lougher's luck ran out and he hit the deck, fortunately without injury and miraculously without taking anyone else off with him. As he went down, fellow Welshman Griffiths went one side and Ulsterman Phil Reid the other. Meantime, Lee was well clear and he seemed a safe bet for victory until the right hand footrest bracket broke off, together with the rear brake assembly, forcing him to retire at the end of the third lap. Griffiths then took hold of the reins, chased by Coates, Reid and Englishman Neil Richardson. Coates very nearly took himself and Griffiths out as he attempted to dive up the inside at Ballabeg on lap five, later admitting he had showed his hand too early. He and Griffiths gradually eased clear of Richardson and Reid, while Tony Duncan had another lonely ride just behind in fifth. Having burned the midnight oil to rebuild the crank on the 250 Honda after a seizure in the previous evening's Junior Founders, Griffiths was determined to make amends this time and he put just enough into Coates on the final three laps to make certain of a comfortable five second victory at the finish. Duncan held on for fifth behind Richardson and Reid, but Richard 'Milky' Quayle got his act together in the latter stages to pip fellow Colby man Decca Kelly for seventh behind 125 TT rostrum man Glen English.

Both winners of the two Sidecar heats went inside the old Formula 2 record in what were ideal conditions for racing on Wednesday evening. Making the most of the extensive course alterations at the Iron Gate and Black Hole over the past winter, Geoff Bell and passenger Lee Farrington tore the record book to shreds in the first six-lapper when they lapped twice at 93.63mph on consecutive circuits. The only crew to stay in touch on the early laps were Richard Crossley and local passenger Karl Ellison, but they lost time on the final lap and eventually finished over half a minute down, still a safe second in front of Greg Lambert and another local chairman Dave Mahon. Kenny Howles and Steve Pointer did a similar disappearing act in the second heat, but although they too went inside the old F2 record on lap three, they were nearly two seconds short of the former winner Bell's 2 minutes 43.4 seconds.

Howles and Pointer finished more than 40 seconds clear of Alan Warner and local passenger Colin Hardman outsprinting course newcomers Vince and Graham Biggs to the line by just four-tenths of a second. The hard luck story of the race belonged to Peter Nuttall and local passenger Nick Crowe, however. Holding onto second place with less than two miles to go the chain snapped on their 600 Ireson Yamaha at Cross Four Ways and they felt the chain whip up through the seat touching passenger Crowe's arm as he leaned over the back of the bike!

Jason Griffiths got his Championship Day off to a good start with a decisive victory over close rival Bob Jackson in the S&S Motors 250/600 race, initially led by Gavin Lee. Denied victory in the previous evening's 250 Junior, Lee shot into an early lead, only to be dragged back by Griffiths on the third lap with a record speed of 101.93mph on the 600 Morris Honda. Griffiths gradually extended his lead, while Jackson ousted Lee for second on the final lap. Richard Coates and Ian Lougher completed the top three in the quarter-litre class.

Out of luck in the qualifying heats, Roy Hanks and Phil Biggs won the Sidecar Consolation race at a canter, after Peter Nuttall and Nick Crowe went out with a broken gearbox on lap two, letting in Mick Staiano with Peter Holmes in the chair into runner-up slot, as Lenny Pallister and Ian Marriner claimed third.

Ian Lougher and Glen English had a race-long battle for honours in the combined 125/400 race, eventually decided in Ian's favour by just one-fifth of a second at the chequered cloth with a record-breaking final lap. Gavin Lee scored his second rostrum placing with another third on the 125 Grant Honda in what was another photo finish with Nigel McCullough of Banbridge. The best of the 400s was ridden by Ulsterman Tommy Diver on the NC30 Honda campaigned by injured local rider Dave Madsen-Mygdal. Phil Gilmour and Kevin Murphy completed the top three.

Welshman Colin Bevan was denied a double victory in the Eurocars Classic Race when he came off his BSA Rocket-3 in the field at Ballanorris on lap six of eight. He was luckily only winded in the incident, the race lead and eventual honours being taken by Karl Bell of Sleaford on the Triumph Trident.
He beat Staffordshire's John Knowles by more than 12 seconds in what by the end of the race was a steady drizzle, the latter taking the 500 class honours. Local man Derek Whalley coaxed his ailing Honda twin to the 350cc class honours in fourth place, ahead of Glen English and the Teece Aermacchi.

Heavy rain delayed the start of the Formula Two Sidecar Championship Race – the heavens opened just as the competitors were about to assemble in the warm-up area prior to the start of the main sidecar event, so the organisers wisely gave them a extra 30-minutes to fit the appropriate wet tyres.
The race duly got underway with the roads awash with water and in a steady downpour.
Ian Ward and Steve Langham of York pulled off the start line after the sighting lap, as three local crews did no more than a token lap before also quitting: Keith Griffin/Peter Cain, Brian and Neil Kelly, and Alan Langton/Tony Pitt all pulling in at the end of the first circuit. Helmut Luneman and Greg Mahon retired at Ballabeg, alongside Steve Sinnott and Dave Corlett, while Greg Lambert and Dave Mahon stopped at Cross Four Ways. Runners-up to Bell the

night before, Richard Crossley and Dave Molyneux's former passenger Karl Ellison stopped at Maggie's Corner.

In a race of attrition, just seven outfits completed two laps, but the conditions appeared to do little to deter the leading two machines ridden at a tremendous pace by Geoff Bell and Vince Biggs. Bell and passenger Lee Farrington held a 13-second lead by one-third distance (three laps), while course newcomers Vince and Graham Biggs were in turn almost a full minute clear of third placed Dick Hawes and Geoff Knight. Clocked at more than 103mph past the start and finish grandstand on the Castletown by-pass, Bell and Farrington were more than 20mph quicker than most of their rivals. Seemingly unstoppable, they splashed to one of the most crushing victories ever witnessed in the 35 years of sidecar racing on the Billown circuit, lapping all bar second placed Dick Hawes and Geoff Knight after the Biggs' were cruelly forced to retire on the final circuit with a broken clutch on the Molyneux framed Yamaha. Geoff and Lee were in the winners' enclosure a full five minutes before the next crew appeared, veteran campaigner Dick Hawes and passenger Geoff Knight, themselves escaping being lapped by just a few seconds. Elevated to third and the newcomers' prize following the departure of Vince and Graham Biggs, Midlanders Roy Tansley and Roy King were quite ecstatic. It was their first meeting together, King's first ever road race and first ride on a Formula 2. They had no wet tyres to fit, so ran on intermediates. Colin Hardman partnered Alan Warner to fourth place ahead of Kenny Howles and Steve Pointer, who suffered throughout with water in the works of their Ireson Yamaha. The sixth and only other crew to finish were Castletown veteran Dennis Proudman and passenger Jamie Scarffe. (97)

Conditions were no better for the start of the Solo Championship race shortly after. Fifth in the opening unlimited race on Tuesday, but out of the reckoning the following evening after overshooting at Cross Four Ways, Peachurst Kawasaki rider Simon Beck was a little too eager to get going and he crept forward from the second row onto the front as the lights changed from red to green signifying the start of what was to be a 12-lap race. He incurred a 20 second penalty from the race organisers as a consequence, but led on the road from pre-race favourites Bob Jackson and Jason Griffiths at the end of the first rain-soaked lap. Jackson went out at the end of the second circuit when the throttle on his McAdoo Kawasaki stuck open at Castletown Corner, leaving Griffiths in the clear overall ahead of Tim Leach and the 600s of Dave Leach and Adrian McFarland. Behind Beck on corrected time, top newcomer Dave Goodley was dicing it out for sixth with the leading 250s of Phil Reid and Ian Lougher. But Reid lost the front end of his Honda on the tight left-hander between the walls at Ballanorris, and went down heavily. A marshal's red coat was apparently mistaken in the distance for a red flag, and the flag marshal at Ballabeg put out the red flag believing the race was to be stopped.

The rescue helicopter, situated within yards of where Reid crashed, airlifted the rider to hospital with a punctured lung and a suspected broken arm, but, with no more than 15 minutes road closing time left, it was not possible to restart the Championship race. The 1996 Solo Championship race was declared as a five lap race. Jason Griffiths, the winner, was over seven seconds clear of former champion Dave Leach when the race was stopped,

(97) 1996 - Geoff Bell and Lee Farrington winners of the F2 Championship.

with Tim Leech taking the final podium

(98) 1996 - Jason Griffiths - Solo Champion

place in third. Ulsterman Adrian McFarland fourth, ahead of Simon Beck and newcomer Dave Goodley completed the top six. The leading 250 was Ian Lougher in seventh, with the injured Phil Reid being credited eighth. The 1996 meeting was marred by the fatal accident, which took place on the Tuesday evening during practice, when local sidecar champions Graham Hayne and Michael Craig were fatally injured in an accident at Church Bends. (98)

1997: Jason retains title!

The 1997 Southern 100 got off to a record-breaking start with both the race and absolute lap records falling in the name of Cumbria's Bob Jackson in the Tuesday evening's Senior Solo Founders race.

Jackson and Preston's Simon Beck had a race-long battle for the honours, finally settled when Bob powered his new McAdoo 750 Kawasaki around the 4.25-mile closed road circuit in 2 minutes 24.7 seconds (105.73mph) on the final lap to break his own previous record set in last year's meeting by two-tenths of a second. Similarly Kawasaki mounted Beck led the charge at the end of the first lap by 0.2 of a second from Jason Griffiths and Jackson, with James Courtney close behind in fourth on the Tillstons Honda. Derek Young, Welshman Steve Ellis, course newcomer Adrian Archibald, big Tim Leech, Tim Poole and Adrian McFarland completed the top ten, with Joey Dunlop languishing in 12th spot on the 500 Honda vee-twin behind leading local Paul Dedman.

Just 5.5 seconds blanketed the top six at the end of the second lap, Jackson setting a new race lap record to oust Griffiths from second spot. Beck continued to hold onto the lead for the next three laps, however, before Jackson finally flew past on the main start and finish straight. By then, Griffiths had lost the tow on John Webb's RC45 but was well entrenched in a safe third place, still followed by the Ulster duo of Courtney and Young. Paul Dedman was slowly working his way through the field, having shaken Joey Dunlop off his tail and taken up the battle for the 600cc class honours with Adrian McFarland. Up front, Beck made another big effort to come onto level terms with Jackson and the pair were side by side running down the Castletown by-pass for the eighth time. But the Peachurst Kawasaki man lost the initiative when he ran wide at Castletown Corner with five miles to go, Jackson stamping his early authority on the meeting with that scintillating final lap to cross the finish line some 4.5 seconds in front of

Beck, breaking the race record in the process. Griffiths slowed up on the final lap to come home almost 20 seconds adrift of the two Englishmen, with James Courtney leading the Irish charge in fourth spot from Derek Young on the over-bored CBR Honda. Tim Leech and Tim Poole both averaged more than 100mph to take sixth and seventh places, while Paul Dedman got the better of Adrian McFarland to take the 600cc honours.

Having blown his RC45 up in the final practice just an hour earlier, Joey Dunlop struggled throughout to keep the front wheel of the 500 vee-twin on the ground, eventually taking 10th spot from course newcomer Adrian Archibald. Richard Quayle had a great ride on his 900 Honda Fireblade to finish 12th in front of New Zealander Blair Degerholm, Crewe's Stuart Jones and Isle of Man Centre Champion Dave Madsen-Mygdal.

Back from injury James Courtney scored a last gasp win in the Junior Solo Founders race, out-sprinting Ian Lougher to the finish line after the Welshman's 250 Honda momentarily cut out exiting the final corner. The race had been a real humdinger from start to finish with up to five riders in with a serious shout of winning up until a couple of laps from the end. Indeed it was Courtney who set the pace on the MSR Honda, but he was reeled-in by none other than Joey Dunlop on lap three, after which it was a five-way dogfight for the honours between those two, Lougher, Gavin Lee and Richard Coates. Lougher moved to the front on lap five, but it was Courtney back at the head of things a lap later with Joey down to third behind Lougher. Gavin Lee retired when the clutch fried on his DTR Yamaha with less than two laps to go, splitting the quintet up. Lougher and Courtney continued to battle it out for first place, while Coates finally got the better of Dunlop for third on the bike he had just finished rebuilding after a big get-off at Scarborough nine days earlier. Into the final corner and Lougher looked to have the race in the bag, but an intermittent cut-out problem, which had plagued him from as early as the first lap, struck again, as he approached maximum revs in second. The bike momentarily stuttered, giving Courtney just the opening he required to zap past to the chequered cloth. Coates was a fine third on his five-year-old Yamaha, some 14 seconds clear of Dunlop at the close, with Tony Duncan completing a lonely ride in fifth spot in front of fellow former Manx Grand Prix winner Decca Kelly. Richard Quayle and Adstock's Neil Richardson had both been well placed in the top seven when they each suffered mechanical problems on lap four and retired, Jason Griffiths having pulled-in after just a single circuit when in eighth spot. Seventh on the road at the finish, Robert Dunlop celebrated his return to the circuit with a comfortable victory in the 125cc class, averaging almost 91mph on Patsy O'Kane's Honda. But the most surprised man on the rostrum was Blackpool's Matt Jackson, who edged out 400 Honda mounted Dave Madsen-Mygdal for second place and was astonished to be shown into the winners enclosure. Two riders shared the quickest lap of the race, James Courtney and Richard Coates both lapping at 100.65mph on the final circuit – Richard's quickest ever lap of his home course, at the time.

Simon Beck held off a spirited late charge from Ulsterman Derek Young to win the Total Oils Senior race in the wet. The big Preston man led the race from start to finish to repeat his only other success on the 4.25-mile Billown circuit four years earlier. Beck fired the 750 Peachurst Kawasaki directly into the lead from the change of the lights, followed by Jason Griffiths and the previous night's winners Bob Jackson and James Courtney. Behind these four the biggest problem for the chasing pack was visibility as a massive plume of spray was kicked up from the rear tyres of the superbikes on the run into the first corner at Ballakaighan. Missing from the bunch was 22-times TT winner Joey Dunlop, who, after suffering a major blow-up with his RC45 Honda in practice, had decided not to try his luck in such tricky conditions with the unpredictable handling 500 vee-twin. Beck arrived at Cross Four Ways, less than three miles out from the start, with a two-second advantage over Griffiths, Jackson and Courtney, followed at another two seconds by Derek Young, Tim Leech and Adrian McFarland. The gap had doubled a lap later as Beck used all his weight to get the power down out of the slower corners, while Courtney took over second spot from Griffiths on lap three and set about halting Beck's runaway charge at the front of the field. By lap four the gap was back down to two seconds, and, at half distance in the ten-lapper, the Irishman had closed right back up with the flying Beck. Derek Young on his 680 Honda now joined Griffiths, while McFarland was in front of Jackson, who was shaking his head in discontent at the unpleasant conditions.

Paul Dedman was having another superb ride and up into the top ten on his 600 Kawasaki. By lap seven, fastest man on the course Young, had jumped clear of Griffiths and caught right up with the leading two to make it a three-way battle for the lead – albeit short-lived as Courtney's Tillston Honda dropped a valve and blew in a big way on the start and finish straight. This left Beck and Young to fight it out over the final 12 miles, and despite all of Young's efforts on the overbored CBR600 he just didn't have the pace to get past Beck's ZXR750, the latter posting the fastest lap of the race on the final circuit at a fraction over 97mph to finish just three-tenths of a second in front. Griffiths remained steady for third, followed by McFarland on the first 600, Jackson, Leech, local ace Dedman, Archibald, and Kiwi Blair Degerholm on Richard Turner's Intersport Kawasaki. David Black had a most impressive ride to finish tenth in front of similarly 600 mounted Paul Hunt, Gary Carswell and Decca Kelly.

There was a double success for the locals in the opening Classic Race when Derek Whalley scored a runaway overall victory and Barry Wood came home fourth and leading 350. After a delayed start due to an oil spillage at Ballawhetstone, Whalley rocketed into the lead on John Turner's Drixton Honda. He was seven seconds in front of Karl Bell's 750 Triumph at the end of the first circuit, and a massive 25 seconds up on John Knowles a lap later following the early departure of Bell's Trident – Alan Phillip's Rocket-3 suffering a similar fate. Welsh veteran Colin Bevan then took up the chase on his Weslake Metisse, but he had no answer for Whalley on the Black Bomber-engined Honda. There was simply no way he was going to be caught, and he turned into the winners enclosure for the second time in successive rides on the Billown circuit over half a minute in front of Bevan at the close – the latter enjoying his first outing since riding in the same meeting last year. Barry Wood tried hard to displace Knowles' 500 Seeley for third, but the G50 just had the extra drive to deny Wood, although the Manxman was the comfortable 350 class winner on Dickie Watson's 250 Suzuki, over 30

(99) 1997-Derek Whalley - 498cc Drixton Honda

seconds
clear of fellow local
Dave Thurlow on a similar mount. (99)

Ian Lougher made up for the disappointment of being pipped at the post in the previous evening's Junior Founders race when he returned the compliment to score a late victory on a gutted James Courtney in the Mann Auto Car Sales Junior race. Buoyed by his win on Tuesday and determined to make amends for a costly blow-up in the Senior race an hour earlier, Courtney led the shortened eight-lapper from the outset on his MSR Honda. He headed Lougher, local man Richard Coates and Southampton's Gavin Lee at the end of the first circuit, followed by Neil Richardson, Owen McNally, Jason Griffiths and Joey Dunlop. Courtney had two seconds on Lougher at the start of the third lap, but Dunlop was an early retirement – still far from happy with his 250 Honda. Lougher had his former mechanic Griffiths as close company for the next three laps as Coates slowly eased clear of Lee and McNally. Local men Richard Quayle and Tony Duncan, who circulated with Joey Dunlop prior to his retirement, now had Adstock's Neil Richardson as the meat in their kipper sandwich. With three to go it was still Courtney out in front, with Lougher a clear second and Coates third as Griffiths slowed up due to a misted-up visor. Into the final circuit and Courtney looked to have a secure enough lead, but luck was not on his side and he coasted through Church Bends with a dead engine after seizing the motor on the rise out of Cross Four Ways. He tentatively bumped the Honda back into life as he exited the bends onto the straight approaching Great Meadow, but Lougher powered by as Courtney's vee-twin finally cried enough and rolled to a halt at Castletown Stadium alongside team manager Davy Wood. It was a complete turnaround of fortune as almost precisely 23 hours earlier he had stepped in to deny Lougher the win when the Welshman's Honda had momentarily cut out on the sprint to the line. After working hard himself to rebuild his 250 Yamaha from a smash at Scarborough, Richard Coates was made up with what was a surprise second place at the close. Still sporting a badly bruised ankle from the flat out in fourth gear fall, Coates finished 3.6 seconds down on Lougher and a little over 10 seconds clear of another Welshman, Griffiths, in third. Owen McNally brought his Aprilia home fourth in front of the local duo of Quayle and Duncan, who not only broke free of Richardson in the latter stages but also got the better of a slowing Gavin Lee on the DTR Yamaha. Steve Richardson of Douglas was the only 350-class finisher.

Greg Lambert and Tony Darby chalked up their first ever Southern 100 victory when they rode Dave Molyneux's 1996 double TT winning outfit to victory in fading light on Wednesday evening. Pushed hard by former solo champion Ian Bell and passenger Neil Carpenter, Lambert and Darby held on well to win the race by a comfortable margin at the close. Run over the full schedule of six laps, conditions deteriorated as the race progressed. Starting on damp roads, the intermittent drizzle turned into steady rain before one-third distance, with the light fading by the minute. Behind the leading two outfits there was a close battle for third between Geoff Bell/Lee Farrington, Kenny Howles/Doug Jewell and Roy Hanks/Robert Briggs. Unfortunately, local cancer victim Mark Fitzgerald's dreams of a top six finish disappeared when he and Alan Warner were forced to retire at mid-distance with mechanical problems. Up front Lambert and Darby were continuing to pile on the coals, holding off Ian Bell's late charge – the latter a newcomer to the course on three wheels despite being a past solo champion. At the chequered cloth he and Carpenter were more than 14 seconds down on Lambert/Darby, in turn some 5.7 seconds up on elder brother Geoff Bell and Farrington, with Hanks and Briggs finally getting the better of Howles and Jewell for fourth. Dave Corlett of Union Mills partnered Steve Sinnott to sixth place, while the first all-local crew were the Kelly brothers Brian and Neil, in eighth spot.

There was disappointment for the local contingent even before the 250/600 race got Thursday afternoon's proceedings underway. Having finished putting a new clutch into the S&S Motors/Done Demolition Kawasaki just half an hour before the race got underway, Paul Dedman was horrified to find that a gasket had been nipped in the rebuild and the bike was seeping oil on the warm-up lap, causing him to pull out. A lap and a bit into the race and there was more bad news for the locals when Richard Quayle was spat off the Mannin Collections/Bullock Honda exiting Ballabeg Hairpin, breaking a collar-bone.

(100) Up front, Bob Jackson and Derek Young were having a close battle for the honours, followed at a discreet distance by Adrian McFarland and Jason Griffiths, with Blair Degerholm holding off the leading 250s of Joey Dunlop and Neil Richardson. There was still nothing in it as Jackson and Young entered the last lap, and, as with two of the races which were to follow, the whole shooting-match was decided on the final corner. Jackson led out of Stadium Corner, but Young had the tighter line into the bridge and ousted Jackson by what was the tightest margin of the day at the line – just one tenth of a second, breaking lap and race records in the process. McFarland also lapped at more than

(100) 1997 - Bob Jackson leads eventual 600cc race winner Derek Young

100mph, while Griffiths was a safe fourth in front of Degerholm, Dunlop, Richardson, Richard Coates and Paul Hunt on Willie Kelly's bog-standard Norbay Builders 600 Suzuki.

Giving his Norton Commando-engined Weslake its second outing in four years, Welsh veteran Colin Bevan exclaimed: 'It runs like a well-oiled watch,' after winning the second Classic race. Leading the eight-lapper from start to finish the Merthyr Tydfil man held off a late charge by Sleaford's Karl Bell on the Triumph Trident to win the race by 2.5 seconds. The pair were neck and neck through the Black Hole on the final lap, but Bell came into the finish with his foot trailing from one of the pegs, albeit well in front of local man Derek Whalley, whose hopes of a double had been partly thwarted by an oil leak on the Drixton Honda. Having retired after just one lap the previous evening, Alan Phillips had a steady ride on his Rocket-3 to take fourth in front of John Knowles and the 350-class winner Barry Woods on the 250 Suzuki. In a race-long dice with Charles Wield and Vin Duckett, Barry grabbed sixth place overall when he out-braked Wield's Seeley Matchless on the final corner after Duckett's similar mount had been pulled up. Dave Thurlow had another good ride to take eighth overall and second in the 350 class ahead of fellow local Ivan Coates.

Robert Dunlop completed his comeback to full-time racing with a superb win in the Steam Packet 125 race. Having last ridden the Southern 100 in 1985 (he rode the Steam Packet Races in 1991 and 1992), Robert had to use all his old daring and determination to beat Owen McNally, Ian Lougher and Gavin Lee in what was a humdinger of a race. Lougher made the early bow waves, but was chased by a swarm of high-revving two-stroke singles as he swept into Ballawhetstone for the first time, most notably Robert who was climbing all over the rear of the Welshman's Honda. After two of the six laps, the leading quartet had broken free of Joey Dunlop and the McCullough brothers, John and Nigel, while Dave Madsen-Mygdal was the leading 400 having his own personal battle with the 125s of Aubrey McCauley and Matt Jackson. With three to go McNally fired up the inside of Lougher at Cross Four Ways, causing the TT winner to stamp heavily on the rear brake and lose vital ground in the chase.

McNally passed Dunlop going into the Black Hole for the last time; Robert trying desperately to draft his way back in front but encountering a backmarker meaning he had to leave his overtaking manoeuvre until the final corner. But Gavin Lee and Ian Lougher had similar ambitions for glory and it was elbows, knees and everything as the four came into Castletown Corner. Dunlop went up the inside of McNally while Lougher stayed left and Lee went straight on up the slip road. Robert was on the gas the quickest and sprinted for the line while Lougher appeared to have the edge on McNally for second. But the 250 winner at this year's North West 200 came across the left-hand side of Lougher's machine, clipping his clutch lever and knocking his Scania Honda out of gear. At the line, 'Micro' Dunlop was over half a second in front with McNally two-tenths of a whisker clear of Lougher and Lee a further 2.1 seconds down on that. It was a cracker of a race and another great ride from Robert. The local trio of Dave Madsen-Mygdal, Michael Cain and Paddy Martin were the first three 400s home, but the race was dominated by the amazing 125s.

A jubilant and thoroughly exhausted Greg Lambert had to be revived by a St John's Ambulance crew when he collapsed just seconds after stepping off the winner's podium at the conclusion of the Sidecar Championship Race. The Catterick man had just completed a Formula 2 double at record-breaking pace with his passenger Tony Darby on the Dave Molyneux-built Yamaha. Having led the previous evening's race in drizzly rain and fading light from start to finish, the pair repeated the feat in somewhat improved conditions in the Championship race. Such was their pace out of the starting blocks that they enjoyed a 4.2 second lead over 1996 champions Geoff Bell and Lee Farrington at the end of the opening circuit, stretching that advantage by another 2.4 seconds before the end of the ninth and final lap. Bell and Farrington never gave up the chase, though, and looked capable of reeling the leaders back in at mid-distance before having a massive fright at Ballawhetstone when their 600 Yamaha went sideways at more than 90mph. The same pair nearly ran into the rear of a slower crew at the Iron Gate in the latter stages and eventually settled for second place, 1.6 seconds clear of Kenny Howles and Dougie Jewell.

Howles and Jewell had their own problems when they discovered the Mistral Yamaha still had no second gear despite a hurried overnight rebuild. They had battled for much of the way with Geoff Bell and TT race winner Roy Hanks, who had Robert Briggs in the chair.

Ian Bell and Neil Carpenter's early promise came to nothing when they first incurred a misfire, then suffered a puncture after clobbering a pavement at Ballanorris with the sidecar wheel. Also going well in the early stages were Alan Warner and local man Mark Fitzgerald who were denied a finish the previous evening by a shredded rear tyre, which ripped a brake pipe off. They were as high as fourth on the opening lap in the Championship race, but then found they had a load of neutrals every time they came into a tight corner, meaning the driver had to hold the clutch in while he changed down through the gearbox. Alan and Mark were overhauled by veteran campaigners Steve Sinnott and Dave Corlett for fifth, while the first all-local crew was that of Port Erin resident Dick Hawes (the day after his 52nd birthday) and the ever youthful-looking 50 year old, Colin Hardman in seventh spot. They just managed to get the better of Brian and Neil Kelly after a closely fought battle. Man of the moment was Greg Lambert, who, quite literally overcome with emotion and exhaustion, praised the efforts of his mechanic for fitting new carbs and refettling the motor to finally cure the elusive misfire which had plagued the outfit all week. Equally delighted on the day were men Doug Jewell and Mark Fitzgerald; Dougie picking up the Paul Fargher trophy for the best local passenger of the meeting; and 'Fitzy' for not only finishing in the top six just a month after suffering an appendicitis, but on the same day as receiving the initial all clear just weeks after completing chemotherapy for cancer.

Ramsey based Welshman Jason Griffith's won one of the most thrilling Southern 100 Solo Championships ever when he smashed lap and race records to pip Bob Jackson by three-tenths of a second. The two, together with Preston's Simon Beck, battled tooth and nail throughout the 50-miler and it was only in the final sprint for the line that Griffiths got the better of Cumbrian veteran Jackson after Beck had been dropped with less than three laps to go. After slightly disappointing rides in the other two open capacity solo races earlier in the week, when Jackson and Beck each had

(101) 1997 - Jason Griffiths and Bob Jackson during the height of the battle for the Solo Championship

a share of the spoils, it was Griffiths who made the early running in the Championship finale. But there were never more than a few bike lengths between the three gladiators as they slugged it out lap after lap over the 4.25-mile closed road circuit. Beck took over the reins on lap two, recaptured by Griffiths a lap later, while Jackson was to the fore on laps six, seven, eight and nine. It was on that ninth circuit that Beck lost the tow on the two former champions when they dived up the inside of a backmarker at Ballabeg hairpin and he ran left onto the straw bales on the exit. Griffiths smashed Jackson's two-day-old absolute lap record on the penultimate circuit with the first ever 106 mph lap of the Southside circuit. But a grimly determined Jackson fought back and the pair were dead-level running down the Castletown by-pass into the final lap. (101)

Jackson led the way into Ballakaighan, but Griffiths was better on the brakes. McAdoo Kawasaki man Jackson fired past on the run down to the Iron Gate, while Griffiths yet again proved the sharper on the brakes to retake the lead at Cross Four Ways. Jackson got his head down on the exit from Church Bends to go back in front on the flat-out run through Great Meadow, but once more Griffiths refused to lie down on the Morris Oils sponsored John Webb Honda. He grabbed the inside line going into the final corner at Alexander Bridge and squeezed Jackson out on the tight right-hander. Jason was quick on the gas coming out and kept his right hand firmly back against the stops in the 300-yard sprint to the line where he was less than a bike length clear of the stalwart Windermere man. Jason Griffiths had regained the Solo Championship he first won in 1994. It was a bitter pill for Jackson to swallow, having also been pipped to the line in the 600 race earlier in the day. Beck was forced to settle for third place, well clear of Derek Young in fourth and Tim Leech in fifth, the latter holding off the late charge from local man Gary Carswell on the Wilson & Collins Kawasaki.

Having missed out on a decent run in the dry with the Chris Mayhew-tuned Ninja, due to a broken exhaust, Carswell finally joined the Southern 100 ton-up club with a lap at 102mph, while other new additions were New Zealander Blair Degerholm on Richard Turner's Intersport 600 Kawasaki, who finished a very impressive ninth in front of Joey Dunlop's 250 Honda, and Neil Richardson, who was the third 250 home behind Dunlop and Gavin Lee. Adrian McFarland was the first of the 600s to finish in seventh spot, just over two seconds in front of Castletown's own Paul Dedman.

1998: Bob regains title!

Bob Jackson punched the air with delight when he won the opening race of the 1998 Southern 100 festival: the Chris Workman sponsored Senior Solo Founders on Tuesday evening. The popular Cumbrian rode well to comfortably beat Honda Britain supported Tillston's man James Courtney in the only ten-lapper of the night. Ramsey's Jason Griffiths nipped inside Simon Beck on the final corner to grab third, while Castletown's Paul Dedman broke the 600cc class lap and race records on his way to fifth overall. Jackson led the way on the opening lap, but the McAdoo Kawasaki man was demoted to second on lap two with Griffiths third and Beck fourth. Steve Ellis held onto fifth place for a while before pulling up the ill-handling Bullock Kawasaki. New Zealander Blair Degerholm was amongst the leading 600s before sliding off at Ballabeg Hairpin, while Gary Carswell was also well placed in the early stages before hitting further gearbox problems with the Wilson & Collins 750 Kawasaki and retiring at Cross Four Ways on lap six.

Bang on form, James Courtney had a 1.7 second lead over Bob Jackson at the end of lap two, and for a while looked capable of extending that advantage. But Jackson refused to let go and when Courtney slackened the pace in the latter stages Bob slipped back in front. There was nothing

(103) 1998 - Winner of first Classic Race - Colin Bevan

Courtney could do this time and, clearly slowing in the latter stages, he crossed the line just over 10 seconds adrift of the Englishman. Simon Beck looked set for third on the Peachurst Kawasaki, but he was caught napping on the final corner at Alexander Bridge where Jason Griffiths saw an opening and slipped up the inside to grab third on the John Webb Honda RC45. Paul Dedman had a relatively quiet time of things and it was something of a surprise to see that

he in fact broke lap and race records in the 600 Supersport class without really being pushed. He was initially part of a group of eight or nine riders chasing the leading quartet, but with the early departure of Ellis, Carswell, Degerholm and Tim Poole, Paul soon pulled clear of the Ulster trio of Richard Britton, Adrian Archibald and Adrian McFarland to finish a lonely fifth on the Done Honda, half a minute behind Beck and Griffiths and nine seconds clear of sixth-placed man Britton on the Schimmel Honda.

Within 300 metres of the finish flag the leading three riders in the Station Garage Junior Solo Founders race were lying spread-eagled on the ground after a dramatic pile-up at the final corner. Having made a last ditch bid for glory, Ulsterman Owen McNally had nipped ahead of Ian Lougher coming into Alexander Bridge, only to be confronted by a couple of backmarkers. Desperate to record his first ever race win on the Billown Circuit, McNally then attempted to squeeze between the right-hand pavement and Wroxham's Michael Blake on the apex of the corner, only to strike the rear wheel of the latter man's 400 Honda. As McNally wrestled to control his own 250 Honda he was then hit from behind by Lougher, sending both men flying to the ground. Right on the pair's heels, Neil Richardson took drastic avoiding action but in doing so dropped his own Honda twin. Marshals were soon on the scene to help sort out the tangle of men and expensive machinery, and while Lougher and McNally were slightly longer getting sorted Richardson was back on his feet in no time. (102)

With Jason Griffiths entering the corner under cautionary yellow flags, Richardson willingly accepted a push-start from one of the marshals and was soon on his way to the chequered cloth. Griffiths managed to slalom his way between the marshals and the remounted figures of Lougher and McNally to snatch a surprise runner-up spot. Decca Kelly overhauled new Manx resident Chris Heath for fifth place in the latter stages after the latter man's Swift Skips Honda went onto one cylinder, but Heath still took the newcomer's award. The hard luck award went to Castletown's Paul Dedman who sensationally led the delayed and shortened race for the first three and a half laps before the clutch on the Paul Bird Honda cried enough.

Damp roads made the going less enjoyable for the buzzy 125 singles, Bob Jackson and Robert Dunlop never quite able to get onto the pace of the Honda 400 of Kiwi Blair Degerholm in the concurrently run 125/400 race. Astride the same Honda Britain-supplied four-cylinder machine which fellow New Zealander Paul Williams rode to victory in the 400cc class of the Lightweight TT, Degerholm led the race from start to finish, crossing the line almost eight

seconds in front of Bob Jackson on the 125 McAdoo Honda, with Robert Dunlop a further two seconds down on the O'Kane machine.

James Courtney smashed the race record and equalled the Total Oils Senior lap record for the Billown Circuit when he stormed to victory in Wednesday evening's opening ten-lapper. The early stages of the race followed a similar pattern to the previous evening's Senior Solo Founders race with Bob Jackson leading Courtney, followed by a second scrap for third between Simon Beck and Jason Griffiths. Paul Dedman once again was a lone figure in fifth. Griffiths went off the pace and eventually retired with a punctured front tyre on the John Webb Honda, leaving Beck out on a limb in third. Courtney got past Jackson's McAdoo Kawasaki on lap four but failed to shake off the determined Cumbrian for another three or four circuits. Lower down the order, there was a good scrap developing for fifth place behind Dedman between New Zealander Blair Degerholm and Ulsterman Adrian Archibald, while Tim Poole, Richard Britton and Adrian McFarland were fighting over the remaining places in the top ten.

By three-quarters distance Courtney appeared to have the race under control on the Tillston Honda and he eventually crossed the finish line some 8.4 seconds in front of Jackson in a new race record time of 24 minutes 29.3 seconds (104.13mph). Beck finished seven seconds behind Jackson, in turn over half a minute in front of Dedman on the Done Demolition 600 Honda, who was slightly short of his record pace of 24 hours earlier. Degerholm won the contest with Archibald for fifth, while Southern 100 regular Tim Poole of Northwich brought his 750 Yamaha home seventh in front of the 600s of Richard Britton and former Schimmel Racing team-mate Adrian McFarland. Just three-tenths of a second split Ronnie McAllister and Dave Madsen-Mygdal for the final place in the top ten.

Welsh veteran Colin Bevan cakewalked the first Island Aviation and Travel Classic Race. Riding a half-faired 830cc Weslake Metisse he led from start to finish to blow the more exotic 750 triples of Karls Wilkie and Bell into the weeds! By half distance he was more than 10 seconds clear, but he opened this up to winning margin of 34 seconds at the close with a fastest lap of just under 89mph. John Knowles rode a steady race to finish fourth and first 500 on his Seeley G50, while Alan Phillips brought his BSA Rocket-3 home a good fifth ahead of the leading 350 ridden by Alan 'Bud' Jackson. (103)

Local hero Paul Dedman smashed the 250-lap record on the final circuit of the Mann Auto Car Sales sponsored

Junior race to snatch glory away from a surprised Ian Lougher. Disappointed after being denied at least the runner-up spot after being involved in a three bike pile-up at the final corner the previous evening, Lougher was determined to make amends on the Scania Honda and he rocketed into an early lead ahead of Junior Founders winner Neil Richardson. Dedman was tucked in tightly on the Vimto Honda ahead of Owen McNally, Jason Griffiths and Richard Coates. Lougher and Richardson soon opened up a small gap on the chasers, which also included the local duo of Chris Heath and Chris Grose.

By half distance Lougher had managed to eke out a five second lead on Richardson, who was coming under heavy pressure from Dedman. Griffiths and Coates, meanwhile, were locked together in a close scrap for fourth. Dedman managed to get past Richardson on lap six and set off after Lougher. By lap eight the gap was reduced to five seconds, but certainly nothing to worry about as far as Lougher was concerned. Going into the final lap the margin was still three seconds in Ian's favour, but Dedman pulled out all the stops on the Paul Bird owned machine and had slashed that lead to just one and a half seconds by Ballabeg hairpin. Dedman had the Welshman firmly in his sights going through the Black Hole and when Lougher looked behind him exiting Church Bends to see the Vimto sponsored machine right on his case he got the shock of his life. Paul slipstreamed the Honda Britain supported rider through Stadium Corner then out-braked him into Alexander Bridge. On the better line he out-sprinted Lougher to the line by just one-fifth of a second, both men averaging more than 100mph on 250s.

Dedman's race average of 100.30mph was impressive enough, but his final circuit of 103.17mph was nothing short of incredible for a rider who had never completed a lap of the circuit on a 250 prior to the start of practice for the 1998 Southern 100! Richardson was third, while Griffiths shook off the challenge posed by Dick Coates in the later stages to finish a comfortable fourth. Chris Grose was sixth, while Decca Kelly had a cracking ride on an ageing TZ350 Yamaha to finish eighth overall and collect the 350-class award.

Ian Bell and Neil Carpenter were the most surprised men in the Southern 100 paddock on Wednesday evening when they came from third to first on the final lap of the first sidecar race. They had trailed race-long leaders Greg Lambert/Lee Aubrey and Dave Molyneux/Craig Hallam throughout, but moved into second place when Lambert and Aubrey stopped at the

Black Hole. (104) & (105)

Bob Jackson started championship day off the way he finished with victory in the combined 600/250 race over Ramsey based Welshman Jason Griffiths. Fired up from his superb win in the previous evening's 250 race, Paul Dedman led a huge field out of the blocks. But a snapped clutch cable, of all things, soon slowed his progress and he dropped almost to the very back of the field by the end of the lap. Onboard adjustments enabled him to continue in the race, but he eventually retired on lap six after fighting his way back up to 12th. Jackson led from lap two onwards, but never looked in serious doubt until the final lap or so when Jason Griffiths got the hurry-up message and got past fellow Welshman Ian Lougher, New Zealander Blair Degerholm and Ulster first-timer Richard Britton, who overshot one of the hairpin corners. But Jason's charge came too late and despite setting a new lap record of 103.31mph for the 600s on lap nine he was still almost five seconds short of Jackson's race-record pace at the close.

(104) 1998 - James Courtney leading the 600cc Race

(105) 1998 - Deputy Clerk of the Course Alan Hampton's tractor 'made a bid for freedom' and held up racing while it was recovered!

Lougher also finished strongly in third spot, winning the 250 class by a comfortable margin from Owen McNally and Neil Richardson. (106)

Colin Bevan's hopes of completing a double in the Classic races were blown when his 830 Weslake Metisse gave up the ghost after he had set the fastest lap of the Eurocars Classic Race. This let the Triumph triples of Karl Wilkie and Karl Bell take the top two podium places, as John Knowles once again brought his faithful Seeley G50 home in third place and top '500', with 'Bud' Jackson filling fourth place in a repeat of the first classic race to claim the 350 award on his 250 Platt Suzuki. (107)

(106) 1998 - Paul Dedman (10) and Owen McNally (9) during 250cc Race - Dedman won

The luck of the Irish was clearly with Robert Dunlop in the Isle of Man Steam Packet 125cc race. Dunlop had been trailing Ian Lougher by a substantial margin, but when the latter man's Honda seized going over Ballanorris Railway Bridge for the penultimate time it left a surprised Dunlop in the driving seat and he duly crossed the finishing

(107) 1998 - Karl Wilkie - Winner of second Classic Race

line as the victor. Behind were the 125s of Bob Jackson, John McCullough, Chris Grose and Matt Jackson, with Mike Cain completing the top six and the first 400 home, quickly followed by the next two 440s – Patrick Martin and Dave Madsen-Mygdal. (108)

As with the TT, Dave Molyneux returned from a year out on the world championship trail to reclaim the Southern 100 Sidecar Championship title he last won, surprisingly, back in 2003 with a scintillating ride. Teaming up with Leicester's Craig Hallam for the second time, having made their debut together at the previous weekend's Oliver's Mount meeting, the pair won the title at a canter after struggling with a broken brake disc in the first sidecar race. Defending champion Greg Lambert and new passenger Lee Aubrey led away from the start again, with Bell and Molyneux tucked in close behind. Molyneux shot out of Bell's slipstream on the run down towards Great Meadow on lap one, and was crawling all over the rear of Lambert down the by-pass. As it was the Sulby ace fired the Honda Britain backed machine he built himself up the inside going into Iron Gate on the second circuit, described by one of the race marshals there as the 'pass of the week!' (109)

Lambert and Aubrey held onto the back of the flying Honda pair for another lap, but the Yamaha chucked a rod out of the crankcase next time down the flat-out run to the Iron Gate and they rolled to a halt with nothing more to show than a lap record for their week's work. But that was soon to be taken away from them as well and within a couple of minutes of their demise Molyneux and Hallam had taken seven-tenths of a second off the record they had set less than 24 hours earlier. Moly and Craig had officially been clocked at 2 minutes 37.1 seconds in practice, which is a tenth of a second inside the ultimate three-wheel record for the course set by Molyneux and Peter Hill on the GP-spec Krauser in 1995. In the race they had to settle for 2m 39.4s (95.98mph) but that was enough. Once they had lost sight of Molyneux and Hallam there was no coming back for Bell and Farrington, and whilst Ian won the solo championship title in 1987, he would have to wait another year at least to become the first man in the history to also win the Southern 100 championship on three wheels. Kenny Howles and local passenger Nick Crowe very nearly repeated the TT 1-2 result when they got past Ian Bell and Neil Carpenter on the final lap, but the latter crew re-passed them at Stadium to take runners-up position at the flag by just three-tenths of a second. Roy Hanks and Robert Biggs who were locked in mortal combat with Howles and Crowe for much of the duration finished fourth, well ahead of back-from-injury Geoff Bell and Lee Farrington. (110)

The Solo Championship race has a habit of throwing up some thrilling encounters, but the finale to the 1998

(108) 1998 - Robert Dunlop - Back to winnings ways at Billown

meeting will live in the memories of all concerned for a long time to come. Wheel to wheel for just about every inch of the 12-lap race, Bob Jackson, Jason Griffiths and James Courtney all had a turn at raising the outright record for the Billown circuit, but in the end it was Jackson, with that final crucial twist of the throttle, who set the new absolute lap record with a speed of 107.07mph on the penultimate tour to clinch the honours. Jackson, who first raced at the Southern in 1975 and claimed his maiden victory two years later, grabbed the holeshot into Ballakaighan on lap one and whilst diving into an early 50 metre or more lead he was soon dragged back by the Hondas of Griffiths and Courtney.

Simon Beck and Welshman Steve Ellis held onto the back of the trio for a lap or so but they soon drifted backwards. Behind them, Tim Poole, Paul Dedman, Ian Lougher, Adrian Archibald, Gary Carswell and Neil Richardson were in the next group. The pace was electric at the front, however, and the big three soon stretched away from the rest of the field. It was obvious the winner was going to emerge from the leading threesome, but which one? Courtney looked to be the dark horse, sitting in neatly behind Jackson and Griffiths. His Tillston Honda RC45 was fitted with the latest fuel injection system and arguably a good match for Jackson's McAdoo Kawasaki down the long fast straights, which are such a feature of the circuit. But Griffiths was determined not to let go of his number one plate easily and he put in his big effort on lap 10. Then Jackson put in that meteoric penultimate circuit, the fastest in the 43-year history of racing on the Billown Circuit. It certainly did the trick, giving him that vital couple of yards going into the final lap. Griffiths tried all he knew, but very nearly came to grief exiting Ballabeg when he put on the power just a little bit early and found himself being kicked out of the saddle as the rear wheel of the John Webb Honda RC45 flicked violently sideways. Somehow, he managed to regain control but Courtney was through into second place for the first time. Meanwhile Jackson had shot into a second or more lead and had the race safely in the bag, barring a disaster. Courtney was still in front of the shaken Griffiths as they sped through Stadium Corner for the last time. Griffiths then executed his favourite passing manoeuvre up the inside going into Alexander Bridge and duly zapped Courtney to cross the line 1.8 seconds down on winner Jackson.

Unable to live with the incredible pace up front, Simon Beck settled for fourth place after struggling for much of the way with a loose fairing bracket on the Peachurst Kawasaki. Tim Poole held off Paul Dedman for fifth and was the first 600 ride home ahead of regular rival Adrian Archibald, with Ian Lougher the leading 250 in eighth spot.

My Domino Story, by Ian Lougher:

I think it was 1998, Owen McNally, Neil Richardson and myself were having a right old scrap for the lead in one of the 250cc races. It was the last lap and as we rapidly approached the final corner, Castletown Corner, Owen was leading, with myself 2nd and Neil in 3rd. We were all bunched really close together and nobody was giving an inch. As we got to the corner, there was a backmarker just where we didn't need a backmarker. Owen decided to make a move in an attempt to get a break from myself and Neil. But as Owen tried to dive up the inside, he had left it a bit late, and the backmarker, who didn't realise we were there, was fully committed to his line. Owen was left with nowhere to go, and catching the backmarker's rear wheel, down he went, right in front of me. With absolutely no room for manoeuvre, I also hit the deck, my front wheel under Owen's back wheel. Meanwhile Neil, who was on a slightly wider line, and for a moment must have thought he had escaped the melee, just clipped the outside of Owen's bike, over-balanced and he and his bike landed right on top of the pair of us.

So there we were, all three of us plus bikes in the road in a big pile.... With the race win still up for grabs there was a

(109) 1998 - Ian Bell (4)- Roy Hanks (6) - Heading towards Castletown Corner

mad dash to get going and take the flag. Neil "Long Legs" Richardson was fortunate to have landed on top and having gathered himself and his bike up he was first away, leaving Owen and me frantically pulling and tugging to get our bikes untangled. Neil eventually took the win, with Owen second and me third,

The backmarker meanwhile, completely unaware of the catastrophe behind him, experienced a bit of a wobble but rode on regardless.

(110) 1999 - Dave Molyneux and Craig Hallam lead the pack

1999: Joey's sixth Solo Championship!

The last Southern 100 of the millennium couldn't have got off to a worse start as eight riders were caught up in an accident in the opening race of the programme. Gavin Lee and Marc McDonald both lost their lives in the incident at William's Bend.

When racing got underway 24 hours later, King of the Roads Joey Dunlop, scored a first and a second on Wednesday evening. The wily Ulsterman powered to the front at the half way point in the combined Senior race, then stepped up another gear to win the ten-lapper by more than nine seconds from New Zealander Blair Degerholm. Dunlop shot past Degerholm going into Ballakaighan corner at the start of the fifth lap. Early on, a battered and bruised Jason Griffiths had led the way for a lap on the O'Kane R1 Yamaha. Then Ulster's Adrian McFarland took the reins for a couple of circuits on his similar mount, before Degerholm shot to the front at the end of lap three.

But there was just no shaking Joey off, and whilst Griffiths and McFarland both slipped back on the Yamahas, the RC45 Honda of Dunlop soon upped the pace. Only Degerholm, on Des Collins' 750 Kawasaki, was able to keep with him, and he eventually lost the fight as the 23-times TT winner disappeared off into the distance. Uel Duncan, who had gone down in the eight-bike-pile-up at Williams' the previous evening, rode extremely well to finish fifth, 16 seconds down on Griffiths, to take the 600 Supersport class honours. Dave Madsen-Mygdal eventually got past old campaigner Paul Cranston and new boy Ryan Farquhar to claim a solid sixth on the older of his two RC30 Hondas.

Derek Whalley won one hell of a scrap for the honours in the Island Aviation Classic race on a G50 Matchless originally belonging to the late Danny Shimmin. Karl Wilkie led the way on the first lap, but he was then ousted by Whalley, who in turn lost the lead to Welshman Colin Bevan. Fellow countryman Jeff Jones took over the reins on lap four, but it was back in Whalley's control with a little of over four miles to go, at which point the luckless Bevan toured in to retire. In the end, Whalley took it by just one tenth of a second from Jones, with new Island resident John Knowles recording the quickest lap of the race to grab third. Barry Wood was the leading 250 on Dicky Watson's Suzuki in his second race back from his TT practice smash at Union Mills.

Ian Lougher was simply untouchable in the combined Junior race, recording lap and race records on his way to a runaway victory on the Sabre Racing Honda. He was already five seconds clear of a three-way scrap for second at the end of the first lap. Richard Coates, Joey Dunlop and Neil Richardson effectively tripping one another up as they shuffled the pack behind them After four laps Lougher was 15 seconds ahead, then 18 and 23 seconds as he continued to stretch the lead. Joey eventually moved ahead of Richardson and Coates, but Lougher and Dunlop went quicker still.

The Welshman heading home the Ulsterman by some 24-seconds, with the Englishman just 1.8 seconds adrift of Joey. Robert, meantime had a good scrap for the honours in the 125 class with fellow Ulsterman Darran Lindsay. Lindsay led early on, but Robert cheekily came alongside him coming onto the Castletown by-pass for the sixth time.

The pair touched hands for a split second, then Robert swung away from his rival and off into a never-to-be-relinquished lead. British 125 champion Chris Palmer made an impressive debut to finish 10th overall and third 125 behind the two Ulsterman.

Craig Hallam battled through the pain barrier of a broken shoulder blade to partner Dave Molyneux to a record-breaking victory in the first sidecar race of the 1999 meeting. They took the lead from Ian Bell and Neil Carpenter on the brakes into Iron Gate on the first lap, and led from there in. But it wasn't easy, as Molyneux explained later: 'We had a misfire with the bike from lap three onwards.' This made his and Hallam's record lap and race speeds all the more amazing.

Hallam was chuffed with the result: 'I'm in pain now, but it wasn't too bad when we were going.' He said. Bell and Carpenter were 2.6 seconds down at the close, well clear of the three-way battle for third – originally a five-way contest until first Rod Bellas and Geoff Knight found the pace too hot, then Geoff Bell and Dave Wells slipped out of the reckoning. This left Roy Hanks/Phil Biggs slugging it out with Kenny Howles/Doug Jewell and Greg Lambert/Lee Aubrey. It was gripping stuff, right up until the finish flag, when Hanks just got the verdict over Howles and Lambert.

Jason Griffiths left it very late on the brakes into the last corner before out-manoeuvring Blair Degerholm and Adrian McFarland for the honours in the combined 600/250 race. Surprisingly, even with Ian Lougher amongst their ranks the 250s didn't get a look in and despite an early flourish from the Welshman he was soon shuffled down the running order. Degerholm soon took up the baton and he appeared to look the marginal favourite on Richard Turner's Intersport Honda as the race began to settle down. But Griffiths, still in considerable pain from his injured right foot, and a rejuvenated McFarland refused to let the Kiwi go. It was the wily Welshman Griffiths who had the final trick up his sleeve and he sling-shot round the outside of the other two exiting Stadium Corner for the last time, grabbing the tight inside line into Alexander Bridge and sprinting off down the by-pass to cross the line just one-tenth of a second in front of Degerholm. McFarland was another tenth behind in third. All three were inside the old race record.

Up and coming Irishman Uel Duncan had a cracking ride to take fourth place on the Allstar Honda in front of the leading 250s of Lougher and Neil Richardson. Best Newcomer was Bob Jackson's protégé Ryan Farquhar, while the battle of the Manxmen went all the way to the wire between the R6 Yamaha of Peter Hounsell and the two-stroke 250 Yamaha twin of Chris Grose, the latter man eventually sneaking eighth place. A short way behind, Andy Jackson beat elder brother Bud for 12th.

Karl Wilkie used the extra grunt of his 750 Triumph triple to deny Derek Whalley a Classic race double. While Derek snatched a late victory in Wednesday evening's eight lapper, Wilkie led Thursday's repeat helping from the second lap onwards to finish some five seconds in front of the G50 Matchless. Jeff Jones and fellow Welsh veteran Colin Bevan had a good battle with former Senior Manx Grand Prix winner Les Trotter for third place, until the latter's 500 Crooks Suzuki twin expired at half distance and the rear sprocket on Bevan's Weslake split in two exiting

(111) 1999 - Ian Lougher and Robert Dunlop read their signalling boards as they flash down Castletown Bypass

Cross Four Ways with a lap and a bit to go. This left Jones a clear third from Alan Phillips' Rocket-3, with G50s of Charles Wield and Vin Duckett completing the top six.

The 250 winner of the previous evening, Barry Wood, completed just a couple of laps before going out on Thursday, leaving Dave Thurlow to battle it out with Bud Jackson. And what a contest it turned out to be, going right the way to the wire before Thurlow got his Suzuki home just a couple seconds in front.

(111) Robert Dunlop recorded his first win of the year when he edged out Ian Lougher by a wheel's length in the Steam Packet sponsored thrilling 125/400 race. Joey Dunlop and Darran Lindsay completed a less than cosy foursome in the early stages of the tiddlers race, but when Robert and Ian made a jump for it on lap three, Joey and Darran were racing for the last place on the rostrum. There was certainly no quarter given between any of the four, and going through the Black Hole for the last time Robert just had the edge of the Welshman. Ian made most of the slipstream effect going into Stadium, and thought he had the job wrapped up coming onto the start and finish line when 'micro' drafted by. Whilst he and Robert were both inside the old race average, Ian had the consolation of setting a new 125-lap record for the Southern. Lindsay edged clear of Joey Dunlop for third, with current British number one Chris Palmer an excellent fifth in his second ever race on the circuit. William Philp of Slough took the 400 class honours from Dave Madsen-Mygdal and Paddy Martin.

(112) 1999 - Ian Bell and Neil Carpenter on their way to making history in the Sidecar Championship

Former Southern 100 Solo Champion Ian Bell made history when he became the first man to also win the Sidecar title on the same course. Runner-up with passenger Neil Carpenter behind Dave Molyneux and Craig Hallam the previous evening, Bell chimed in on all of his Yamaha R6's four cylinders in the Championship race when Molyneux's Honda CBR fizzled out. The race was restarted after just one of the original nine circuits when 1997 winner Greg Lambert and stand-in passenger Ivan Murray crashed out spectacularly at Ballawhetstone, fortunately without suffering major injuries. Their outfit apparently hit the

(113) 1999 - Joey Dunlop on his way to winning his sixth Solo Championship

outside hedge, then rebounded across the road upside down, above the heads of Roy Hanks and Phil Biggs. Another outfit piloted by Mike Ibbotson and Mark Fitzgerald, ran over Murray's legs. Hanks and Biggs played no further part in the proceedings as their Yamaha's brake master cylinder was damaged. (112)

In a retake of the original start, Molyneux led Ian Bell and Kenny Howles through Church Bends on the first lap of the shortened six-lap race, followed at a wider margin by Geoff Bell, Rod Bellas and Keith Walters and Gary Masterman. Little changed on the second tour, but heading onto the top gear Great Meadow straight there was a distinct misfire emanating from Molyneux's Honda, a repeat of the previous evening's problem which plagued them from lap three onwards, but even more severe. It was the last the crowd saw of the TT winners. They eventually diagnosed the problem as a faulty ignition. His and Craig Hallam's departure left the way clear for Bell and Carpenter to mop up, but when they had a bit of an overshoot it enabled gritty campaigners Kenny Howles and Doug Jewell to catch right up, and they in fact led by a marginal distance with two laps to go before Bell and Carpenter regained command. At the flag, the latter crew were over four seconds to the better, with Southern 100 regulars Rod Bellas and Geoff Knight a good third in front of Geoff Bell and Dave Wells. The only newcomers to complete the distance were John Potts and Roy King in sixth spot. (113)

Plumping for the identical compound rear Dunlop tyre as Jim Moodie did in the Senior TT, Joey Dunlop almost suffered the same fate as his Honda Britain team-mate when rubber from the centre of the slick started to peel away in the latter stages of the Solo Championship. The tyre was in fact the very same spare Moodie had in the pits on Senior day but never used, fitted to a smaller than standard 16 and a half inch wheel.

'The tyre works superbly for about 40 miles, then it just starts to rip up,' said Dunlop, after his sixth championship win in 23 glorious years at Billown. He hadn't realised the tyre had almost worn through until he stepped off the bike in the winners enclosure. After winning three titles in a row from 1976-1979, Dunlop only contested the Southern on a couple of occasions in the 80s during the peak of his F1 and Honda Britain career, but he bounced back with another win in 1991 and another two years later. Such is the experience and supreme confidence of the 47-year-old that he never seems to panic, even when he appears to be out-sprinted by riders almost half his age in the early stages of a race. It happened in the Senior Founders race on Wednesday evening when he appeared to be slipping off the back of the leading trio for a few laps, then suddenly there he was at the sharp end. It was much the same on Thursday in the main race of the week when Blair Degerholm made the early running, with Adrian McFarland and Jason Griffiths both elbowing for space alongside the 23-times TT winner. Two laps into the race, though, and Joey was out in front, and charging. From thereon in he was in full control. Ready to up the pace when necessary, but demoralising the opposition in the meantime as he continued to steam away into the distance. McFarland broke free of the similarly R1 Yamaha-mounted Griffiths after three or four laps, eventually reeling in Degerholm's Wilson & Collins Kawasaki. He was in front of the New Zealander with four laps to go, but Blair finally got back ahead as McFarland suffered problems from, of all things, tennis elbow! (114)

Professional despatch rider Blair admitted later he needed a few good work-outs in the gym to get fitter if he was to make any serious inroads on Dunlop – Joey's definitely the boss! Behind Griffiths, fellow Ramsey man Gary Carswell gained his only finish of the week in fifth place. Sixth, and producing one of the rides of the day on a nine-year-old TC30 Honda, was Dave Madsen-Mygdal. For much of the race he had been in a five-way scrap for seventh place with young guns Ryan Farquhar and Uel Duncan, the number 17 Kawasaki of Paul Cranston, and the 250 Honda-twins of Ian Lougher and Neil Richardson. But Dave eventually wore them down, and with a final sprint he pipped Lougher for that last place on the top six leaderboard. (115; 116; 117; 118)

(114) 1999 - Joey receives the winner's laurels from Jack Yardley, Managing Director of Ronaldsway Shoe Co.

two successes in the Corlett's Trophies sponsored Senior Founders. Astride the same Hector Neill R71 Yamaha he rode in last month's F1 and Senior TTs, he soon made his way to the front of the field. But Degerholm was never far away on the Wilson & Collins 750 Kawasaki. The pair were nose to tail for much of the 10-lap race, and when the New Zealander made his move into Cross Four Ways on the final circuit it looked as though he had timed his bid to perfection. But the New Zealander had been a little over zealous with his late breaking and admitted later he out-braked everyone in the race – including himself. To avoid a close inspection of the straw bags he had to slam everything on at the last second, enabling Lougher to nip through on the inside and retake the lead he had held for all but a few yards of the entire race.

Jason Griffiths was initially on the pace, but slackened off after a couple of laps to finish a lonely third on Ray Cowles R1 Yamaha. He was no way slow enough to allow Ulster's rising star Ryan Farquhar to squeeze into the winners; enclosure, however, as the Ulsterman only moved up into fourth place in the latter stages when Paul Hunt firstly overshot Ballakaighan corner, then Cross Four Ways in a similar way to Degerholm. To that point, 'Big H' had ridden an excellent race on Kevin Cringle's R1 Yamaha, but clearly cracked under the pressure as Farquhar made a late charge on the McAdoo Kawasaki. Adrian McFarland took the 600cc class honours in sixth place, breaking local man Paul Dedman's lap record in the process. Seventh across the line, Ulsterman John Donnan was the leading newcomer – indeed doing extremely well to average more than 100mph in his first ever race on the Billown circuit.

Dave Madsen-Mygdal had a start to finish battle with Bud Jackson. Both similarly mounted on RC30 Hondas the pair were at it hammer and tongs lap after lap before Dave

(115) 1999 - Solo Championship Presentation-1

(116) 1999 - Solo Championship Presentation-2

(117) 1999 - Solo Championship Presentation-3

(118) 1999 - Solo Championship Presentation-4

2000: First Kiwi Solo Champion

Ian Lougher got the first Southern 100 of the new millennium off to a flying start with a brace of wins in back-to-back races on the opening evening of racing. He broke Bob Jackson's two-year-old race record in the Senior Solo Founders after a great scrap with Slough based Kiwi Blair Degerholm, then he notched up his 18th Southern 100 victory in a slightly more leisurely fashion in the Junior Founders. Separate class wins went to the Ulster duo of Adrian McFarland in the 600 and Darran Lindsay in the 125 – both breaking existing lap records in the process. (119)

Welshman Lougher had to work very hard for the first of his

finally got the better of the Cumbria man in the closing stages to grab eighth. Victor Gilmore, another newcomer from Ulster, finished 10th in front of the local trio of Gary Carswell, Peter Hounsell and Paul Duckett.

(120) Darran Lindsay's pit crew gauged his record-breaking ride in the 125 class of the Station Garage sponsored Junior Founders race to perfection. His Honda ran out of petrol as it crossed the finish line! The very much on-form Ulsterman led his class from start to finish, shaking off an early threat from former British Champion Chris Palmer. With the Nibbles Catering Honda running on fumes, Lindsay came down the Castletown by-pass for the final time with an 8.7 second advantage over the Englishman to grab a fine sixth

place overall in the combined field of 125s and 250s. Matt Jackson was third of the tiddlers in eighth spot, but there was no luck for Chris Grose who dropped out on the final lap when in striking distance of a top four finish. Out in front at the head of the field throughout was Ian Lougher on the Manton Honda, notching up his second win of the night with consummate ease. He grabbed the advantage in the 250 class from the drop of the flag and never looked back. Almost six seconds clear at half-distance, he relaxed the pace in the closing stages to finish 2.6 seconds in front of the titanic battle for second between Gary Dynes and Neil Richardson.

Originally a three-way contest, until Jason Griffiths retired on lap three with a slipping clutch on the Trollope Yamaha Dynes and Richardson were never more than a couple of bike lengths apart. Richardson finally got past his rival with two laps to go and for a while appeared to be stretching clear. But Dynes had other ideas and he equalled the 250-lap record of 100.29mph with a huge push on the final circuit. Whilst Richardson kept the tighter line into the right-hander at Alexander Bridge, Dynes took a wider faster sweep and powered his way across the line just one-tenth of a second in front. Blair Degerholm made the right tyre choice in what was a wet start to the second evening of racing at the 2000 Southern 100 to notch up his first outright win on the Billown Circuit. The Slough-domiciled New Zealander made up for a sluggish start to win the reduced Total Oils Senior race by some 15 seconds from Adrian McFarland. He was third into Cross Four Ways on the first lap behind Ian Lougher and Darran Lindsay, but soon moved ahead of both men into a never-to-be-relinquished lead. Having put a full wet on the front of Des Collins' Kawasaki and a hand-cut slick on the rear, the Kiwi soon knew he'd made the correct choice. Blair remarked that it was very wet and he was getting wheel-spin over the brow before the Black Hole.

Without the R1 Yamaha he rode so well last year, Adrian McFarland made full use of the softer power of his smaller capacity R6 to record a best ever result on the Billown Circuit in second spot. He came from fourth place on the first lap to overhaul fellow Ulsterman Lindsay and Tuesday night's open class winner Ian Lougher. Gary Carswell rode well for sixth in front of Victor Gilmore and Dave Madsen-Mygdal.

(119) 2000 - Ian Lougher leading the 250 charge into Ballakaighan

Local riders scored a clean-sweep of class wins in the Island Aviation & Travel Classic race. Dave Madsen-Mygdal led the race from start to finish on Pete Tyer's 750 Triumph Trident, while Derek Whalley was the 500cc class winner and Barry Wood the first 350 across the line in sixth spot. Madsen-Mygdal was very nearly caught napping in the latter stages of the race when Ulsterman Karl Wilkie made a late bid for glory on his similar Rob North-framed Triumph. He and Rocket-3 mounted Jeff Jones had enjoyed a close contest for the number two spot, until – with a little more than four miles to go – he broke free.

Unaware that Wilkie was closing in on him until he heard the distinctive sound of a second Trident right on his case at Ballabeg hairpin on the final lap, Madsen-Mygdal had to put his skates on through Williams corner and the Black Hole to keep ahead of his rival. Having glanced over his shoulder again at Cross Four Ways he knew that Karl was still close enough to mount a challenge at the last corner and kept his head down to take his first outright victory at the Southern 100. At the line the gap was four-fifths of a second between the first two, with Jones at a further seven seconds. Seeley G50 mounted Derek Whalley rode a lonely race in fourth to take the 500cc class honours by a clear margin from Cumbrian veteran Les Trotter, while Willaston's Barry Wood rode a 250cc version of the Suzuki twin to sixth place and first 350.

Ian Lougher took his Manton Honda to its second win in as many nights, this time in the Mann Auto Car Sales Junior race – the fifth on the programme for the Isle of Man Steam Packet sponsored Southern 100. Buckingham's Neil Richardson ran a close second to Lougher for the first three or four laps, but once Lougher got the jump there was no holding him. Fellow Welshman Jason Griffiths rode a steady race to finish third on Dennis Trollope's Yamaha, while rejuvenated Bud Jackson finally got the better of Sulby's Brian Kneale for fourth. Both men beat Gary Dynes, who had a couple of scares on the wet roads after plumping for a slick rear. Leading 400 was Martin Sharpe, repeating his success of twelve months earlier. Dave Madsen-Mygdal was second riding Monica Floding's 400, with Kevin 'Ago' Murphy third.

Roy Hanks and Dave Wells split the Bell brothers in what was a ding-dong contest in the Agrimark sponsored Formula 2 Sidecar race – the final event of Wednesday evening. Ian Bell and Neil Carpenter led the race from start

(120) 2000 - Darran Lindsay record breaking 125cc race winner

to finish, but it was without a doubt the most exciting race of the evening with close battles right the way down the order. In fading light, but rapidly drying conditions, Ian Bell and Carpenter won the six-lap affair in a race time of 16 minutes 24.6 seconds, almost 13 seconds ahead of the titanic struggle for second between Ian's brother Geoff Bell and fellow veteran Roy Hanks. No more than a few feet apart throughout, Bell and Hanks swapped places on several occasions. Bell was passengered by Craig Hallam, the former Dave Molyneux ballast man. Phil Dongworth and John Luebke made a flying start and were a close second to eventual winners Bell and Carpenter in the early stages. They eventually finished a good fourth ahead of another amazingly close battle for fifth.

This was settled in Rod Bellas' and Geoff Knight's favour, although they were in fact accredited with an identical time to Kenny Howles and Dougie Jewell. The first all-Manx crew home were Brian and Neil Kelly in eighth spot.

Kiwi ace Blair Degerholm kept his other local sponsor Richard Turner happy with a record-breaking win in the combined 600/250 race, which opened the five-race programme on Championship day.

Having notched his first outright victory on the course the previous night, Degerholm clearly had the smell of victory in his nostrils again when he left the start at a rapid rate of knots in the 10-lapper.

But it was Ulsterman Darran Lindsay who made the initial bow waves at the head of the field on his 600 Yamaha. Fourth into the first corner, Degerholm had muscled the Intersport Kawasaki into the lead by midway round the second lap and there he stayed. Two very quick laps at mid-distance, which saw Degerholm establishing a new lap record of 103.518mph, successfully broke a four-strong Ulster rearguard action and despite a lack of any pit boards around the course he came home some six seconds in front of Adrian McFarland at the close, with Lindsay third and Ryan Farquhar fourth.

Gary Dynes won the 250 class, fifth overall, making up for some disappointment of a wrong tyre choice the previous evening. And local man Brian Kneale made it onto the podium as the third of the 250s behind Ian Lougher.

Karl Wilkie of Millisle in Northern Ireland won the second Classic race of the meeting when local man Dave Madsen-Mygdal's Trident blew up at mid-distance. Wilkie got the better of starts, but when Madsen-Mygdal manoeuvred into the lead on lap three it looked as though he was on his way to a double. However, when Pete Tyer's 1971 triple cried 'enough' a lap or so later at Great Meadow, Wilkie was nicely placed to retake the reins. Welsh veteran Jeff Jones applied the pressure in the latter stages, but at the finish it was Wilkie by 2.6 seconds, with Derek Whalley a very steady third across the line – winning the 500 class for the second race in succession on the Seeley G50. Kirk Michael resident John Knowles won a close contest for fourth place with Les Trotter after Kewaigue's Alan Phillips retired in the latter stages. First 350 to finish was the 250 Suzuki of Bud Jackson, but he again had to contend with the 350 Honda of Tony Cawte who once again rode extremely well.

Darran Lindsay's turn for glory came in the 125cc race when he led the charge of the tiddlers from start to finish. Ian Lougher was right with him initially, but in the end he had no answer for the on-form Lisburn man. At the close, Lindsay was over six seconds clear with former British Champion Chris Palmer a good third behind the Mannin Honda of Lougher in what was only his second year at the Southern. Sulby's Chris Grose was a good fifth behind Blackpool's Matt Jackson, followed home by the leading 400s of Martin Sharpe and Dave Madsen-Mygdal.

Ian Bell and Neil Carpenter led the Sidecar Championship race from start to finish, establishing a new race record despite the loneliest of rides. Whilst another titanic battle raged behind for the minor placing on the podium, Bell and Carpenter ploughed a lonely furrow at the head of the field on the Molyneux-chassised Yamaha. They completed the nine-lapper in a winning time of 24 minutes 11.5 seconds, 4.6 seconds inside the time set by Dave Molyneux and Craig

(121) 2000 - Ian Bell and Neil Carpenter once again collect the Championship honours

Hallam in the 1998 championship race, but slower than the average speed set by the same pair in the shorter F2 race last year. On this occasion, Hallam was passengering Ian Bell's brother Geoff, and it was they who took second place ahead of the previous night's runners-up, Roy Hanks and Dave Wells. Hanks and Wells had a real scrap with Phil Dongworth and John Luebke until the latter crew went out with a suspected blown motor on the final circuit. A lap earlier, Rod Bellas' and Geoff Knight's race had come to an end on the approach to Great Meadow when they were slugging it out with Kenny Howles and Dougie Jewell for fifth place. This late reshuffle left Howles and Jewell a clear fourth in front of Keith Walters/Lee Aubrey and the first all local crew of Centre Champions Brian and Neil Kelly. Veteran charioteers Billy Quayle and Dennis Proudman had their own private battle for honours, which eventually went to Quayle and passenger Gareth Lacey from Proudman and Glyn Jones. (121)

Glyn Jones jumped straight out of the chair of the Swift Skips Yamaha onto his own SP1 Honda for the solo championship race, which followed. Blair Degerholm became the first antipodean to win the Southern 100 Solo Championship title in the 32-year history of the race. But the New Zealander had to smash the outright Billown lap record on his 12th and final circuit of the main feature race of the week to deny an equally determined Welshman, Ian Lougher, what would have been his first championship.

The race was a fitting climax to the first Southern 100 of the millennium, sponsored as a whole by the Isle of Man Steam Packet Company.

With a win apiece in the two open class races going into the final day of the meeting, it was always going to be a close affair. Few thought it would be quite so thrilling. Lougher took the early lead on the Hector Neill R71 1000cc Yamaha, with Degerholm and Jason Griffiths tucked in close behind.

(122) 2000 - Solo Championship first lap charge

(123) 2000 - Blair Degerholm first Kiwi to win the Solo Championship

Griffiths held on for the first couple of laps, but the pace up front between the lead two was a little too hot to handle for the three times former champion on this occasion. Lougher continued to keep his nose in front, but Degerholm grabbed the lead for the first time at Ballawhetstone on lap five. (122)

Two laps later Lougher got him back, but Degerholm refused to lie down and he had another turn at the front at three-quarter distance. Lougher retook the lead from the 750 Wilson & Collins Kawasaki man at Castletown Corner on the penultimate lap and it was all square going into the final 4.25-mile circuit. Degerholm was right beside the Welshman as they went over the hump-backed railway bridge at Ballanorris, but he wasn't able to find a way past until he managed to again get the better drive out of Ballabeg and dive into the lead entering the first right hander at Ballawhetstone. Once ahead this time he was determined not to let it slip, managing to block Lougher's efforts on the final two tight right-handers at Cross Four Ways and Alexander Bridge. He crossed the line three-fifths of a second in front of his rival to register one of the closest ever finishes in the championship race, but that final lap was a scorcher of 107.217 mph – two-tenths of a second quicker than Bob Jackson's 107.068mph set on the penultimate lap of his wining ride in 1998. Jason Griffiths was third some 22 seconds back. (123)

Fourth place went to Ryan Farquhar on the Winston McAdoo Kawasaki. In only his second year at the Southern, he finished some six seconds in front of fellow Ulsterman and leading newcomers John Donnan, with Darran Lindsay the first of the 600s in sixth place. He had a race long dogfight with fellow countryman Adrian McFarland, but top Manxman Paul Hunt eventually split the pair. 'Big H' started strongly and held onto fourth place behind Griffiths for most of the way, until he was forced to slacken the pace

(124) 2001 - Throughout 2001, work parties were in progress

in the latter stages due to an injured right hand. Gary Dynes was the best of the 250s in ninth spot, just in front of another Ulsterman, Victor Gilmore.

2001: No Southern 100

November 2000 and the Southern 100 committee were well ahead with planning the 2001 Southern 100 Road Races, scheduled for 16th, 17th, 18th & 19th July 2001. Then early in the New Year came the news of the foot and mouth epidemic in the UK. The TT races were the first meeting to be cancelled, only the third time in their illustrious history that they would not run. After much consultation with competitors, government officials and the like, the Southern 100 committee made the decision to postpone the July event until Friday, Saturday and Sunday, September 14th, 15th & 16th, after emergency legislation had been passed in Tynwald. New Regulations and Entry Forms were sent out and other preparations put in place. (124)

Then in July, ironically during the week that the 'Southern' should have been run the decision was made to call off the 2001 meeting. Club officials met Department of Agriculture, Fisheries and Forestry, prior to the monthly Committee meeting and the decision was made to cancel the Southern 100 Road races for 2001. Club Chairman, at the time, Derek Nicholson said: *"It is regretted that we, as a club, have had to call off this year's events, especially so with all the efforts put in by the committee to safeguard racing on the Billown Circuit. But having due regard for all the co-operation the club receives annually from the farmers, landowners, as well as the government agencies and in the best interests of the Manx community as a whole, to lose one year for their continued long term support is a small price to pay."*

Secretary George Peach added: *"It is perhaps more disappointing that the new dates had to be abandoned as such a wonderful response had been received from competitors wishing to enter. All we can ask them is to keep their enthusiasm intact until next May for the Pre-TT Classic and the Southern 100 again in July."*

Both Castletown MHK Tony Brown and Tourism and Leisure Minister David Cretney were disappointed at the news. Transport Minister Mr Brown, who marshals at the event, said: *"We must acknowledge and praise the organisers for acting responsibly in dealing with this year's races. I fully support them in this matter and look forward to 2002's races with great eagerness."*

Mr Cretney said: *"I am obviously disappointed but felt the decision may have been becoming inevitable. I will work with the organisers to ensure next year's season is bigger and better than ever."*

Chief veterinary officer Eamon O'Donnell believes farmers will feel a 'great deal of relief'. He said: *"The organisers have an excellent relationship with the farmers and they realise the debt of gratitude they owe them and they did not want to put that relationship in jeopardy. They did not even ask the question of them and the club did not get to the situation where they would bulldoze the running of the event through. I am sure the Manx National Farmers Union and the farmers do feel a great deal of relief."*

2001 saw a complete wipe-out of racing on closed roads in the Isle of Man. Only the two world wars prevented the TT and the Manx Grand Prix taking place. It was the first time the Southern 100 had been cancelled since the first meeting in 1955.

2002: Back in business & it's Lougher again!

Ian Lougher opened his 2002 Southern 100 account in scintillating fashion with a brace of record-breaking wins. Now based in Dromore, Northern Ireland, the popular Welshman was in a class of his own in the two Solo Founders races. Astride the same 1000cc TAS Suzuki he finished runner-up to David Jefferies on in the Senior TT, he won the opening race of the 11-race programme by almost 15 seconds from Ryan Farquhar. None of his rivals really saw which way Lougher went. He was a couple of seconds clear in little more than a lap and six seconds to the good after four of the 10 circuits. But the best was still to come and on lap six he bettered the outright course record set by New Zealander Blair Degerholm in that memorable dogfight with Lougher for the 2000 Solo Championship title.

Three-tenths of a second inside that standard, Ian's speed of 107.44mph was a full 2.3seconds better than Bob Jackson's long-standing class lap record from 1997. Despite negotiating a number of backmarkers, Lougher threw in another lap of 2 minutes 22.4 seconds on the penultimate circuit to equal his earlier standard, crossing the finish line almost 15 seconds in front of Farquhar. Jason Griffiths looked strangely off the pace en route to third place. Fast starting Chris Palmer was ousted by fellow local Paul Hunt for fourth place, while Victor Gilmore rode steadily for sixth in his comeback ride after breaking a pelvis in the TT. Fellow Ulsterman Darran Lindsay picked up the prize for the best 600 rider, which surprised him – he didn't know there was a class for 600s in the race! He finished 10th overall and well clear on the road of Jeff Tansley and local newcomer Tom Clucas of Peel.

Barely an hour later Lougher and Lindsay were both back on the rostrum after finishing first and second in the Junior Founders race. This time Lindsay got the drive off the line while Lougher's 250 Honda bogged down. There was little between the two at the end of the opening lap, but Lougher was soon past and off into the distance again. A class lap record of 102.34mph on the third circuit gave him a clear lead of almost six seconds at half way. By the end of the penultimate lap the margin had grown to 11 seconds and Lougher was able to trim down the wick to coast home a fraction under eight seconds clear at the finish. It was the first time the race had been won at an average of over 100mph. Lindsay had a good scrap for second place with Stoke-on-Trent's Derek Welch, the latter making his return to the Billown circuit after an 11-year break. The gap was almost four seconds at the close, but for much of the race there was a matter of only a few yards between them. Griffiths had another lonely ride, this time to fourth place, some way in front of Richard Coates. Robert Dunlop was sixth overall, first in the 125 class. Palmer got caught up in a race-long scrap with 250-mounted Bud Jackson, and it was only when he broke free of the latter rider in the final couple of laps that he started to reel Dunlop back in. At the close, the gap was 2.4 seconds but both men were inside the old lap record for the 125s in this particular event.

Ian Lougher celebrated his 38th birthday in style with another double victory and a new outright lap record for the Billown Circuit during the second evening's racing of 2002. Recording a carbon-copy of the previous evening's big bike win on the 1000cc TAS Suzuki, he beat Ryan Farquhar by an increased margin of 19 seconds, with Ramsey's Jason Griffiths a further 20 seconds down in third. In pulling away from the Yamaha pair, Lougher upped his own new outright lap record to a staggering 108.587mph on the third lap – a time of two minutes 20.9 seconds for the 4.25-mile course.

His race record of 106.813mph for the Total Oils sponsored race wasn't too far short of the lap-record-previous-sun-kissed meeting. Farquhar and Griffiths were left to fight over the crumbs from Lougher's birthday celebration bash. They had a good tussle for a couple of laps, but with Lougher out on his own, Farquhar slowly edged clear of Griffiths for the runner-up spot. Farquhar's pace was similarly just out of Griffiths' reach, while Victor Gilmore had a good ride to hold off Castletown resident Chris Palmer for fourth – the pair battling it out for most of the distance. Maughold's Gary Carswell was the leading Manxman in sixth place, Paul Hunt having endured a number of problems before eventually retiring.

Dave Madsen-Mygdal, the veteran local campaigner had a golden hour on Wednesday evening when he scored back-to-back wins. He had his rivals well and truly licked in the Davison's Ice Cream sponsored Classic race when he won by precisely 10 seconds from the leading 500 of Mike Hose, then scored a tremendous victory over rising Ulster star Ryan Farquhar in the 400 class of the Junior race. A regular supporter of road races in the Isle of Man and Ireland, Madsen-Mygdal was in vintage form. He led the eight lap Classic race from the word go, later admitting it took him a couple of laps to get dialled in after stepping off his RC30 Honda from the previous Senior race onto the 1971 Triumph Trident for the Classic. Once clear, there was no stopping him and he went on to record a comfortable victory on Pete Tyer's big triple. Hose rode gallantly, but John Turner's Honda twin didn't have the lungs of the Trident and despite some heroic cornering he had to settle for a comfortable win over the Seeleys and Beezers in the 500 class. Karl Wilkie brought another Triumph triple home in third, while Barry Wood overcame gearbox problems to secure a class double for sponsor John Turner in the 350cc category.

Win number two for birthday boy Lougher came in the third race of the evening, the Mann Auto Car Sales Junior race. This was a lot tougher as Darran Lindsay initially refused to lie down, despite Lougher getting the cleaner start. Lindsay's bike was quicker on the long straights and he managed to get back in front when the Welshman accidentally hit the kill button on his 250 Honda exiting Church Bends.

Lougher simply sat behind Lindsay and picked his spot, on the brakes into Ballabeg Hairpin for the fourth time. Once in front, Lougher again stamped his authority on the race and was soon away into the distance. The gap was just under 18 seconds at the close, but it was another new lap and race record for the flying Welshman. Griffiths was again third, in front of fellow locals Richard Coates and Brian Kneale, with Laxey's Adam Nowell the best newcomer in seventh spot. The real contest was for the 400cc class honours, where Dave Madsen-Mygdal produced one of his best rides of his long racing career to eventually see off Ulster ace Ryan Farquhar.

In their first ride together for three years, former TT winners Dave Molyneux and Craig Hallam scored a thrilling victory in the DHL Formula Two sidecar race. Aboard the Slick Bass-tuned Honda Britain machine, the pair looked as sharp as ever – leading the race from the word go. Ian Bell and Neil Carpenter were never far away, pushing the lead pair throughout and eventually setting the fastest lap. Both crews were lapping consistently inside Moly and Hallam's 1998 record, but it was Bell and Carpenter who ended up the quickest. After dropping a second or so behind, former Southern 100 solo champion Bell charged round the 4.25-mile circuit in 2 minutes 36.2 seconds on the fifth circuit to raise the three-wheel best to 97.951mph. It still wasn't enough to get level with Molyneux and Hallam though and the gap remained 1.3 seconds in the latter crew's favour at the chequered cloth. Phil Dongworth and John Luebke broke away from Geoff Bell and Jake Beckworth to grab the final podium spot, while Kenny Howles and Doug Jewell were fifth in front of Greg Lambert and Daniel Sayle.

Jason Griffiths, a regular winner on the Billown course since 1993, scored his only success of the 2002 Southern 100 in the combined 600/250 race. Riding the Road & Track 600 Yamaha, the Ramsey Welshman led the race from start to finish to win by a clear margin of 13-and-a-half seconds from Darran Lindsay. Griffiths made a reasonable getaway and was first into Ballakaighan Corner, leading Ian Lougher and Ryan Farquhar through Ballabeg. Farquhar had a troubled race and eventually retired, while 250-mounted Lougher was forced to give second best to Lindsay. It was still classified as a class win for Lougher, but for once he wasn't on the pace of the lead two. Lindsay was pleased enough with his second place, considering he was riding a fairly stock-based Regal 600 Suzuki.

Local Fireman Paul Hunt chalked up his second fourth place of the week, just seeing off Mark Parrett. Dave Madsen-Mygdal recorded one of the narrowest victories in Southern 100 history when he came from nowhere to pip Mike Hose by one-tenth of a second in the Eurocars Classic Race. Struggling with the three-cylinder Triumph which ran intermittently on two pots in the early stages, the local garage mechanic was about to call it quits after a couple of laps, as it wouldn't rev over 6000, but then it chimed back in on all three. Mike Hose was well away with it by half distance on John Turner's 500 Honda twin. He soon disposed of Karl Wilkie and was looking set for a runaway victory when the bike sprang a leak. With oil over his boot and back wheel, he nevertheless held on to win the 500cc class. Madsen-Mygdal only just got the verdict in the final few yards of the race. Coming over the brow onto the Castletown by-pass the pair were neck and neck, but the big Trident just snatched it on the line. Derek Whalley was well clear of Alan Brew for fourth place and second in class, while Chris McGahan just held off Barry Wood for the 350 honours.

Robert Dunlop smashed lap and race records to deny Ian Lougher a clean sweep of all main solo classes at the 2002 meeting. The pair were at it hammer and tongs throughout a thrilling 125 race. Lougher set off like a scalded cat and

was a couple of seconds clear of his friend and rival within six miles. But Robert fought back tenaciously to take out four seconds in the space of one lap on the third circuit to turn a two second deficit into a two second lead – smashing Lougher's three-year-old lap record in the progress.

It was then Lougher's turn to do the chasing and he re-caught Dunlop with two to go. They rode the last nine miles nose to tail, but canny Dunlop kept all the doors closed on the final lap to snatch it by three-tenths of a second on the line. Dunlop had borrowed some engine bits and a Bridgestone tyre off his rival before the start. Former British Champion Chris Palmer had another lonely ride to third in front of the leading 400 of Dave Madsen-Mygdal. With Ryan Farquhar an early retirement on this occasion, Madsen-Mygdal was able to take things a little easier once he had got past fast-starting Swiss Peter Jarmann. John Crellin had his best result of the week to finish seventh overall and third in class ahead of leading newcomer Alastair Bayley of Skelmersdale.

Dave Molyneux clinched his sixth Sidecar Southern 100 Championship with consummate ease. With Craig Hallam in the chair once again, the Honda Britain pair won by some 22 seconds from Roy Hanks and Dave Wells after Ian Bell and Neil Carpenter stopped at two-thirds distance. Moly and Hallam pulled out a 3.5-second lead after just one lap of the circuit, stretching it by another couple of seconds in the next two laps. Going into the seventh lap the gap had grown to over eight seconds, but when Bell and Carpenter pulled up at Cross Four Ways with a burst water pipe on the Yamaha it was all over bar the shouting. The lead gap immediately shot to 24 seconds over Hanks and Wells, so Moly was able to slacken the pace over the final couple of circuits. Not only did Molyneux and Hallam set a new race record for the Championship race, they also wrestled the outright sidecar lap record away from Bell and Carpenter – set only the previous evening. At two minutes 35.6 seconds it means the pair are only three seconds short of the first 100mph lap for the chairs at Billown.

The brace of wins makes Molyneux the most successful driver of all time in the Southern 100. He is now top of the pile with 14 wins, one more than Ulsterman Lowry Burton. Moly has won the championship title twice with Hallam (1999 & 2002), three times with Karl Ellison (1991, 92 and 93) and once with Paul Kneale (1986).

One brother's misfortune was another's gain and Geoff Bell stepped in to fill third place with Jack Beckworth after the demise of his younger sibling. As ever with the sidecars there was a high rate of attrition on the bumpy closed roads circuit. Phil Dongworth and John Luebke were dicing with Hanks and Wells for much of the way, before retiring with three laps to go. Greg Lambert and Daniel Sayle went out of sixth place at mid-distance and Nick Crowe and Darren Hope recorded another non-finish after initially showing so much promise. Doug Jewell partnered Kenny Howles to fourth place, but the best all-local crew were Glyn Jones and Jamie Scarffe in sixth.

From the outset of this year's Southern 100, only one rider looked like getting his hands on the main solo championship trophy. Such was his dominance of the big bike classes on the Temple Auto Salvage 1000cc Suzuki, Ian Lougher was always the red-hot favourite. He duly won the 11th and final race on the calendar at a canter from Ryan

Farquhar, with Jason Griffiths completing a carbon copy 1-2-3 of the other two superbike races. Surprisingly, it was the joyous Welshman's first-ever Solo Championship race. (125)

Only in recent years has Lougher concentrated more seriously on the bigger machines, finishing a very close second to Blair Degerholm in the 2000 event. Nevertheless, he is now the clear second-most-successful rider of all time on the 4.25-mile Billown Circuit. His tally of six wins equalled Joey Dunlop's similar record from 1991, and leaves him just seven short of the great man's all-time record number of 31 wins. He had a lead of three seconds over Farquhar after two laps, seven after five and 18 going into the final circuit. Having cracked the 108mph barrier on Wednesday, Lougher reeled off another couple of laps at a similar pace but fell short of the blistering 108.587mph he set the previous evening. Farquhar and Griffiths were again left in his wake, Ryan admitting that he would have crashed if he'd gone any quicker. Griffiths made a poor start and had to battle his way through the slower riders in the early stages. Chris Palmer, like Griffiths a relatively new resident, had a lonely ride to fourth, followed by Ulsterman Victor Gilmore and fellow countryman Darran Lindsay on the first of the 600s. Best of the Manxies was Paul Hunt in seventh spot, after the retirement at mid-distance of Gary Carswell. Brian Kneale of Sulby was the best of the two-strokers, picking up the 350cc class award on the ex-Jeremy McWilliams 250 Honda in 15th spot.

Nelson Gill

The funeral of a great stalwart of the Southern 100 Motorcycle Club took place on a bright and sunny day in May 2002. It was decided to give Nelson an official send-off and it was arranged with the undertakers for him to do a lap of the Billown circuit in the hearse, with Club officials gathered on the start line, where the chequered flag would be lowered as the hearse went past.

The officials were all dressed in Club paddock jackets and were on the inside of the circuit on the start line with Phil Taubman and Gordon Clague on the other side of the road on look out for the cortège to appear over the rise from Castletown Corner. After a shout from them "Here it comes!" the assembled officials all stood to attention with heads bowed – as the local plumber, who has a black van, drove past, much to the amusement of everyone involved. As time was pushing on we were starting to get worried if Nelson was actually going to get his last lap, when over the brow of the hill his hearse arrived. It slowed down at the start line and our respects were paid. Then it took off like a rocket.

As we were designated to carry the coffin into the church at Arbory, we crossed the road and got into our cars and set off to Arbory. Rounding Ballakaighan Corner there was no sight of the hearse on the long straight. When we arrived at the church, having to park a good 800 yards away and walking up, we saw the hearse waiting for us to carry Nelson in. We are sure Nelson would have enjoyed his last lap, and, as someone said, he would be saying Phil Taubman was a nuisance when he started in the club as a boy and he still is!

Rest in Peace Nelson.

(125) 2002 - Unbeatable on the 1000cc TAS Suzuki - Ian Lougher

2003: It's Ryan's year!

Dungannon's Ryan Farquhar smashed lap and race records in the opening race of the 2003 Southern 100 meeting, but very nearly came to grief in the second race when he clipped the rear end of the 125 TT winner Chris Palmer's machine. Farquhar led the G H Corlett Senior Solo Founders virtually from start to finish on the big McAdoo 1000cc Suzuki, lapping at 107.746mph on lap seven before cruising to a safe 6.7 second victory margin over Ramsey's Jason Griffiths. (126)

Ian Lougher, who had nabbed the early break with a cracking start on Mark John's GSX-R, had to settle for third behind the Yamaha UK R1 of his fellow Welshman, but the talk of the race was the dual performances of course newcomers Guy Martin and Martin Finnegan. Two of the up-and-coming talents of real road racing, the pair battled it out for most of the 10 laps before Englishman Martin just got the edge over Finnegan's Round Tower Suzuki in the latter stages. Three former Senior Manx Grand Prix winners occupied sixth to eighth places, with Mark Parrett the filling in the Manx sandwich between Paul Hunt and Gary Carswell. Scotsman Bob Grant took the 600 class honours in 11th spot, with Castletown's Chris Palmer next home on the Irish Racer sponsored R6 Yamaha. (127)

Palmer took second place in the Station Garage sponsored Junior Founders race, which followed, but was very nearly taken out by Farquhar at half-distance at Castletown Corner. With Lougher out in front on the Berwick 250 Honda, Palmer and Farquhar were dicing for second place when the latter man cut sharply into the rear wheel and seat

(126) 2003 - Ryan Farquhar negotiates Church Bends, followed by Jason Griffiths

(127) 2003 - Newcomers Guy Martin and Martin Finnegan were spectacular

of Palmer's machine. It was amazing how he stayed on as he set off in the direction of the slip road in Malew Street. But stay on he did to narrowly pip Neil Richardson for third place at the flag, with first and second places settled between Lougher and Palmer. The leading 125 of Robert Dunlop, who rode a lonely race on his Crossan's Honda, split Paul Owen and fellow newcomer Norman Rank of Germany at the finish.

In a carbon copy of the previous evening's two opening races, Ryan Farquhar and Ian Lougher won the Total Oils Senior and Man Auto Car Sales Junior races. The two riders were literally side-by-side as they powered down Castletown by-pass at some 150mph to complete the first lap of the open-capacity Senior race. But Lougher, far from happy with the handling characteristics of his Mark John's 1000cc Suzuki, was soon forced to back off the pace and it was fellow Welshman Jason Griffiths who eventually took up the gauntlet as Farquhar's main challenger.

Before that, Lougher and Griffiths had a good dice on the road until Lougher slowed and ultimately pulled in to retire, complaining that the silver-coloured bullet refused to keep its front wheel on the road – even in top gear! Farquhar, meantime, had built up a substantial lead and looked a sure winner until he was baulked by some backmarkers with two laps to go and his advantage came tumbling down. Heading into the final lap, Ramsey resident Griffiths had slashed the Ulsterman's lead back to 1.9 seconds. Griffiths continued to slash away at the Dungannon man's lead, which was just 0.21 of a second going into the final 4.25 miles. Farquhar appeared to have it covered and had opened the gap to about 20 metres at Cross Four Ways with about two miles

(128) 2003 - Dave Madsen Mygdal - winner of first Classic Race

to run to the flag. Griffiths' last hope was an inside overtaking manoeuvre at Alexander Bridge, but Farquhar had the tight line well protected and he exited well to seal the win by two-tenths of a second – Griffiths equalling Lougher's absolute lap record for the course on that final circuit with a speed of 108.587mph.

Griffiths admitted it had been a tough race and when Farquhar got away in the early stages he concentrated on the second-place battle with Lougher. Northern Ireland based Englishman Guy Martin finished a very impressive third place in only his second ever race on the course. Martin had edged clear of fellow newcomer Martin Finnegan prior to the latter man pulling out with mechanical problems on lap six. Finnegan and Lougher's departures on consecutive laps moved Castletown's own Chris Palmer up to fourth place on the ICR Suzuki, with Ulster's Victor Gilmore fifth and Maughold's Gary Carswell rounding off the leader board in sixth.

Dave Madsen-Mygdal won his third Southern 100 Classic race in as many years when he rode Pete Tyer's Triumph Trident to a clear victory. Initially involved in a four-way battle for the lead with similarly mounted newcomer Simon Walsh, 500 class winner Allan Brew and Seven Oaks veteran Chris McGahan, Madsen-Mygdal soon opened up a substantial lead. Just half a second in front at the end of the first lap, he was 7.24 seconds clear by mid-distance and 9.13 seconds to the fore with a couple of laps to go. He was to slacken the pace on the final two circuits and still cruise home with 7.5 seconds to spare over McGahan's BSA Rocket-3. Andreas man Allan Brew rode an excellent race on his G50 Matchless to finish third overall and first in the 500 class. He was catching McGahan up on the slower corners, but losing out to the 750 triple on the faster straights. Grantham's Simon Walsh made an impressive debut to finish a clear fourth overall. Barry Wood and Decca Kelly had a good scrap for the 350 class honours. Both 250 Suzuki mounted, Kelly got past his rival on lap two when Wood missed a couple of gears. (128)
But Wood pegged him back to retake the advantage at half distance in the eight lap race, going on to finish ninth overall some 11 seconds in front of his fellow Manxman.

Ian Lougher just made it home on a raucous-sounding Berwick Honda in the Mann Auto Car Sales Junior race after the 250 twin's silencer came off with three laps remaining. Fortunately for him, he had built up a safe enough lead over close friend Chris Palmer and the win was never really in serious doubt. At the close the winning margin was 5.2 seconds in Lougher's favour. Ryan Farquhar, fresh from his second win of the week in the preceding Senior race, led the concurrently run 400 class from start to finish, but despite achieving a class lap and race record he was never on the pace of the leading two-strokes. He finished 0.2 of a second in front of newcomer Paul Owen at the finish, the latter man having enjoyed a close scrap with Roy Richardson (400) and German first-timer Norman Rank on the fourth 250 home.

The opening sidecar race was abandoned after sidecar crew Andy Brown and passenger John Dowling died when their Yamaha machine lost control and crashed at Ballawhetstone during the third lap of the race.

Ian Lougher won a close scrap with rival Ryan Farquhar to

(129) 2003 - Lougher leads Farquhar into Cross Four Ways during their hectic 600cc race

take the honours in the opening 600 solo race on Championship Day. Held on wet roads in a steady drizzle, the race saw another grudge match battle – between the two men – that left the rest of the field in their wake. Initially Lougher cleared off, having settled for full wets on his Manton Honda as opposed to intermediates. He built up a four second lead in as many laps but then, as the rain

(130) 2003 - Madsen-Mygdal took the second classic honours

stopped and a dry line appeared, Farquhar started to haul the Welshman in. The gap was down to 1.8 seconds with four laps remaining, then virtually nothing at all as they raced down the by-pass side by side. (129)

It nearly all ended in tears when Farquhar twice attempted to go up the inside of Lougher on the brakes at Cross Four

(131) 2003 - Ramsey's Alan Brew took the 500cc Classic Race

Ways. On the first occasion he very nearly rammed the Manton machine but just managed to turn the nose to the right to avoid what looked like a certain collision. The pair were still neck and neck going into the final corner at Alexander Bridge, where Farquhar exited just in front only to be outgunned over the brow of the by-pass by Lougher who took the flag by just three-hundredths of a second. On his 39th birthday, Lougher admitted his choice to stick with wet tyres undoubtedly won him the race. Farquhar rued his choice of intermediates back and front, admitting he was unable to get the power down out of the final corner.

Peel's Tommy Clucas had a cracking ride to finish third, by some way his best result on the Billown Circuit. Jason Griffiths was black-flagged at the end of the penultimate lap due to an oil leak, leaving new boy Guy Martin to finish an impressive fourth in front of Victor Gilmore and Mark Parrett. Chris Palmer had a steady ride for seventh and the first 250 home.

Home riders won all three classes of the Eurocars Classic race – a complete stencil of the first Classic race. Dave Madsen-Mygdal led this one from start to finish on Pete Tyer's big Trident to cross the line some 42 seconds in front of Allan Brew's Seeley 500 Matchless, while Barry Wood rode a brave race on Dicky Watson's little Suzuki to take the 250 honours. In damp conditions, Madsen-Mygdal was never in any serious threat, nor for that matter was Brew in second place, who had Chris McGahan well beaten. Allan immediately dedicated the double victory to his father and former racer Dennis Brew, who was listening to the race commentary from a hospital bed in Ramsey Cottage Hospital. Wood actually held on to fourth place for a lap or two before conditions started to improve and the larger capacity machines were able to outgun his T20 Suzi. Nevertheless, sixth place was an excellent result, over half a minute in front of the next bike. (130) (131) (132)

Roy Richardson was the surprise winner of the Steam Packet combined 400/125 race. In the rapidly improving conditions he in fact established new lap and race records on a Honda which was originally prepared for the TT but had broken down on the opening lap of the Mountain Course. Ryan Farquhar made the early running but as his wet front overheated on the drying roads he was ousted by Blackpool man Richardson, who led from lap three onwards. Dave Madsen-Mygdal broke free of the 125s of Chris Palmer and Ian Lougher on the final lap to finish third on the road, Palmer just ousting Lougher for the smaller capacity honours after grabbing the slipstream behind both men going through Great Meadow for the last time. (133)

Dave Molyneux waved goodbye to the Southern 100 with a seventh Sidecar Championship title. Twenty years after making his debut appearance on the 4.25-mile Billown Circuit as a 19-year-old, the Regaby ace revealed that he will not be returning to defend his title next year. Thursday's championship race was a very low-key affair. Ian Bell had packed his truck and left for home on the morning of the race. His brother Geoff was nursing two broken arms from the previous evening's crash at Ballawhetstone, while other notable non-starters included Roy Hanks/Dave Wells, whose DMR Yamaha stopped on the warm-up lap at Cross Four Ways. Molyneux and passenger Craig Hallam were just seconds away from being non-starters themselves as their Honda refused to fire up in the holding area. Molyneux admits it was his own fault as he had taken the clutch cover off after the abandoned Wednesday race and had forgotten to reconnect an electrical wire. With the wire reconnected, they just managed to get the outfit back together in time for the warm-up lap. The all-local crew of Nick Crowe and Darren Hope led the opening lap before Molyneux and Hallam powered through the twists at the end of the by-pass straight going into the second circuit. Once ahead they never looked in trouble and pulled out two seconds or more a lap on their nearest rivals. Fancied runners Greg Lambert and Daniel Sayle, on Molyneux's 2002 outfit, retired on lap three leaving Phil Dongworth and Kenny Howles in a real scrap for third with their respective local passengers, Gary Partridge and Doug Jewell. That battle became a contest for second place after Crowe and Hope were forced out at Church Bends on lap five when the sidecar tyre deflated. (134)

The battle went all the way to the wire with Howles and Jewell beating Dongworth and Partridge by just over one second. Newcomers Steven Coombes and Stuart Castles rode very well for fourth place in front of the first all-local partnership home of Brian Kelly and Jamie Scarfe.

Ryan Farquhar came to within seventh-tenths of a second of the first ever 110mph lap of the Southern 100 circuit, when he scorched to victory in the Ronaldsway Shoe Co. Solo Championship race. The race was initially halted at the end of the first lap following an incident at the Iron Gate corner in which star newcomer Guy Martin broke an ankle. He had made a strong start and was attempting to go underneath early leader Farquhar at the tight right-hander when he ran out of road, sat upright and went straight into the straw bales lining the solid stone walls on the left. Martin's 750cc Suzuki bounced back across the track, but mercifully hit none of the following riders. Nevertheless, with the rider requiring immediate attention and wreckage from the bike and bales strewn right across the road the decision was made to red flag the race. (135)

At the restart, 25 minutes or so later, Farquhar again forged his way to the front on Winston McAdoo's GSX-R. The only rider ever in any real contention was Ramsey's Jason Griffiths on the Yamaha Motor UK R1 entered by Road & Track Motorcycles. He admitted being very lucky not to have been caught up in the initial incident at the Iron Gate and had purposely taken a tight line on the right-hand side to avoid the machine which he knew was likely to bounce across the road in front of him. But to say he settled for second place would be a misleading statement for he indeed began to make inroads into the Ulsterman's lead as the race drew to a close

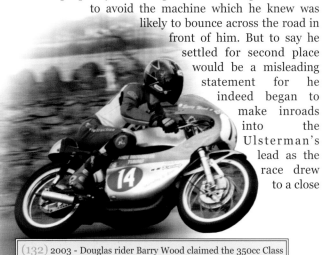

(132) 2003 - Douglas rider Barry Wood claimed the 350cc Class

(133) 2003 - Roy Richardson - surprise winner of the 400cc race

– in much the same way as he had the previous evening. Farquhar knew that Griffiths was on a late charge and he ran wide at Cross Four Ways on the final lap as he came under increasing pressure, but the young Dungannon ace held on to record what he admitted was his best ever victory. He smashed the absolute course record on lap eight with a time of 2 minutes 20 seconds precisely (109.285mph), 0.9 of a second inside the standard set by

(134) 2003 - Dave Molyneux said farewell to the Billown Circuit with his seventh Championship victory

Ian Lougher last year but equalled by Jason Griffiths in Wednesday's Total Oils Senior race. Griffiths also went inside the old record with a time of 2.20.3 on that final lap and admitted to being pleased with second place on the day. Newcomer Martin Finnegan finished a fine third, having started the week on his backside following a fall during

(135) 2003 - Ryan Farquhar sweeps through Church Bends on his way to the Solo Championship

practice. Maughold's Gary Carswell rode a solid race on his near standard GSX-R 1000 to finish a good fourth after a close initial dice with Victor Gilmore, Ian Lougher and Chris Palmer. Lougher had opted to ride the Manton Honda he rode to victory in the 600 race instead of Mark Johns' big 1000 Suzi, which had simply refused to behave itself over the bumps and jumps of the 'Southern' course. Mark Parrett made up for the disappointment of a non-finish in the Senior race by getting the Wilson & Collins Kawasaki home in sixth place.

Newtownards man Bertie Payne, a long time 250cc sponsor of the late great Joey Dunlop has donated a new trophy to be presented annually at the Southern 100. The Joey Dunlop Trophy, together with a cheque, will be awarded to the fastest competitor at the Southern. Bitmac contractor Bertie explained: (136)

(136) 2003 - Bertie Payne presents Ryan Farquhar with the Joey Dunlop Trophy

"The Billown Circuit was one of Joey's favourites and one where he achieved some of his most memorable successes, breaking lap records on many occasions. The trophy is a fitting tribute to the man himself and to a great meeting – one he was always proud to be associated with."

2004: Ian regains Solo Championship!

The conditions for the opening two races of the 2004 Southern 100 meeting couldn't have been wetter, but the racing could hardly have been closer! With impeccable timing, a light drizzle turned to a steady downpour as riders came to the line for the Corlett's Trophies Senior Solo Founders race. Clerk of the Course, Phil Taubman,

immediately despatched the riders back to the Paddock to enable them to fit intermediate or full wet tyres, but some – including fancied runners Martin Finnegan, Paul Hunt and Tom Clucas – failed to return. The reduced field reassembled some 25 minutes later and the race was run over a reduced distance of six laps. Guy Martin was the early leader, but his reign was short-lived as problems with the clutch on his Uel Duncan Racing 1000cc Suzuki caused him to pull up at Ballanorris on lap two.

Farquhar, fourth at the end of opening lap, was at the head of the field a circuit later, shadowed by Ian Lougher, Darran Lindsay and Adrian McFarland. But the riders were only tiptoeing their way around the circuit and conditions on the back section of the course in particular were not pleasant. Leading local hope Gary Carswell was another early retirement, leaving the lesser-known Gavin Feighery to fly the flag on his 600 Suzuki. Farquhar built up a seemingly safe lead on fellow Ulsterman Lindsay, but the latter closed right back up on the final two laps and the two were nose to tail going into Castletown for the last time. Lindsay lapped a full second quicker than Farquhar on that final lap, recording the only 100mph average of the race, but it wasn't quite enough to get the better of the McAdoo Kawasaki man in the sprint to the line. At the chequered cloth Farquhar was .25 of a second in front, with McFarland making it a 1-2-3 for the Northern Ireland contingent. Ian Lougher had a steady ride on the Mark Johns Honda Fireblade to finish fourth, over six seconds in front of the leading 600 ridden by Tim Poole of Northwich. (137)

(137) 2004 - Ryan Farquhar on his way to winning the wet Senior Solo Founders Race

Despite the rain backing off slightly, conditions were only marginally improved for the start of the Station Garage Junior Founders race. One lap into the race there was still nothing between the 250 Hondas of Farquhar, Lindsay and Lougher, but as the race progressed back came the rain and the rapidly failing light made the conditions borderline. Farquhar and Lindsay continued with another race-long battle and at the finish this time there was an even tighter margin of .22 seconds between them. Lougher played it safe again in third, with local man Chris Palmer fourth and newcomer Yarno Holland impressing in fifth. The battle for the 125cc class honours went right the way to the wire and while the eventual outcome may have been predictable the leader going into the final lap certainly wasn't. With little more than four miles to go, Crosby's Tony Cawte had a slim advantage over five times TT winner Robert Dunlop. But the wily Ulsterman just got it back on the final run-in to the flag to pip his young Manx rival by just over six-tenths of a second.

(138) Guy Martin scored his first of what looks like many Southern 100 wins with a start to finish victory in the Total Oils Senior race. The colourful Drumahoe-based ace, who only made his Billown debut last July, made up for the disappointment of a non-finish in the previous evening's rain-hit open class race with a clear victory over Uel Duncan Racing/Robinson Concrete team-mate Darran Lindsay. Martin had half-a-second in hand on Ian Lougher at the end of the first circuit, but that advantage was extended to 3.6 seconds after just two laps when Lougher came off at Cross Four Ways after a leak from his Mark Johns Honda put water on to the rear wheel. He was unhurt in the incident, but the general scatter enabled Martin to grab an early lift and jump clear of the chasing pack. The advantage continued to grow and by half-distance he enjoyed a more than comfortable 13.6-second lead over the Irish trio of Ryan Farquhar, Martin Finnegan and Lindsay.

Farquhar's race came to an end one lap later when he pulled his McAdoo Suzuki in to the pits, leaving Finnegan and Lindsay to slug it out for second place. But up front, Guy Martin was experiencing problems with his GSX-R 1000 Suzuki and it started to surge out of the slower corners. He was almost pitched over the front of the bike exiting Ballabeg on a couple of occasions and the question was, could he hold on to take his first win? The gap reduced to less than six seconds at one point, but the problem mysteriously cleared on the final lap and he cruised home to a 7.07 second victory over Lindsay, who just got the better of Finnegan on the final run-in. Lindsay scored his third second-place finish in as many races and admitted he had been happy enough to sit behind his team-mate for a safe second before Martin Finnegan put the pressure on. It wasn't a particularly good race for the local contingent. Gary Carswell and Tom Clucas were both early retirements, while Paul Hunt was dicing for a possible fourth place with Adrian McFarland and Mark Parrett when he slid off at the final corner. He was unhurt and eventually remounted to tour across the line in 17th place. This left Chris Palmer as the best local finisher in sixth spot, two ahead of Southern newcomer Nigel Beattie, while Mike Crellin and Gavin Feighery both had good rides for 12th and 13th respectively.

(139) 2004 - Darran Lindsay during the Mann Auto Car Sales Junior Race, which he won

Manxman Alan Brew recorded his first out-right win on the Billown course when he steered his Seeley-framed Matchless to victory in the opening Classic race. Initially third, he soon got the better of the 750 BSA Rocket-3 of Chris McGahan and took over the lead reins when the Bullock Honda twin ridden by Roy Richardson stopped at mid-distance. Richardson had been running away with it to that point, but the 1968 Drixton-tuned motor spat out a lot of oil before giving up the ghost altogether. From therein Brew had the race well under control and he crossed the line almost 20-seconds clear of the leading 750 ridden by Ron Soar of Loughborough, following the demise of McGahan on lap five. Southern 100 newcomer Paul Coward, who was in fact a double race winner at the Pre-TT Classic this year, finished third overall and first 350 on his Honda.

After three second places in as many races, Darran Lindsay finally stepped up to the top step on the podium with a well-deserved victory in the Mann Auto Car Sales Junior race. He admitted later that he had seen how good Ian Lougher was on the tricky back section of the course in training and knew he would have to get that stretch right if he was to get the better of the Welshman. And that is precisely what he did. Lindsay grabbed the hole-shot ahead of the other evenly matched 250s and had a 0.3 seconds lead at the end of the first circuit. He extended that by a further half a second on lap two as Lougher was briefly sucked in by Castletown resident Chris Palmer. Showing no ill-effects from his fall in the earlier Senior race at Cross Four Ways, Lougher fought back hard in the latter stages but was unable to make any serious inroads into Lindsay's lead. Lindsay who prefers the Southern 100 to the TT, bettered Lougher's previous race record with a speed of 102.49mph, and finished 4.48 seconds in front of the multiple former winner. Palmer finished a lonely third, well clear of Southern 100 first timer Nigel Beattie. (139)

At one point there were no fewer than five Irish newcomers in the top ten, but in the end Yarno Holland was the best of the bunch in sixth spot. Roy Richardson led the 400 class from start to finish on a 1995 model Honda. Richardson's race time was seven seconds inside Ryan Farquhar's record from last year. Derran Slous of Ramsey was somewhat

(140) 2004 - Nick Crowe and Darren Hope on their way to their first race win and first time reaching the chequered flag!

surprised with second place, he simply had no idea how he was placed, while fellow local Dave Madsen-Mygdal was third of the 400s.

(140) Nick Crowe and Darren Hope won the first Sidecar race, revealing that it was in fact their first ever finish on the Billown Course! The Jurby pair grabbed the lead going into Ballakaighan on the first lap – scraping their way past fast-starting Kenny Howles and Doug Jewell – and soon built up a commanding lead. By lap four they were 12.5 seconds clear, extended to 20.18 at the finish. Greg Lambert and

(141) 2004 - Guy leads Ryan in the very wet 600cc Race

In his only island appearance since 2000, he proved just what a good road racer he really is with a clear victory in the Gary Dynes Foundation championship race and the Steam packet Company 125 race one hour later in marginally drier conditions. Despite very wet roads for the Clarehill Plastics-sponsored 250 race, it was a real cracker for most of the way between Lindsay, Ian Lougher and Ryan Farquhar. Lindsay and Lougher both had a share of the lead, while Farquhar looked equally capable of taking the honour if it went to a last lap sprint to the line. (142)

But his race came to an end with just one circuit to go with seized wheel bearings on his Honda, and a similar retirement for Chris Palmer just a couple of seconds later promoted Barry Davidson up to a surprise third in front of Southern 100 newcomers, Yarno Holland, Andrew Neill, William Dunlop, Nigel Beattie and Robert McCrum. The fact that the race was arguably the closest of the week and that five newcomers were placed in the top eight proves that 250 racing is far from dead and buried yet.

Ivan Murray were runners-up, eventually shaking off Howles and Jewell. Seasoned campaigners Howles and Jewell were happy with their result, but not as much as local newcomers Neil Kelly and stepson Jason O'Connor who produced a cracking ride to finish fourth, whilst fellow locals Alan Langton and Stuart Graham were a best-ever fifth.

Guy Martin was a 'happy camper' after winning the S&S Motors 600 race from Ryan Farquhar. The pair traded places half a dozen times in the early part of the race, on glass-like roads, but when the steering damper on Farquhar's Kawasaki broke at Ballabeg Hairpin on lap five he had little choice other than to back off. Registering his second win in less than 24 hours, Martin was more than satisfied with his success, having come through from fifth on lap one. Tommy Clucas brought his Bullock Honda into a good third spot in front of Bob Grant, Darran Lindsay and course newcomer Kevin Mawdsley. (141)

Darran Lindsay took his tally of wins for the Southern 100 to three with an impressive double on Championship Day.

(142) 2004 - Close action in the Clarehill Plastics 250cc Race between Ian Lougher, Ryan Farquhar and Darran Lindsayo

Alan Brew completed a double in the Eurocars Classic race, fending off a strong challenge from Ulsterman Adrian McFarland on the 500 Honda-twin. Without Roy Richardson in the line-up for the rain soaked event, the race always looked like being a two-bike affair at the head of the field between first Classic race winner Brew and leading modern bike rider Adrian McFarland.

Brew made the stronger start on his Seeley Matchless, but McFarland refused to let go and turned around an early 2.4 seconds deficit to lead the Andreas man by 0.98 of a second at the end of lap three. Brew was simply biding his time, however, and with three and a bit laps to go he retook the lead to cross the finish line at the end of lap eight almost six seconds to the good for his second win of the meeting. Paul Coward was again the leading 350 rider in third place, struggling a bit with the gearshift after putting the lever back on in the wrong place following problems in scrutineering. Local rider, Graham Taubman had a good ride on a G50 to finish third in the 500 class and fourth overall, while Ron Soar was clearly delighted with back-to-back wins in the 750 class on his Spondon-framed Norton. Only ten riders finished the race in pretty awful conditions.

Darran Lindsay left things a lot later in the 125 race, as he was still trailing Chris Palmer with a mile to go. After dicing with the former British Champion for much of the way, he draughted him going past Great Meadow for the final time and got past him into Stadium Corner to just hang on for a win by 0.6 of a second. Ian Lougher was third in class, but only sixth in the combined race after his machine suffered intermittent misfires with what he thought may have been a problem with the battery. Dave Madsen-Mygdal won the 400 race in third place overall, with Mark Parrett claiming second and Darren Slous third. (143)

Nick Crowe and Darren Hope won their first ever Southern 100 Sidecar Championship in what were the best conditions of the final day of the Steam Packet – sponsored meeting. Steady rain for most of the

(143) 2004 - Darran Lindsay at Cross Four Ways on the Nibbles 125 Honda

afternoon meant that most of the roads were still wet, but a brief better spell of weather meant that the crews at least enjoyed improving conditions as a dry line started to appear over most of the course. Having won the previous evening's race at a canter, the Jurby pair were always the clear favourites and they never looked in serious doubt, extending an initial lead of 1.2 seconds to 11.59 after five of the nine laps.

That gap was 14 seconds over Greg Lambert and Ivan Murray going into the final lap and just over 19 seconds at the chequered flag. Strangely, runner-up Lambert regretted his decision to switch to intermediates. Kenny Howles and Doug Jewell made a flying start on their Ireson Yamaha, but problems with the driver's helmet visor misting up meant they were unable to maintain the pace and they soon slipped to third – well clear of Welshmen Keith Walters and Andrew Webb. After a slightly disappointing week by his standards, Ian Lougher came up trumps with victory in the main feature race of the 49th Southern 100 in dire conditions, bring the 2004 meeting to a close.

Having come off his Mark Johns 1000cc Honda Fireblade exiting Cross Four Ways the previous evening, the 41-year-old Welshman won the race which really mattered when he led the reduced-in-distance Ronaldsway Shoe Co. – sponsored race from lap four onwards. Another heavy shower of rain just before the start meant for very treacherous conditions all around the course. Keen to make up for the lap one crash which put him out of the championship race a year earlier, Guy Martin's 1000cc Robinson Suzuki slithered sideways as he applied the power getting off the start line, but he was making up ground nicely when he crashed at Church Bends right on the tail of Darran Lindsay, Lougher and Ryan Farquhar. He appeared to be bang on line on the right-hander going

between the two graveyards, but the front wheel of his machine tucked beneath him and the bike cannoned into the straw bales lining the left-hand wall before skidding across the road into the opposite wall. (144)

(144) 2004 - Early action in the Solo Championship race - Lindsay leads Lougher, Farquhar and Martin

It was another disappointment for the young Lincolnshire ace, but at least this time he walked away from the incident. Meanwhile, his Uel Duncan Racing team-mate Lindsay headed the lead trio into lap two, although it was very tight with less than one second covering the top three. Lougher made his move going down the Ballakaighan straight for the fourth time and just managed to outbrake Lindsay into Iron Gate Corner. Defending champion Ryan Farquhar also managed to get past Lindsay, but he never really got close enough to his great rival Lougher to pose a serious threat. The gap was two seconds after seven laps, 2.2s after eight and 3.7s by the end of the 10th and final circuit. Lindsay was content with third place, at the end of what had been a highly successful comeback to the Southern for the likeable Lisburn man. (145)

Fellow Ulsterman Adrian McFarland lost the initial tow when he was slowed by the Guy Martin incident on lap one, so he had a relatively lonely ride to fourth, while yet another Ulsterman – veteran campaigner Paul Cranston – had a very good ride for fifth in front of Mark Parrett and first local Tommy Clucas on the leading 600 fending off newcomers Kevin Mawdsley and Bob Grant.

(145) 2004 - Ian Lougher heads Ryan Farquhar through Church Bends on his way to victory in the Solo Championship Race

(146) 2005 - Guy Martin leads Ian Lougher in the early stages of the opening race of the Golden Jubilee Meeting

Chapter Six

Fifty Years of the Friendly Races 2005

2005: Ian retains Solo Championship!

Ian Lougher electrified the Golden Jubilee Southern 100 by winning the opening race and setting the fastest ever lap around the Billown Circuit. Riding a 1000cc Slingshot Honda Fireblade, the Dromara-based Welshman beat Kirmington's Guy Martin (1000cc Robinson Concrete Uel Duncan Racing Suzuki) by just over 10 seconds after a thrilling battle throughout much of the 10 laps. Ryan Farquhar (1000cc MSS Discovery Kawasaki) snatched third from Jason Griffiths (1000cc Yamaha) when the latter got boxed in by a backmarker at Cross Four Ways on the last lap. (146)

(147) 2005 - Chris Palmer just ahead of Ian Lougher in the Junior Solo Founders Race

Lougher led from start to finish, but Martin and Farquhar chased him hard in the opening stages. Lougher went through the 110mph barrier at 110.39mph on lap three, with Martin doing 110.35mph. Lougher then pushed it to 110.83mph on lap four to pull out a slight lead. Farquhar and Griffiths disputed third most of the way, with Manxman Paul Hunt (1000cc Cringle Construction Honda) holding off Martin Finnegan (1000cc Vitrans Ten Kate Honda) for fifth until the engine went pop on

lap eight. Fellow local Nigel Beattie was also out of luck when the clutch of his 1000cc Rockett Evomoto Yamaha failed on lap six when running eighth. A third Manx competitor, Paul Dedman (1000cc Wilson & Collins Kawasaki), was forced to tour in. That let Castletown man Chris Palmer (1000cc DSC Racing Yamaha) into the top six, followed by Paul Cranston (1000cc P&J Suzuki) and newcomers Davy Morgan (1000cc Touchwood Kawasaki) and John Burrows (1000cc Sports & Motorhomes Suzuki). They were followed by the leading 600cc machine, the Roberts Scrap Metals Honda ridden by Tim Poole of Northwich.

Lougher zoomed home at a race record 109.115mph, with Poole taking the 600cc class at 102.452mph. Lougher's new outright lap record was two minutes 18.044 seconds, taking over from Farquhar's previous two minutes 20 seconds (109.285mph) set in 2003.

Just 10 minutes after his terrific outright lap-record-winning ride in the Senior Founders Race, Ian Lougher was back out to try to make it a double by taking the Junior Founders on his 250cc mount. But this time he had to give second best to Palmer, who pushed very hard to win by about three seconds. The pair had raced close through most of the 10 laps, joined originally by Darran Lindsay (Roy Hanna Honda) until he crashed out on the left-hander at Church Bends on the second lap having just taken the lead. Lougher (Stewart Smith Honda) tried very hard to win his second race within an hour, but former British 125cc champion Palmer just sneaked away towards the end. The pair were well clear of the rest of the field, led by Barry Davidson (Honda) then Yarno Holland (McAdam Yamaha). (147)

That duo see-sawed third place, but Holland grabbed it on lap eight and held it to the finish. Nigel Beattie and newcomer Davy Morgan were next in line with the concurrent 125cc class headed by Crosby's Tony Cawte on the Domicilium Honda. Cawte came under severe pressure as the exhaust began to blow in the final stages. But he withstood the pressure to finish just ahead of the feuding pair of Nigel Moore and William Dunlop – son of former winner Robert. Lougher

(148) 2005 - Jason Griffiths heads Ryan Farquhar going into Ballakaighan

claimed to be satisfied with second, having not ridden the bike much recently, with Cawte delighted to win the 125 class.

Ian Lougher (Honda) and Guy Martin (Suzuki) staged a repeat of Tuesday evening's record-breaking tussle when they rejoined battle in the Total Oil Senior race. Time and again they shattered the outright lap record set by Lougher less than 24 hours earlier, as they fought for supremacy on the Billown Course. At the end Lougher pulled away to win, with Martin backing off as it again dawned on the youngster that he still has a thing or two to learn from the old master. Lougher won by nine seconds and kept his name on the ultimate lap record at an amazing 111.83mph as he broke Martin's challenge on lap eight. The pair raced wheel-to-wheel thrilling a large crowd gathered in perfect conditions. Lougher led for the first two laps, Martin took over on lap three, Lougher was in front on lap four, Martin on five and six. On one or two corners the riders almost touched in their bid to be first but, just as the night before, Lougher found a little bit extra when it mattered and knocked more than 40 seconds off the race record speed. Jason Griffiths (Yamaha) ploughed a lonely furrow in third, with Ryan Farquhar (Kawasaki) fourth until he retired on lap three. Martin Finnegan (Honda) took over but was pressed hard by Darran Lindsay (Suzuki), who appeared little worse for his spectacular fall at Church Bends the previous night. Paul Hunt (Honda) and Chris Palmer (Yamaha) contested sixth most of the way, with 'Big H' moving clear towards the finish. Nigel Beattie (Yamaha) was seventh with last year's Senior MGP winner Davy Morgan (Kawasaki) winning a four-way battle for eighth in a close dice with John Burrows (Suzuki), Paul Cranston (Suzuki), Victor Gilmore (Honda) and Tim Poole (600 Honda). (148)

The first Classic race of the 50th anniversary meeting saw victory for Alan Oversby from Blackpool on a 500cc Manx Norton, but what a race he had with Dave Madsen-Mygdal on a 750cc Triumph Trident. It didn't matter that they were running in separate engine-size classes, as they fought tooth and nail throughout the six laps, with 41-thousandths of a second separating them at the line. Oversby's Craven Manx Norton frequently nosed ahead along the bumpy backstretch to Cross Four Ways, but the Triumph's slight power advantage gave Madsen-Mygdal the edge on the fast out-run through Great Meadow. But as they roared out of Castletown Corner for the final time, Oversby somehow kept the single ahead of the three to squeeze home as a matter of honour between two pure road racers. After stalling on the start line and having to be bump-started, Roy Richardson ran second for three laps, but his Honda twin went sluggish and he fell back a long way.

Chris McGahan (BSA) finished a distant fourth, Allan Brew's misfiring Matchless kept him back in fifth, with Ewan Hamilton doing wonders to finish sixth overall on his 250 Suzuki Super Six. A delighted Oversby reflected that it had been a great race and it had made no difference whatever that they were in different classes – it was a straight race to the flag!

Chris Palmer (Honda) claimed his second successive 250cc win in a race reduced by two laps after a frightening pile-up at the original start. Tim Poole, John Schyma and Roy Richardson were involved with Richardson stretchered off with back and leg injuries – thankfully they were not too

serious. A shaken Schyma and Poole got to their feet unharmed and the riders were held up at Ballabeg while the crash was cleared. From the re-start Palmer simply vanished into the blue yonder while expected challenger Ian Lougher (Honda) went out at Castletown Corner on the first lap. Palmer pulled away at the rate of over a second a lap, with Darran Lindsay unable to respond and finishing seven seconds in arrears. Lindsay had to defend second from Nigel Beattie, whose bike was going much better than the night before. Beattie tried hard and was on Lindsay's tail at one time, but wisely settled for third as the clutch began to slip. (149)

Clouting the kerb on the final corner could have cost Nick Crowe and Darren Hope victory in the opening Sidecar race of the Golden Jubilee, but they laughed it off and notched up victory by well over half-a-minute. The Honda outfit sponsored by Andy and Jenny Faragher, rocketed off the line and picked up a lead of three seconds on the first lap. Thereafter they were always totally in command, with the rest left to battle for runner-up. Evergreens Roy Hanks and Dave Wells (Molyneux Rose Honda) were going well and repelled any designs on second place that Glynn Jones and Ivan Murray (DSC Yamaha) may have entertained. Mick Harvey and Fiona Baker-Milligan (Shelbourne Suzuki) ran fourth to start with, but soon gave way to Greg Lambert and Jamie Winn (DMR Honda). And Harvey and Baker-Milligan were edged out of another place on the last lap by the surge of Ben and Luke Beckworth (Jacob Yamaha). Reflecting on their Castletown Corner pavement touch,

(149) 2005 - Nigel Beattie through Church Bends

(150) 2005 - Charge of the Chair Brigade headed by Nick Crowe and Darren Hope

the winning crew declared: 'It's only a wheel!' Adding that it had been a faultless run otherwise. (150)

The eight-lap race for competitors who had not been able to secure a ride in the main races saw Tim Maher from Templemore clinch a start-to-finish victory. Davy Clarke from Dungannon ran second until the last lap, when Mick Charnock displaced him.

Liverpool's Carolynn Sells became the first woman to win a Southern 100 race outright when she took her Martin Bullock 400cc VFR Honda to victory in the combined Classic and Junior Support race. (151)

She led all six laps to win by 10 seconds from Mick Moreton,

(151) 2005 - Carolynn Sells leads the pack through Church Bends on her way to victory in the Junior Support Race

who opted for his modern machine rather than his classic Matchless. Third was Jules Ray (Honda) with the first Classic home Malcolm Kneale's TS1C Yamaha in 12th place. Elle Forest was the first female to win at the Southern, and like Carolynn it was a class win. The difference is that Carolynn actually also won the race outright. It was also the last-ever race for 77-year-old Denis Christian, who had competed in the very first Southern 100 50 years earlier. He signed off from racing with 18th place at 65.202mph on his 500cc ESO.

It took a record last lap for Ian Lougher to beat Ryan Farquhar in the S&S Motors 50th Anniversary race.

Farquhar led on six of the eight laps but Lougher led when it mattered – as the chequered flag came down on a very close race with the top three averaging more than 105mph. Farquhar led first time round, and then Lougher took over. But from laps three to seven it was the Kawasaki just in front. Coming out of Church Bends on the last lap, Lougher got the better drive and forced past, barrelling down through Great Meadow at maximum revs. (152)

(153) 2005 - Ian Lougher took the 250cc race honours on Championship Day on Stewart Smith's Honda

At Castletown Corner he defended the lead by scuttling down the inside, then dragged the Honda to the line for victory by three-tenths of a second. Farquhar couldn't quite believe it! Guy Martin stayed in the hunt for five laps but faded over the last three to trail in four seconds adrift, but comfortably clear of the pack fronted by Jason Griffiths, who disposed of a challenge by Tim Poole. Martin Finnegan dealt likewise with Darran Lindsay to claim the final leader-board position. Ian Lougher had little trouble winning the Clarehill Plastics 250cc race on the Stewart Smith Racing Honda vee-twin, romping home by nearly 10 seconds. (153)

The expected challenge from Chris Palmer never quite materialised after a sluggish start. He dropped back about a second a lap but enjoyed a good scrap with Darran Lindsay until the latter retired on lap five, the engine dramatically seizing on Castletown by-pass with Palmer right in his slipstream. That promoted Neil Richardson to third, but only after he had fought off the attentions of Nigel Beattie, with Yarno Holland not far back either. Alan Oversby and Dave Madsen-Mygdal finished first and second in the Eurocars Classic race, but there was no repeat of the fantastic finish they produced in the first race. Having been separated only by the electronic transponders in the first race, this time Oversby's 92-bore 500cc Craven Manx Norton ran well clear of Madsen-Mygdal's 750cc Triumph Trident in spite of a bad misfire which caused him to change up the gears early. Chris McGahan on his 750cc BSA version of the Meriden triple was also unable to keep up with the lighter single cylinder machine, but again put it over Allan Brew whose Seeley Matchless still seemed somewhat out of sorts. Ewan Hamilton again did wonders on his 250cc Suzuki, finishing fifth overall ahead of a host of larger capacity machines. (154)

A five second penalty for jumping the start prevented Derren Slous from winning the 400cc section of the six-lap Steam Packet Company sponsored race combined with the 125cc bikes. Although he was first over the line, the Andreas rider was only two seconds ahead of Chris Palmer, who was therefore promoted to the overall win. And such was the closeness of the finish, Slous didn't even have the satisfaction of winning the bigger

(152) 2005 - Close action at Ballabeg during 600cc race - Farquhar, Lougher and Martin

(154) 2005 - Dave Madsen-Mygdal collected the 400 laurel wreath on Thursday

engined class. Dave Madsen-Mygdal and Mark Parrett were also within five seconds to knock Slous down to third in class and fourth overall. Palmer led every lap except the last, when Slous's endeavours to get more than five seconds clear pulled him past the Mannin/Lloyds TSB machine. Tim Poole headed the rest but was hauled back by Madsen-Mygdal on lap three and overtaken next time round. Mark Parrett, who was back riding for the first time since breaking his left shoulder also passed Poole, who soon retired with power loss. Classic specialist Alan Oversby then took over fifth place, followed by Ian Lougher on the other Mannin/TSB 125.

With a start-to-finish victory, Nick Crowe and Darren Hope (DMR Honda) enjoyed further glory by repeating last year's Sidecar Championship win. The Manx crew were never threatened and put nearly five seconds on their rivals, headed by the evergreen Midlands pairing of Roy Hanks and Dave Wells (Molyneux Rose Yamaha). Such was the local pair's superiority that they were three seconds clear at Cross Four Ways three miles out on the opening lap. And their second-a-mile advantage was maintained and reflected in their eventual win by 34-seconds after the 34 miles. Avoiding clipping kerbs as they had done in the first sidecar race, they kept a tight rein on their CBR Honda as they entertained the crowd with brutal slides round the corners, particularly at Castletown Corner, where their technique was to slide in a semicircle then wind on the power. By contrast Hanks and Wells were sedate, but sufficiently experienced to get out early and avoid the battles behind. Leading these were Glyn Jones/Ivan Murray, who almost threw it all away when they got hopelessly out of gear at Castletown Bridge on lap six and were gobbled up by Mick Harvey/Fiona Baker-Milligan (Suzuki) and Alan Langton/Stuart Graham (Yamaha). With amazing verve they forced back past both crews to re-establish third spot within the next lap, making sure they kept tight on the inside to

(155) 2005 - Glynn Jones and Ivan Murray in a hurry through Church Bends

repel any last-minute invaders. Ben and Luke Beckworth (Yamaha) made up the top six. Alan Warner and Mark Fitzgerald (Kawasaki) crashed at Church Bends and the medical helicopter was summoned. Luckily they were not seriously injured. (155)

(156) 2005 - Ian keeps Guy at bay rounding Ballabeg Hairpin in the early part of the Solo Championship Race

Precisely 50 years to the day since the running of the first Southern 100 the Welshman from Northern Ireland, Ian Lougher, won his third Southern 100 Championship by 10 seconds at record lap and race speeds. For his efforts he won the Ennett Memorial Trophy, which was fitting as Derek Ennett, in whose memory it is named, won that original Southern 100 race. It was Lougher's fourth win of the meeting and proved once again there is no substitute for experience. (156)

Younger contender, Guy Martin challenged for half of the 10-lap distance but again had no real response when Lougher upped the ante. Lougher (Honda) tailed Martin (Suzuki) for three laps before slipping past and putting four seconds between them by lap seven. Next lap

(157) 2005 - Ian Lougher Solo Champion 2005 negotiates Church Bends on the Slingshot Honda

Lougher lapped at 111.688mph, which completely destroyed Martin's challenge. In fact, it was not quite as fast as Lougher had gone the previous evening when again repelling Martin's brave attempt. That had established a new outright course record of 111.883mph, the difference being just over a fifth of a second. Ryan Farquhar (Kawasaki) ran third for three laps before being overtaken at Stadium Bend by Jason Griffiths (Yamaha), but two laps later the Irishman was back in place. Griffiths again got his nose in front on the penultimate lap and held it to the final corner on the last lap only for Farquhar to snatch it back in a demon move, including weaving away down the finishing straight. Darran Lindsay (Suzuki) and Martin Finnegan (Honda) enjoyed a battle for fifth place in similar fashion. Lindsay was ahead on laps one and two but once Finnegan got past he was able to stay there, though not by much.

Another good dice was between Chris Palmer (Yamaha) and Paul Hunt (Honda). Palmer led to halfway then Hunt squeezed by. Palmer got back in front a lap later and they traded places lap by lap until Hunt claimed it last time round. Mark Parrett (Yamaha) and Paul Dedman (Kawasaki) were early mechanical casualties, while Tim Poole (Honda) fell at Cross Four Ways trying to keep up on his 600cc machine. He was not hurt. That left Kevin Mawdsley, who had survived a hairy spill at Church Bends in an earlier race, to take the Alan Hampton Cup for the best 600cc bike.

Lougher said: *"I am amazed that a bike which was completed only a week ago and tested only briefly has carried me to three wins, the main one, of course, the solo championship. I followed Guy for a couple of laps then decided to get my head down and go."* (157)

Martin commented: *"I'm gutted. I thought the changes we had made to the bike would be enough, but they weren't. It's simply not quite right."*

Farquhar admitted that his 'spoiling tactics' by weaving on the final straight probably upset Jason Griffiths, but said: *"I was determined to get a rostrum position after all the hard luck we've had this week."*

My memories of 50 years of the Southern 100

Can it really be 50 years since I sat on the wall at Cross Four Ways watching the first ever Southern 100? Well, yes, it is, but it certainly doesn't seem so.

Over the years there have been some fabulous races, and I am pleased to say that I am one of those who can truthfully claim to have seen at least a part of every year's Southern. At the outset the main race was over 24 laps, which gave the meeting its title of Southern 100 from the 100 miles that distance entailed. In 1954 Derek Ennett and George Costain had won their respective classes at the Manx Grand Prix, and it was in their honour that the South created its own event, though never intended to be anything but races totally in their own right.

That's how it started, and much has stayed the same ever since. The main race distance may have been reduced by 50 per cent, but is no less demanding for that. Indeed, the shorter event provides a level of excitement that simply didn't exist over the 24 laps. It is interesting that the organisers readily acknowledged that and adjusted to contemporary thinking, but they could have hardly have envisaged that the time spent on 12 laps would eventually prove to be about a third - rather than half – that of the 24 laps as speeds rocketed.

When I think of the Southern, I can pinpoint individual instances, though am no longer able to recall all the years totally precisely. More particularly, I can easily recount the vast range of highly talented competitors the meeting has always been able to attract. That first Southern in 1955 saw victory going to Terry Shepherd, which was fine by me as he was a particular favourite. His dices with Bob McIntyre in later years were certainly among my highlights of the early days. McIntyre's speed in the wet during a 350cc race still is a wonder to me so many years later. The Glaswegian had done the TT double in 1957 on the four cylinder Gileras but appeared just as happy mastering the Billown Circuit on private Nortons.

There was Alan Shepherd and Phil Read, who along with Ron Langston and company provided many fine races including a 350cc dead-heat between Read and Shepherd I had the privilege of seeing right on the line. The appearance of John Hartle on a 250cc four cylinder Honda came later, but was no less memorable for me, as he was another of the favoured. Although it was a long

way from an exciting race, the sight and sound of this rider/bike was a definite "must" of my reminiscences. So many names – all have special Southern memories for me. As early as 1968 (only four years after Manx Radio started) I was broadcasting the event and have been involved with that on-and-off ever since. I also reported and photographed it for Motor Cycle News from 1971 until 1997. It sometimes involved taking the film to the airport between races!

Joey Dunlop, Philip McCallen, Chas. Mortimer, Charlie Williams, Ian Lougher, Robert Dunlop, Dave Chadwick, Brian Reid, Bill Smith, Tom Herron, Bob Jackson, Simon Beck and Rob McElnea are a few who spring to mind, with sidecar stars led by Bill Currie and the novelty of the John Worthington three-wheeler Scitsu. Later came Roy Hanks, Geoff and Ian Bell and the modern Formula Two crews.

Ian Bell is one who graced Billown on two and three wheels, while prominent local sidecar performances I recall include those of Dave Molyneux. Talking of which there were many sterling performances by the local element in the solos, too.

Danny Shimmin, Kenny Harrison and Roger Sutcliffe always rode well there, with the latter associated with the great Ray Cowles, who has been such a strong supporter of the Southern and saw his riders Selwyn Griffiths, and later son Jason Griffiths, take so well to the 4.25 mile road course The emergence of the powerful two-stroke Yamahas forever changed the face of the Southern from its original AJS/Norton domination, and provided heart-stopping races as the missiles launched skywards over the Billown bumps.

In recent years, the club has expanded into the pre-TT Classic and post-TT national events, and even though these are really nothing to do with the actual Southern 100, it is a mark of the respect the July meeting has developed that the May and June events are often referred to as the Southern 100!

It is a great tribute to the work started out all those years ago, and my own association goes right back to the days when I was occasionally among those who filled the straw bags and struggled to attach them to the unforgiving stone walls. Names such as Jimmy Taubman, Bob Clarkson, Arthur Bridson, Percy Quayle, Theo Watterson, Jack Bridson, Arthur Jones and company were gods to me. In later years I acted as the Southern 100's press officer, churning out results on a duplicator at George Costain's.

Nowadays, timing is by automatic transponder and results are instantaneous. There's been triumph and tragedy at the Southern, but it rightly remains one of Britain's foremost short circuits, with a deserved reputation for friendly organisation.

I hope I shall be around for many more years enjoying the pleasure of racing pioneered so many years ago. Before the split into the Southern 100 MCRC, the

Southern Motor Cycle Club, who also ran trials and scrambles, of which I was also a part, ran the early events. The Spirit of the Southern is the same as it always was. Long may it remain so.

Geoff Cannell.

(158), (159)

(158) 2005 - Montage of Riders in Parade Laps

(160) Pre-TT - 1993 - Bob Heath splashes his way to victory in the 500cc race

Chapter Seven

Pre-TT Classic Road Races

(159) 2005 - 50th Anniversary Special Events

The Pre-TT Classic Road Races came into being in 1988 at the request of the then TT organisers, the Auto Cycle Union; Classics having first appeared on the Billown course twelve months earlier at the popular Southern 100 Road Races.' The first TT Classic Races were held on the 31st May 1988, the meeting consisting of four races: 250cc/350c; 500cc; Unlimited; and Sidecars, and attracted 115 entries in all.

Honour of being the first race winner went to Graham Godward of Royston in Hertfordshire, riding a 350cc Aermacchi, whilst the 250cc category was dominated by 'local' classic man Mike Cain from Onchan on his 250cc Suzuki. Dave Pither, (Seeley Matchless) took the 500cc race from Richard Swallow on Syd Lawton's Aermacchi with Alan Dugdale third. Riding a BSA Metisse, Stroud's Robert Price finished first in the Unlimited race, whilst the controversial MV Agusta sidecar outfit of Mark Kay and Richard Battisson took the chequered flag in the final race of the day. The Classics had arrived at Billown!

The following year saw a similar programme being run. 1990 and the combined 250cc/350cc race was split into two separate races, Mike Cain making it a hat-trick of wins in the Lightweight class, as Bill Swallow completed a double in the Junior event.

The race programme was increased to six races in 1991 when a Vintage Class was introduced, Steve Linsdell, riding a 1950 346cc Royal Enfield, won the race.

Bob Heath won his first race at the Pre-TT Classic Meeting, which was to extend to 15 before he hung up his competitive leathers at the end of 1998.

The 1993 races were run on the wettest day in June (2nd) since records began, as Bob Heath splashed his way round to repeat his 500cc victory of 12-months earlier. Bob Jackson repeated his 250cc win of 1992 as Mike Hose took the 350cc honours, Dave Pither the 1300cc class, and Stuart Digby and Nick Cutmore received the Sidecar laurel wreaths. Frenchman Bernard Guerin took the Vintage race on his 1939 348cc Velocette. (160)

Just two months after undergoing a specialist eye operation, Manxman Kenny Harrison was chasing victory in record-breaking style in the 1994 Classic races. At the end of the unlimited race his 850 Triumph Trident was almost half a minute clear of Bob Heath on his ultra light 499 Seeley. Heath however won the 500cc race, achieving a hat trick of victories in the Senior class. Lancastrian Stuart Marshal won the 350cc clash from Derek Whalley, when the latter's brakes failed towards the end of the race. What is good enough for one Bob (Heath) was certainly good enough for the other (Jackson), as he too completed a hat trick of wins in the 250cc class. Father and son newcomers' John and Andy Smith won the Sidecar race by eight seconds, as Bernard Guerin again claimed the chequered cloth for the Vintage race.

1995 saw the introduction of a Single Cylinder race, which replaced the Vintage class. Bob Heath dominated the race with two convincing wins in the opening Single Cylinder race and the Junior Classic. Heath was always in control of the Singles race, streaking away on his 349 Seeley to win by 18 seconds from Mike Baldwin and Chris McGahan. The 47-year-old's win in the Junior Classic, aboard the same Seeley, was almost a carbon copy of the first, as he rocketed away again to lead from start to finish in a race record speed of 84.82mph. (161)

Heath's hopes of a hat trick were dashed in the Unlimited Classic when he pulled out on his 499 Seeley at the end of the first lap . Last year's winner Kenny Harrison looked certain to repeat his 1994 performance until his 850 Triumph engine exploded spectacularly while he led along the start and finish straight. It left his bike with a gaping hole in the crankcase. His demise left the way clear for Stuart Jones on a 1972 Triumph to take the victory, followed by Bill Swallow on a 499 Seeley and Jack Gow on a 1962 Manx Norton – the last one to be built. Father and son combination John and Andy Smith retained their sidecar title on a 998 Imp. The Lightweight Classic went to Graham Larkins on a 246cc Yamaha. (162)

Bob Heath once again splashed his way to an impressive full house of four wins in the 1996 races. With all six races on the programme reduced in length due to the atrocious conditions, Midlander Heath started the day off with victory over Scottish veteran Jack Gow in the Single Cylinder race, Gow just four-tenths of a second in front of a similarly Aermacchi-mounted Bill Swallow. Win number two came Heath's way in the 500 race shortly afterwards, when he finished almost one whole minute in front of Bob Jackson and Jack Gow, but still managed to average an amazing 80mph despite the torrential conditions. (163)

The Sidecar race was won for the second time by Dave Stone and Owen Dyke on the 950 Norton, from the Yamahas of Jim Silver/Barry Pepperell and Albert Price and Dickie Dale. Conditions improved considerably over the hour lunch break and it was Bob Heath who came out fighting when the action recommenced. Rocketing away from the start, 7R AJS replica-mounted Heath was almost ten seconds clear of the 350cc pack at the completion of the first circuit. He continued to pile on the coals, and was some 38 seconds up on Windermere's Bob Jackson and the Suzuki twin at the close. Derek Whalley had another good ride to snatch third away from Bill Swallow and Jack Gow.

Despite his dominance in the first three solo races, a question mark did hang over whether Bob Heath's single-

(161) Pre-TT - 1995 - Stuart Jones leads the pack into Ballakaighan

cylinder Seeley would have the steam to live with the triples of Dave Pither and Glen English in the Unlimited race. But another flying start gave him the early jump on

(162) Pre-TT - 1995 - Father and son John and Andy Smith took the sidecar honours on their 998 Imp

the 750 multis, and they quite simply never saw which way he had gone. Glen English was an early retirement on Norman Mile's Trident after clipping a bank, and former winner Dave Pither was never on the pace as he struggled to get the power down on his similar

(163) Pre-TT - 1996 - Bob Heath shows his mastery of the rain once again

(164) Pre-TT - 1996 - Bud Jackson took the 250cc race victory

marque, leaving Heath and fellow regular Bob Jackson clear on their 500 singles.

(164) The 250 Lightweight race, turned out to be the best of the day with a real scrap in the early stages between the Jackson brothers, Alan (Bud) and Bob and Deeside's Terry Kermode. Kermode retired with two laps to go, leaving the Cumbrian brothers to dice it out for the honours in the Suzuki-dominated race. Bud Jackson eventually crossed the line some three seconds in front of his brother, with Barry Wood a superb third.

Bob Heath achieved yet another double in 1997 in the Senior and 750cc races; Bill Swallow took the honours in the Single Cylinder race; Derek Whalley the Junior; Bob Jackson the Lightweight and Alistair Lewis and Bill Annandale the Sidecar honours.

1998 Saw Bob Heath repeat his four wins tally of two years earlier, with Bob Jackson lifting the 250cc laurel wreath and husband and wife pairing Geoff and Ruth Hands claiming the sidecar victory.

Bill Swallow set a new outright lap record of 93.35mph when he clinched the third of his hat trick of wins at the 1999 meeting, where a Post Classic class was added to the Unlimited race – the two classes running concurrently. It took a last lap, last corner passing move to give Swallow the 1000cc win after Decca Kelly (350 Yamaha) had led all the way. On only his third outing on John Oldfield's 750 BSA-3, Swallow kept up his 100 per cent record that started at Killalane in Eire and continued at Chimay in Belgium. Fifth at the end of lap one, Swallow took six laps to get up to second. As the temperature of Kelly's Yamaha soared from 65 to 90 degrees, he eased back just at the moment that Swallow attacked. Swallow had scraped his boot down to his bleeding toes before he grabbed the lead for the first time at Castletown Corner, leaving Kelly in second spot and Kenny Harrison's six-year-old lap record in tatters.

Swallow had earlier had an easy win in the Singles race, taking more than six seconds a lap out of the opposition in the early stages before easing back on the Aermacchi he jointly owns with John Poyner. Swallow, who won the same class two years before, won by 40 seconds from Blackpool's Vin Duckett, who was second throughout and clear of

another veteran, Glasgow's Denis Gallagher on Bob Pearson's 350 Seeley-BSA. Gallagher was only three seconds ahead of Dorset's David Smith on the best of the 250s, having overtaken Derek Whalley on the last lap. Smith grabbed his second class win in three years when local ace Whalley slowed with a spluttering Ducati. Swallow's second win was in the 500, in which he stormed into the lead only to be reeled in by Jason Griffiths – having his first classic race and mounted on Fred Walmsley's Manx Norton – and John Loder (Weslake). Loder hit the front on the seventh lap with Swallow and Griffiths right up his pipes. Swallow had his act together but his Dick Linton 450 Aermacchi doesn't have the steam of the full 500s. Loder nearly ran into the back of Swallow at Iron Gate and then messed up the next Ballabeg hairpin to put him out of contention. On the last lap, Griffiths got ahead going to Ballakaighan then Swallow regained the lead at the Iron Gate to hang on and win by three-tenths of a second. Ulster newcomer Colin Rodgers set a new race record of 85.14mph as he won the 350 race on his Drixton Honda. He took the lead with two laps to go and went on to win by 18.5 seconds from Manxman Barry Wood. Paul Coward won the 250 class

(165) Pre-TT - 2002 - Decca Kelly finished sixth in the Lightweight Race

which he had led throughout on his ex-Peter Padgett/Jim Lee Yamaha. He won by 5.1 seconds from Decca Kelly with newcomer Karl Hayes third on an over-rich Suzuki.

Four different crews led an eventful sidecar race before German newcomers Bernd Tittler and passenger Andre Hohensee won on a sit-up-and-beg 1211cc Guzzi. Stuart Digby was the first leader to retire. Then husband and wife Geoff and Ruth Hands stopped with a stripped belt drive on their Imp after they had built up an 18 second lead. Alistair Lewis was next leader to go out, his NRE-Triumph expiring at Ballabeg, leaving the German crew to give Guzzi a first win in the Island since Ken Kavanagh won the 1956 Junior TT.

Millennium year, 2000, brought with it a main sponsor for the Pre-TT Classic Races, the De Montfort Group, as the popular race programme remained the same. Millisle publican Karl Wilkie celebrated a memorable victory when he won the Post Classic class of the combined Unlimited/Post Classic race. Astride his 750cc Rob North Trident triple, Karl finished third overall and topped his class in perfect conditions. And aboard a 500 Seeley Matchless, Karl was also sixth in the Senior Classic race. Third in the Unlimited Classic last year, his victory in the Post-Classic race was Wilkie's first win at the Pre-TT Classic meeting. The only other Irish rider to have won at the meeting is Colin Rodgers from Comber, who made a winning debut on his 350 Honda in the Junior race last year – but Colin was out of luck this time around, posting an early retirement. Manxman Brian Kneale lead the nine laps 1000cc/Post Classic race from the start to finish on his RG500 Suzuki, with John Loder second and leading the Open class on his 750 Nourish Seeley until he retired with two laps remaining. Huddersfield's Bill Swallow had been second in the class and posted the fastest lap at 89.78mph before he retired his 750 BSA Rocket-3 at the end of lap four. Shortly before Loder's premature exit, Glaswegian veteran Denis Gallagher overtook Loder and he finished overall runner-up and second in the 1000cc class on Bob Pearson's 900 Seeley Weslake. Wilkie had been catching Loder before his premature exit and passed the Birmingham rider at Cross Four Ways on the penultimate lap to move into third position on the roads and secure victory in the Post Classic class.

Earlier, Wilkie, placed sixth in the Senior Classic race, won by Mike Hose from Wallasey on his 500 Honda from Loder, who had a difficult ride after the throttle stuck open on his 500 Nourish Seeley from the second lap of nine. Fresh from his victory in the Classic race at the Tandragee 100, Huddersfield's Bill Swallow couldn't repeat last year's hat trick of wins, and nevertheless, he scored a double. Astride his 350 Aermacchi, Swallow won both the Single Cylinder and Junior 350cc races, the former from Hose on a 350 AJR Bultaco and Loder on a 350 Greeves Oulton, and the latter from Steven Elliott on his Rutter Honda and Cumbrian Bud Jackson aboard his Suzuki. Roy Richardson took the Lightweight 250cc victory ahead of fellow

(166) Pre-TT - 2002 - Out of retirement (again), Richard Coates took the winner's laurels in the 750 Classic Race

Suzuki rider Bud Jackson, with Matt Jackson third on a Yamaha. Husband and wife team Geoff and Ruth Hands smashed both race and lap records en route to victory in the Sidecar race in their Hillman Imp-powered outfit.

Of course 2001 was a year to be forgotten with the loss of most of all pure road races due to the foot & mouth crisis in the UK.

An alteration to the schedules was made in 2002 when the Singles Race was run on the Saturday afternoon, towards the end of the final practice session. Local riders scored a brace of wins, with Derek Whalley securing victory in the opening Singles race and Richard Coates winning the final race of the programme. Only a fifth of a second separated Whalley and newcomer Tim Stephenson at the end of a dramatic opening to the Southern 100 club's Pre-TT meeting. Whalley, on Fred Walmsley's 7R AJS, nearly slid off at Castletown Corner but he held on to win the 350 Single Cylinder class from Stephenson, who set the fastest lap of the race (83.79mph) on the final circuit. Harold Bromiley of Andreas finished an excellent third on the 350 Bultaco. Poole's David Smith was the 250-class winner on an Aermacchi from veteran Ted Fenwick and the Greeves of Norman Williamson. Liverpool policeman Steven Elliott won the 500 race by 9.1 seconds from former 125 Grand Prix star Gustl Auinger and Stephenson. Yorkshireman Paul Coward from Hebden Bridge led all the way in the Junior 350cc race, followed home by Barry Wood, who had suffered a slipping clutch throughout the race, with John Leech third. Coward was robbed of a double after his 750 Triumph-3 ran out of petrol when in a comfortable lead on the last lap of the Post-Classic Superbike race. Coward's retirement gave victory to Ulster's Karl Wilkie from Tim Stephenson. The Yorkshireman also finished third in the

(167) Pre-TT - 2003 - Age is no barrier to Ted Fenwick, his racing number is equal to his age!

250 race behind Karl Hayes and Scottish newcomer John Leech. Decca Kelly had a cracking ride on his comeback to the circuit after a big crash in 1999 at William's corner. The popular Colby man was sixth. (165)

Geoff Hands and Andy Smith won the Sidecar race for the third time with the rapid Imp-engined outfit beating Alistair Lewis and Bill Annandale by 11.1 seconds. With the locals mostly out of luck, home honour was maintained by Eddy Toombs and Bob Dowty who rode a very good race on the 980 BMW to finish third ahead of Greg Lambert and Stephen Taylor. Richard Coates came out of yet another racing retirement to win the 750 Classic from Ian Pattinson. (166)

Riding the TZ350 Yamaha, which was bought new for him in 1983 by Baldwin farmer Kenyon Crowe, Coates led the race from the second lap onwards. Early charger Brian Kneale soon went backwards with a slipping clutch on the RG500 Suzuki, leaving Coates well clear at the head of the pack. The real battle was for second place where Decca Kelly, new resident Adam Nowell, Ian Pattinson and the leading three Post-Classic bikes had a battle royal. Kelly's 350 nipped through on lap six, leaving Nowell and Pattinson to fight it out over the final few miles. In the end it was Weakdale's Pattinson who edged home second from Laxey's Nowell on Roger Owen's RG.

(167) Ted Fenwick knocked road racing records into Kingdom Come when he won the 2003 250 Single Cylinder classic race. Six years after he won the race for the first time, the York veteran snatched victory on the last lap and won – at the age of 75. Fenwick, who's been racing since the Fifties and once passengered world champion Max Deubel at Scarborough, took the lead when runaway leader Paul Coward's Greeves ran out of fuel. In only his second race of the season Roger Birkenhead finished 17 seconds ahead of Graham Taubman.

Mike Hose broke race and lap records in the concurrently run 350 Singles race. On a notably volatile Bultaco two-stroke that owners Paul and Lynn Wilkinson have been trying to win with at Billown for five years, Hose trailed local rider Derek Whalley throughout the eight laps until he shot up the inside at Stadium and nicked the lead which he held to the flag. In beating Whalley by 0.3 of a second, Hose

(168) Pre-TT - 2003 - Chris McGahan-Steven Elliott-Derek Whalley- 1,2,3 in the Junior Classic Race

Ruth as passenger. Last year, she was recovering from a big crash at Cadwell Park and was replaced by Andy Smith. This year, she made her racing comeback and they won the race again. They led all the way, though they did come under big-time attack from Scots Alistair Lewis and Bill Annandale for the opening two-and-a-half laps, when they were nose to tail all the way until Lewis' Triumph gave up the ghost on lap three at Church Bends. That left Hands with a massive lead and they slowed and still won by 31 seconds from Stuart Digby and Paul Thomas on another Imp. They had taken second place from Eddy Toombs and Bob Dowty, who were well pleased to finish third on their 980 BMW, the first of the big-wheel machines to finish. (169)

(170) Pre-TT - 2004 - Bill Swallow leads through Church Bends

took 17 seconds off Bob Heath's eight-year-old race record. He also took two seconds off Heath's class lap record, also set in '95. In a race affected by occasional showers and cold conditions, Hose and Whalley were in a class of their own in their two-stroke/four-stroke Bultaco/AJS battle. They quickly disposed of Bill Swallow, whose Aermacchi had a persistent misfire. Swallow went on to take third, 29 seconds down on the leaders and half a minute ahead of fellow-Yorkshireman Tim Stephenson, also on an Aermacchi.

(168) Chris McGahan won a thrilling 350 race. On a rapid Kenny Garfield-tuned Drixton Honda sponsored by enthusiasts Tony and Suzy Hales, McGahan took command of what had been a terrific race at halfway. From the moment he opened a two-second gap, he was never headed and he went on to win by 2.8 seconds from Liverpool policeman Steven Elliott. Before that McGahan, Elliott, Mike Hose, Bill Swallow and Derek Whalley had a seriously intense battle for the lead, which changed at almost every corner. Elliott went up the inside at Ballakaighan, the first corner, and he led across the line for four laps. When Swallow went out with a broken exhaust on lap five, the action got hotter. Hose scored the shoulder of his new leathers when he got too close to the wall at Church Bends. In the last couple of laps he slowed and dropped back to fourth. Whalley took third place, only a second down on Elliott and 35 seconds up on Hose, who was being caught late on by local rider Barry Wood.

For the fourth time in the last five runnings, Geoff Hands won the Sidecar race. On the same Imp-powered Windle chassis, Hands has won three times with his wife

For the second year in succession, Steven Elliott won the 500 Classic race. Leading from start to finish, he proved last year's victory was no fluke as he finished 21 seconds ahead of Allan Brew, who was second throughout on his Conister-backed Seeley. Elliott, was in command from the start. His lead extended when Mike Hose's Honda seized on lap three. Brew, fourth on lap one, then took over the No.2 spot and finished 17 seconds ahead of Preston's Colin Dally for third. When Ewan Hamilton started the 250 race, he didn't know if he'd be able to coax his Suzuki round the warm-up lap. He knew a cracked cylinder head could mean early retirement, even though he was setting off in pole position. In effect, it didn't matter, he led from start to finish and won his first Classic race at Billown by 36.8 seconds from Mike Hose, who raised more than a few eyebrows when he got Pete Coogan's Ariel Arrow into second place by a whisker from Barry Wood.

2004: due to the demand for entries the organising club has once again re-scheduled the race programme to include a seventh race to accommodate over thirty entries that otherwise would have had to be turned away – depriving not only them of the experience of riding the Billown Course, but also the thousands of enthusiasts, young and old, who line the hedgerows to watch and enjoy the races, take in the atmosphere, and applaud the winners and all who participate. Bill Swallow and Mike Hose scored two wins apiece. Swallow, won the Senior and Singles races on Dick Linton's immaculate Aermacchis. Hose won the Junior on a Honda K4 and the Lightweight on a 250 Ariel Arrow. Stuart Digby and Paul Thomas took their 998 Imp-engined outfit to victory in the Sidecars over ex-World Champion Ralf Englehardt and passenger Winfried Viencenz, while the honours in the 750 Classic/Superbike solo race went to Paul Coward of Hebden Bridge on a Mk5 RG500 Suzuki.

Despite a poor forecast, conditions turned out to be absolutely perfect for what proved to be an excellent day's racing. The Singles race provided a start to finish victory for Huddersfield ace Swallow, who smashed lap and race records en route to beating Greeves-mounted John Loder by very nearly a full minute. Mervyn Stratford of Aylesbury took the 250 class honours from 76-year-old Ted Fenwick

(169) Pre-TT - 2003 - Three times winners of the Sidecar Classic, Geoff and Ruth Hands

after early leader Paul Coward retired with a puncture on lap three. Mike Hose got off to a poor start in the nine-lap Lightweight race, but slowly ate into Scotsman Ewan Hamilton's lead. With a lap to go it was down to 3.8 seconds and then there was drama on the final corner when Hamilton's lost the front end on his 250 Suzuki twin and slid off at Alexander Bridge, handing the win on a plate to Hose. Bill Wark rode very well as a newcomer to the course to finish runner-up in front of former winner Bud Jackson. Alan Oversby was the early runaway leader of the Senior 500 race but he eventually slid off at Ballabeg hairpin. Although he quickly remounted he was forced to retire back at the paddock. This elevated Bill Swallow into a 10-second lead on the 444cc Aermacchi, a margin he defended all the way to the flag over Hose. (170)

(171) Pre-TT - 2004 - Popular Sidecar crew Ralf Englehardt and Winfried Viencenz take Castletown Corner in style

The Sidecar race was led from start to finish by Stuart Digby and Paul Thomas on the 998 Imp, eventually lapping all bar the second, third and fourth finishers in a race of high attrition. Popular runners-up were Ralf Englehardt and Winfried Viencenz of Germany on the big Busch BMW. (171)

Due to the ever growing popularity of the Billown event, an overspill race opened the proceedings after the lunch break and while Alec Whitwell of Blackpool was the convincing winner of the Senior class, Glaswegian Eleanor Forrest made history by becoming the first ever female solo race winner on the course with success in the 350 Junior category. The race of the day was the Junior proper where, despite Mike Hose leading from start to finish at race and lap-record speed, the real contest was for the runners-up spots. Four riders fought it out for the final two podium places, eventually decided in Chris McGahan and Bill Swallow's favour over local man Derek Whalley and Carnforth's Alan Oversby. Midlander John Loder led the combined 750 Classic/Post-Classic Superbike race from the gun on his 750 Nourish Triumph. He was over five seconds clear at half distance, but this was rapidly reduced by Paul Coward on the comparatively modern Mk5 RG500 Suzuki. Going into the final lap the margin was just 0.23 of a second, and Coward more than reversed this in the final four miles to win by five clear seconds. Loder still took the Classic honours from Bill Swallow and Steve Elliott. (172)

The 2005 saw a new main sponsor arrive, Blackford Financial Services, who have pledged their support for a number of years, which is very much appreciated by the Southern 100 Club. As the opening event of the '50th Anniversary year', the Pre-TT Classic provided some exciting racing, no more so than when Huddersfield's Bill Swallow won his 12th Pre-TT Classic race, being made to work every yard of the way. Riding a 350cc Aermacchi owned by Dick Linton, he took victory by a bike length from Derek Whalley aboard a 350cc 7R AJS. The six-lap Single Cylinder race, which opened the meeting, was run

(172) Pre-TT - 2004 - John Loder at Ballabeg Hairpin

in dry but very windy conditions, and gave the crowd a thrilling 25-mile joust. Swallow headed the field until the fifth lap when Whalley overtook coming out of Church Bends. But as they came up on backmarkers going into Iron Gate for the final time, Swallow blasted back into the lead and held on to the chequered flag. Both riders concurred that there was little between the two very different machines' performance and heartily agreed they had thoroughly enjoyed the race-long dice. Quite some way behind, battling alone, came newcomer Luke Notton on another 350 AJS.

(173) In the 250cc class run concurrently there was a rare Greeves one-two-three, with victory going to Paul Coward. After three previous attempts at winning had ended in retirement, he took victory on the Silverstone model manufactured in 1965. Runner-up by five seconds was David Spencer and third Mervyn Stratford. Blackpool's Roy Richardson repeated his 2000 win by taking Martin Bullock's T20 Suzuki twin to victory in the Lightweight Classic race. He eventually won by 25 seconds, but that far from told the full story. Wallasey's Mike Hose pushed him extremely hard for the first half of the nine laps, but slipped back when his Ariel Arrow twin developed gearbox trouble and he ran wide a few times attempting to change down. The pair scampered away from the rest of the field, pulling 10 seconds out even on the first lap. Kirkconnel's Bill Wark and Kendal's Tom Jackson slugged it out for third, but it all ended in tears when Tom tweaked the Super Six just a mite too hard exiting Cross

(173) Pre-TT - 2005 - Paul Coward took the Lightweight Race on this Greeves

(174) Pre-TT - 2005 - Mike Hose had a start to finish victory in the Junior Classic - the race of the day

Four Ways on the last lap. Down on his ear he went and Wark was left wondering how he'd managed to miss colliding with him, crossing the line to take third.

Lap and race records went by the board as Chris Palmer and Roy Richardson battled out the Senior Classic. Palmer was having his first ride on the Fred Walmsley Manx Norton, while Richardson had a 450cc Honda twin from the stable of Martin Bullock. Palmer took the advantage off the line, although Richardson stuck with him like glue, but at Cross Four Ways on the sixth of the nine laps, he came into the right-hander too fast and almost stood the Honda on its nose, almost dropping the plot. It was all Palmer needed and he pinched back the lap record his rival had just taken from Bob Heath, leaving it at 2 minutes 45.159 seconds, an average speed of 92.638mph. Richardson recovered to come home second with Carnforth's Alan Oversby having a lonely ride on his Craven Manx Norton to take third. Hillman Imp engine-powered three wheelers finished one-two in the six-lap sidecar race. Once again the ex-works flat twin BMW failed to deliver sufficient power to overcome the more modern outfits. Stuart Digby and Paul Thomas were harried by course newcomers Eddy Wright and Neil Wheatley on the first lap, but settled for a steady drive to second as the temperature of the water began to climb.

Klaus Enders's veteran former passenger, Ralf Englehardt thrilled the crowds with his right-hand chair with Winfried Viecenz as passenger and was happy enough with the final place on the podium. Roy Richardson's 61-year-old father Peter made it a family double when he won the 350cc class of the Solo Support race by some 50-seconds from newcomer John Leech and last year's victor Elle Forrest third. Brian Nichol of Dalkeith near Edinburgh took the 500cc honours from Harold Bromiley and Ron Brown.

(174) Wallasey's Mike Hose smashed his own lap and race records en route to victory in the Junior race. Astride local sponsor John Turner's 350 Drixton Honda, Hose admitted he became a bit complacent in the latter stages of the nine-lapper enabling Bill Swallow to close down the gap. He upped his pace on the final circuit with a new lap record to see off the Yorkshireman's determined challenge. Newcomer Luke Notton took another place on the podium, edging out Steve Elliott by the narrowest of margins at the line. Castletown's Chris Palmer rounded off his first ever Classic meeting with further success on the Walmsley Norton in the combined Post-Classic / Superbike race, the final of the meeting. (175)

Guy Martin set the early pace on the ex-Alec George Trident, but retired at Ballabeg on the opening lap when the triple let go rather expensively. Paul Coward was elbow to elbow with Palmer down the by-pass on lap two, as the Island resident used his superior course knowledge to edge clear of the Yorkshireman. Coward's Post-Classic TZ350 Yamaha eventually seized at Cross Four Ways on lap four, letting Decca Kelly through for a surprise win after what had been a sluggish getaway for him. Up front, Alan Oversby piled on the coals in the latter stages, setting the fastest lap of the race in the process, but Palmer still had almost two seconds in hand at the chequered cloth. Swallow, who had a bit of a moment at Ballakaighan, was third, ahead of Kelly and Chris McGahan on the first of the triples.

(175) Pre-TT - 2005 - Chris Palmer won two races on his 'Classic debut'

Chapter Eight

Isle of Man Steam Packet National Road Races

991 saw a new event added to the annual TT Festival, which effectively extended the competitive TT period by one day. The 'Isle of Man Steam Packet Company National Road Races' were introduced to provide entertainment for enthusiasts who were staying on the Island after the end of the TT Races, as it was at the time proving impossible to 'evacuate the many thousands of bikers in a day or two', as once was the case.

So what better way to keep the fans of road racing occupied, than to promote an event that would achieve this aim, along with providing the chance for the competitors, who had pitted their skills around the most famous 37.73 mile ribbon of road in the world for the past two weeks, to attempt to recoup some of their expenses with a generous prize fund.

The Steam Packet Company asked the organisers of the Southern 100 Races and the Pre-TT Classic Races, held on the 4.25-mile Billown Circuit, in the south of the Island, if they would be prepared to run an extra meeting. The discussions resulting in the inaugural event being run on Saturday 8th June 1991.

Southern 100 Racing devised a three-race programme catering for machines ranging from 125cc to 750cc, with practising taking place in the afternoon and racing, early evening. The calibre of the entry was first class for the three classes: 125cc and 400cc Supersport; 250cc and 350cc; followed by the 750s, competing for a prize fund which stood at over £5,000. In all ninety-nine entries were received.

The 'weathermen' must have known that the Steam Packet was sponsoring the event, for such were the conditions that the sponsors could have almost sailed their fleet around the course! Driving rain forced a 50-minute delay in the proceedings, resulting in the race distances being reduced in length, however, the waiting was worthwhile for the surprisingly large crowd considering the conditions.

Joey Dunlop made a welcome return to the Billown Circuit after a break of 14 years and showed he had lost none of his course knowledge. First event of the evening was the six lap combined 125cc and 400cc Supersport race – Joey led the pack into Ballabeg, but water in the 'works' caused problems at Church Bends, however he coaxed the little Honda into life on the run to Great Meadow, although

down in tenth place. Leading the race was newcomer James Courtney, who was also second overall on the roads, Dave Leach having put his 400 Yamaha into a commanding lead. Courtney was the '125' sandwich between the 400s of Leach and Ian Lougher and that was the way they crossed the line. Joey Dunlop finished fourth overall and second in the 125cc category. Richard Mortimer completed the top three in the smaller class, as David Madsen-Mygdal took third position in the Supersport class.

Next up was the 250/350cc race reduced from ten to eight laps – Joey Dunlop had no problems on his 250cc Honda Britain machine, taking a start to finish victory at 85.57 miles per hour. Ian Lougher, Dave Leach, Gary Radcliffe, Richard Coates and James Courtney created the excitement. Coates excelled in the latter stages with an impressive ride, overhauling Leach for sixth place, then 'Raddish' for fourth, then, appropriately for the conditions, dived inside Courtney at Alexander Bridge on lap six and set about catching Lougher (the Junior TT winner), ousting him on lap 7 to take second place at the chequered flag.

The feature race of the evening, the 750cc class, saw Joey Dunlop, Kenny Harrison, Dave Leach and Gary Radcliffe on the front row. When the lights changed, once again it was Joey who led into Ballakaighan, although Kenny's cheer was short lived as he overshot at the tight right-hander. At the end of the lap it was Leach, Dunlop and Radcliffe filling the leader-board positions. Amazingly, Dave and Joey averaged over 90 miles per hour as they powerslid their big 750s around the 4.25-mile circuit, with the Yamaha rider (Leach) controlling the pace, his Honda rival seemingly content with second position and taking the flag 13.2 seconds in arrears to Dave Leach. David Madsen-Mygdal (Honda) just got the better of Gary Radcliffe (Kingswood Honda) for third place and the end of eight very wet laps where they were credited with the same time!

So ended the inaugural 'Steam Packet National Road Races', everyone having enjoyed the outstanding racing in what was appalling weather conditions and looked forward to returning in 1992, hopefully with improved weather conditions. Such was the success of the 1991 meeting, that the Steam Packet had no hesitation in sponsoring the races in 1992. A similar race programme was witnessed by record crowds who witnessed one of the best meetings held on the Billown Course!

The Dunlop brothers won three of the four race classes, but it was new star, Phillip McCallen who proved to be a revelation in the 250cc race, setting the first 100 mph lap on a quarter-litre machine on the 4.25-mile circuit. Unknown Scot, Bob Grant, riding a 400cc Shirlaw Yamaha was the surprise winner of the 400cc Supersport race with a start to finish victory. Run concurrently with the 400s, the 125cc class produced a race-long battle between Denis McCullough and Joey Dunlop, which only ended when Denis dropped the plot at Alexander Bridge after the front end went away. The Banbridge man remounted and chased after the Ballymoney rider to finish 12 seconds in arrears at the flag, taking third overall and second in the smaller class. Both Denis and Joey set the fastest lap of the race – Denis on the sixth lap at 92.72 mph, with Joey equalling the time and speed on laps 8 and 9. The time of 2 minutes 45.0 seconds was a new lap record.

The 250cc race proved to be a cracker, with a ten-lap race-long duel from when the lights changed to green-between Robert Dunlop and Phillip McCallen. Robert was in a very determined mood to win, he led the race on the Ray Cowles 250cc Yamaha, until McCallen on the Turkington Honda made his move at Iron Gate on the penultimate lap, receiving the same 'medicine' on the last lap from Robert who managed to keep his nose in front to the line! A consolation for Phillip was his new record lap on the eighth lap in 2 minutes 32.2 seconds, equal to 100.52 mph.

All eyes were focused on Joey Dunlop and Phillip McCallen for the feature race, the ten lap 750cc, but surprise leader for the opening laps was another Ulsterman, Derek Young on his RC30, before being gobbled up by the 'works' machines of his rivals. Joey had the upper hand throughout, although his team-mate watched the maestro's every move, looking for a minute mistake, which never came. Even so, Joey was forced to up the lap record on the final lap to 104.65 mph to stay ahead by just two-tenths of a second at the chequered flag, as Jason Griffiths on another Honda pipped Derek Young for third place. Another first class meeting was seemingly over so soon.

1993 provided a major dilemma for the race organisers, as atrocious weather conditions during the TT forced the postponement of the Senior Race from the Friday to the Saturday morning, thus necessitating organisers, officials and last but not least the competitors to complete their duties on the Mountain Course before heading down to Castletown! The Race Committee set to rescheduling practice and race times and the meeting went ahead, albeit with race distances being shortened to ensure compliance with road closing and opening periods.

The same programme of races were planned, except that the capacity for the premier race was increased to 1000cc although only two competitors took advantage of the extra ccs available. Derek Young, Bob Jackson and Johnny Rea provided the fireworks in the 400cc class, with Rea on the Millar Yamaha leading the race from start to finish, with Jackson looking to take second place until he was black-flagged. Young then took up the challenge reducing the gap to 1.5 seconds at the flag, also setting a new lap record at 94.09 mph. The Cumbrian rider was allowed to restart and finished 7th overall and third in the Supersport class.

In the competitive 125cc class, once again it was Joey Dunlop who dominated the race from the flag, setting a new lap record for the tiddlers at 93.63 mph – Denis McCullough, nephew of his great rival in the Ballymoney man's early career, Ray McCullough, claimed second place with Glen English slotting into third after seven hectic laps. It was the turn of Welshman, Jason Griffiths to dominate the two remaining races, the 250 and 1000cc events. Firstly in the 'smaller' class, although Richard Coates led from the start, he overshot at Castletown Corner leaving Griffiths and Dave Milling to dispute the lead for the next few laps, until Milling overshot at Cross Four Ways. Jason took the chequered flag 3.2 seconds ahead of the Cumbrian rider, who held off fellow Cumbrian Bob Jackson, who in turn kept Coates at bay, having spent much of the race dicing with McCullough and Gary Dynes. Changing his 250 Cowles Yamaha for the 750cc Bob Heath Honda, he controlled the shortened eight lap race from the change of the lights from red to green, to win by 19 seconds from Derek Young and local man Gary Radcliffe. Certainly an impressive ride by Jason, who had earlier in the day finished in fourth place in the Senior TT!

Twelve months later saw the first major change to the race programme, still maintained at three races. Race one was to cater for 125cc and single cylinder machines of unlimited capacity, whereas race two was for machines 175cc to 400cc. The final race remained the same at 1000cc. One word sums up the 1994 Steam Packet event – Dunlop – having achieved two wins on the Mountain Course earlier in the week, the Ulster Legend scored a 'maximum' at the Steam Packet Races a hat trick!

Riding his McMenemy Honda in the opening race he set a new lap and race record heading home Ian Lougher by half a second, with James Courtney third. The 'new' single cylinder class provided a victory for Jason Griffiths on the 680cc Spondon Yamaha. Gary Radcliffe took second and Derek Young third. Lougher and Dunlop were the main protagonists in the 250cc race, dicing furiously in the early stages of the race, until the Ulsterman nosed ahead, eventually winning by nearly ten seconds. Once again it was Courtney who took third despite the efforts of Phillip McCallen, who eventually settled for fourth.

The atmosphere was electric as the riders lined up on the grid for the final race of the evening – would Joey achieve the hat trick having already earlier in the day ridden six laps of the Mountain Course, followed by eighteen laps of the Billown Circuit? Jason Griffiths and Phillip McCallen swapped the lead several times on the opening laps, while Joey settled in on the big Castrol Honda machine, then on lap five he outgunned the pair of them into Ballakaighan Corner. By the end of the lap he was 2.7 seconds clear of the duelling duo. Joey took the chequered flag at the end of the nine laps 1.5 seconds ahead of his Honda team-mate with Jason on the Webb Kawasaki 17.7 seconds adrift of Phillip. Phillip had the distinction of setting the first 105 lap around the Billown as on his seventh circuit he lapped in 2 minutes 25.7 seconds equal to 105.01 mph.

The same programme format was retained for the 1995 races, Bob Jackson took the honours in the Single cylinder race, on his 800cc MHD machine setting a new race record at 92.75 mph, along with a lap record at 94.09

mph, whilst Denis McCullough claimed the laurel wreath for the 125cc class, ahead of Joey Dunlop and another Ulsterman Owen McNally. Fourth was Gary Radcliffe, on the 600 DTR Yamaha in what was 'Raddish's' last ever race, having decided to hang up his leathers after a very commendable career.

The Lightweight race gave Joey his seventh victory at the Steam Packet Races, some 12.6 seconds ahead of James Courtney, with Gavin Lee third.

All was set for the final race of the evening, but the competitors got no further than Ballakaighan on the opening lap when an accident occurred. Chris Day sustaining serious injuries, the race was abandoned, bringing the 1995 meeting to a premature close.

1996 was once again a record-breaking meeting, Gavin Lee improving the 125cc race record to 92.75 mph, on his way to victory in that class, as Joey Dunlop increased the 250cc record to 99.30 mph and equalled his own lap record as he took victory in the quarter-litre class from fellow Ulstermen Gary Dynes and Derek Young. The feature race of the programme, the 1000cc once again provided a fitting finale to the meeting, with Jason Griffiths and Bob Jackson dicing determinedly for the chequered flag – Jackson leading until the last corner of the last lap, Griffiths nipping underneath the Cumbrian and going on to take the flag two-tenths of a second ahead of his rival.

1997 saw a second change to machine capacities in two of the three classes. Firstly the opening race would now cater for 200cc – 400cc in Class A and for 401cc – 600cc in Class B. Race 2 was now to cater for 125cc machines only. A nip-and-tuck battle ensued during race one in the 600cc class between Derek Young and Bob Jackson, with Young winning by one-tenth of a second on his Anderton Honda from Jackson on the McAdoo Honda. Third was Jason Griffiths who was apparently biding his time for later in the early evening! Manxman Richard Coates rode a tremendous race in the 250cc class, taking victory over Welshman Ian Lougher by 1.5 seconds, with Joey in third place.

The 125cc race may have been small in numbers, but there was no shortage of quality of riders or racing as the top six jostled for position throughout the nine-lap race. It was all down to the last lap dash to the line, or so the spectators thought. As Glen English led through Church Bends, McCullough, making a final bid for victory, overdid it a little coming into Castletown Corner and went down, handing victory to the Southampton rider. Ian Lougher took second place, with Gavin Lee third. Denis remounted to finish fourth, ahead of Joey Dunlop and Chris Richardson.

Despite Joey Dunlop being a non-starter in the feature race, there was still a good four-way contest at the head of the pack between Derek Young, Simon Beck, Jason Griffiths and Bob Jackson. Ulsterman Young on the Tillston Honda took an early lead with Beck second, followed by Jackson and Ramsey-based Griffiths. As Griffiths gained confidence on his RC45, he passed the men in front one by one, eventually taking over from Young on lap six. On lap eight he broke the lap record, upping it to 105.29 mph and ensuring victory, taking the chequered flag next time round by 1.6 seconds from Derek Young, with Bob Jackson third.

A fitting end to the seventh running of the 'Steam Packet National Road Races' on the Billown Circuit.

1998 brought another first for the 'Steam Packet Races', the organisers making the decision to postpone the three-race programme for 24 hours due to the dreadful weather. The delay meant that most of the visiting riders were unable to ride, having left for home on the early morning boats – this also caused the 125cc Race to be scratched from the programme – leaving just two nine lap races, the 250/600 and the 1000cc events.

Castletown's Paul Dedman still on a 'high' after his TT rides pushed Jason Griffiths all the way in the first race, so much so that the Ramsey-based Welshman broke Derek Young's existing 600cc lap record improving the speed to 102.62 mph, taking the chequered flag by a mere 1.4 seconds. Both Jason and Paul broke the old race record. Behind them, Slough-based New Zealander Blair Degerholm had a lonely ride to take third place making it a Honda 1-2-3. Simon Beck took the initial advantage at the start of the 1000cc race on his Peachurst Kawasaki, but Jason on the John Webb Honda RC45 got past the green machine and eventually opened up a five second lead to take his third Steam Packet victory in a row! Gary Carswell and Paul Dedman had a race-long duel for third, with the former achieving his best ever result on the Billown circuit.

The eighth running of this popular meeting might have been postponed and shortened, but the riders present certainly showed their metal, and their racing prowess delighted the large number of spectators present. Every lap and race record was shattered during the 1999 'Steam Packet Road Races', which provided some of the most thrilling racing ever seen on the Billown Course. The opening two races were won by just two-tenths of a second, whilst the 'premier' race, the 1000cc, saw Joey Dunlop get to within six-tenths of a second of the outright lap record for the 4.25-mile closed roads course.

Entered in all three races, the Ballymoney publican failed to make the line in the opening 250cc/600cc race after an engine seizure during practice, leaving Ramsey-based Welshman Jason Griffiths and Slough-based Kiwi Blair Degerholm to battle for the initial honours and some battle it proved to be! Both on 600cc machines, Griffiths on the O'Kane Yamaha and the New Zealander on the Intersport Honda, the pair went off together at the change of the lights. Jason took an early advantage, but Blair slipped through at Alexander Bridge on the sixth lap to take the lead. However, the Welshman was not going to give up, retaking the lead on the penultimate lap and eking out a two-tenths of a second advantage over his rival as he took the linen cloth. Degerholm set a new lap record on the final circuit at 103.659 mph, as both finished inside the old race record.

Ulsterman Adrian McFarland rode a good race to take third place on the Splash-in-the-Pan Yamaha ahead of fellow Ulster rider, Denis McCullough on the 250cc Sanyo Honda setting 250cc lap and race records in the process. Another Welshman, this time Ian Lougher, was well away with the 125cc race, that was until one Joey Dunlop got his act together at half distance and started to reel in the similarly mounted Honda rider. After four laps the margin was two seconds in the Welshman's favour – a lap later it was down to three-quarters of a second. The pair were inseparable for the next two circuits and going into the final lap it was either rider's race. Still nose-to-tail as they exited Alexander Bridge towards the awaiting chequered flag, Lougher was ahead, then Dunlop dived out of his opponent's slipstream to gain the honours by just two-tenths of a second. As in the previous race, both riders were inside the old race record, whilst Joey's penultimate lap at 96.897 mph was a new lap record for the 125s. Third was close neighbour of the winner, Owen McNally on the Bob Mullan Honda with Dave Madsen-Mygdal fourth and first of the 400s ahead of Blair Degerholm on the 400 Intersport Honda, some 20 seconds adrift.

The 1000cc race brought the curtain down on the 1999 TT Festival, as Joey wheeled out the Honda Britain RC45. His rivals included Jason Griffiths on Patsy O'Kane's R1 1000cc Yamaha and Blair Degerholm on the Wilson & Collins 750cc Kawasaki. Also in contention were the two Adrian's – McFarland on the Rendezvous R1 Yamaha and Archibald on the 900 Dowd Honda. The Honda Britain man made a somewhat sluggish start, allowing both Griffiths and Degerholm to take an early advantage, with the Kawasaki ahead for the first two laps.

Joey had by then picked off Jason and set off in pursuit of the flying Kiwi, whom he picked off two laps later to eventually win by four seconds with yet another record-breaking average speed of 104.89 mph and setting a new lap record for the Steam Packet Meeting at 106.620 mph. Jason Griffiths claimed second place – three-tenths of a second ahead of Blair Degerholm with Adrian McFarland

(176) Steam Packet - 2002 - Ryan Farquhar holds off Adrian McFarland in the 600cc race

taking a fine fourth place ahead of Archibald.

After the thrills and excitement of the 1999 races officials, competitors and enthusiastic spectators looked forward to a repeat programme in 2000 – the meeting's tenth anniversary. Alas, it was not to be as the weather turned sour preventing the Senior TT being run on its traditional Friday afternoon and being moved to the Saturday. The postponement meant that, very reluctantly, the organisers, after consultation with the Senior Officials and Medical Services, decided in the interests of safety to cancel the meeting.

2001 proved to be a year of non-events, with all road races on the Island and throughout most of the British Isles being cancelled due to the foot and mouth crisis in

England. Thankfully it was full steam ahead at Billown for the 2002 meeting, and it was not one for the faint hearted! The three-race event saw Ramsey's Jason Griffiths and Ulster's Ryan Farquhar dominate the closely fought and incident-free racing. Dungannon's Ryan Farquhar came out on top in two thrilling dices in the 600cc and 400cc honours, then for good measure followed Welshman Griffiths home in the 1000cc race.

(177) Steam Packet - 2002 - Jason Griffiths took the feature race victory

Jason was unable to maintain the pace of either Farquhar or fellow Ulsterman Adrian McFarland in the opening 600cc/250cc race over nine laps of the Billown circuit. The three were pretty close on the opening laps, but once Griffiths lost the tow he had to settle for a somewhat lonely third place – more than 20 seconds behind the leading duo. McFarland enjoyed two or three laps at the helm on the Rendezvous Suzuki, however Farquhar's McAdoo Kawasaki appeared to just have the edge. Going into the final corner he kept a tight line to close the door on his fellow countryman and at the flag the margin was only two-tenths of a second. (176)

The concurrently run 250cc race was led from start to finish by local man Richard Coates, who was fifth on the road at the chequered flag, as he completed the course 12 seconds ahead of Bud Jackson. Farquhar took up where he left off in the previous race by leading at the start of the first lap of the 400cc/125cc race, although he had the 125s of Robert Dunlop and Chris Palmer snapping at his wheels, together with the second 400 of Dave Madsen-Mygdal. Palmer took the reins on lap two and Dunlop moved to the front next time round. At Alexander Bridge on the fourth lap the former British 125 Champion again took the lead and held it for another lap before Farquhar surged ahead on the 400 Kawasaki, then drama struck as Palmer toured in to retire with a broken fairing bracket.

Farquhar, Dunlop and Madsen-Mygdal remained together for the final three laps with the Ulsterman taking his second chequered cloth of the day, followed by the 125 of Robert Dunlop who was the filling in the 400 sandwich as Madsen-Mygdal brought his NC30 third across the line. The final race of the evening proved a convincing victory for Jason Griffiths on his R71 Yamaha. Farquhar took the hole-shot as the field headed towards Ballakaighan, but once the Ramsey man got past him on the brakes into Iron Gate it was virtually all over. (177)

The gap at the end of the second lap was 5.1 seconds in

Jason's favour and he continued to pull out an average of five seconds a lap, to win by a margin of 44.7 seconds at race record speed. It was Griffiths' fifth Steam Packet race victory as he set a new lap record for the meeting at 106.918 mph. Ryan Farquhar took runner-up spot, as local rider Gary Carswell produced a best-ever individual performance on the Billown circuit when he grabbed third place on his 1000cc Suzuki, after surviving a big scare on

(178) Steam Packet - 2004 - Farquhar chased by Clucas through Church Bends

the exit of Cross Four Ways, as he averaged over 100mph for the race to hold off Chris Palmer and Adrian McFarland for the final podium place.

2003 and once again the weather was not kind to the organisers of the 'Steam Packet Road Races', with the event being delayed for twenty-four hours and run on Sunday afternoon. After his outstanding performances at the TT, Ryan Farquhar won the main event of the day, being the only Ulster competitor at the Castletown circuit. He was only able to compete in one of the three races, as Winston McAdoo's Gortreagh Printing machinery is not available to him on Sundays. Nevertheless he scored a start to finish win astride his fellow Dungannon man Kenny Harker's GSX-R1000 Suzuki, in production racing trim. In the Senior race, the anticipated challenge from Ramsey-based Jason Griffiths failed to materialise.

Griffiths opted to ride the Road & Track Motorcycles 600cc Yamaha R6, in preference to the Yamaha R1 on which he practised, but the Welshman pulled out of the race while in contention after just two of the six laps. Starting from pole position, Farquhar was never headed, although he did have a 'moment' when he overshot at Cross Four Ways on the second lap. That delayed him only temporarily, and he paced himself to a six seconds victory over fellow former Manx Grand Prix winner, Englishman Mark Parrett, aboard the Wilson & Collins ZXR750 Kawasaki, with Manx fireman Paul Hunt third on his GSX-R1000 Suzuki.

Griffiths led the combined 600cc/250cc race from start to finish, to win by half-a-minute from Manx resident Chris Palmer on Nick Woodman's RS250 Honda. Tom Clucas was third despite sliding off his 600 at Ballabeg hairpin on the opening lap, skittling Parrett in the process – there were no hard feelings between the pair – Parrett finishing fourth. After his Ultra-Lightweight 125cc TT victory, Chris Palmer romped to the chequered flag in the combined 125cc/Supersport 400cc race. Astride Blackpool man Nick Woodman's Honda, the 1998 British 125cc Champion came

home 21-seconds ahead of Dave Madsen-Mygdal, on his 400 Honda taking the '400' honours.

The 2004 TT came to a fitting finale with an excellent evening's racing at Billown.
The Isle of Man Steam Packet sponsored National Road Races have been run since 1991, but there has never been a meeting to rival this meeting for all-round entertainment, beautiful weather and thrilling, serious, accident-free racing. The crowds came out in their thousands to line the 4.25-mile closed road circuit, and there was no shortage of talent on the track with a number of TT podium men topping up their sun tans and their bank balances at the end of a hectic fortnight. Little more than 29 hours after registering his maiden TT win, Ryan Farquhar rode the same Kawasaki which carried him to victory on the Mountain Course to further glory in the opening 600/250 race.
He led from start to finish on the production-based ZX6, opening up an initial lead of eight seconds over the battling Guy Martin and Tom Clucas after just three laps. (178)

By the end of the ninth and final lap he had extended that lead to a winning margin of 13.08 seconds with a new race record average speed of 103.04mph.
Farquhar's penultimate lap was also a record at 103.99mph. Martin and Clucas battled all the way to the flag where Derry-based Englishman Martin was half-a-second ahead. Mark Parrett got the better of Paul Hunt mid-distance and Ian Lougher led the 250 class throughout on Pete Berwick's Honda, after main rival Chris Palmer retired early on. Ryan's game plan was to get away at the start and it worked perfectly, although he felt sure he could have added an extra

(179) Steam Packet - 2004 - 125cc winner Ian Lougher through Church Bends

couple of mph onto the record on a fully tuned bike.
Guy Martin, at the end of a highly impressive TT debut, admitted how much he enjoyed the dice on the roads with local man Clucas.
His last experience of the Billown course ended with a broken leg when he crashed at the Iron Gate last July, and his return was barely a mile-and-a-half old when he went through the wide-open 'Joey's Gate' at Ballanorris on the opening lap of practice!
Clucas regretted having too tall a gear on the front – the bike was bogging down out of the slow corners.

Race two saw an impressive ride from Ian Lougher on Alan and Mike Kelly's Lloyds TSB Offshore 125 Honda. (179)

Chief rival Chris Palmer made a poor start and suffered

(180) Steam Packet - 2004 - Superbike Race winner Ian Lougher on the Mark Johns Honda

problems throughout after a new set of brake pads in the front of his Woodman Honda caused the bike to chatter badly. The problem caused him to run wide at Cross Four Ways on the first lap, clouting the bales. He then had to reverse the bike out and paddle it to get it started.

The race was lost as far as first place went and within the space of just two laps he was 6.3 seconds behind Lougher who went on to win by a comfortable margin of 20 seconds at the close.

Sandwiched between the two leading 125 pilots was Dave Madsen-Mygdal, who duly notched up his third 400 class win in four years on Billy Wood's Honda. He and Palmer were right together going into Castletown Corner for the final time, but Palmer had further braking problems and went straight on towards home before doing a quick turnabout in Malew Street and heading back out onto the by-pass.

Ian Lougher was relieved to get a result, as it had not been the best of TTs for the Ulster-based Welshman. Madsen-Mygdal admitted he made a bad start himself, whilst Palmer said the bike was a sick as a dog at the finish.

Third place in the 125 class went to Blackpool's Matt Jackson, while Kiwi surprise Paul Dobbs and local driving instructor Dave Corlett filled the final two podium spots in the 400cc class.

The final race of the sun-kissed programme was another Ian Lougher benefit.

The nine lap 1000cc Steam Packet race saw a stinger of a race between Lougher and fellow Welshman Jason Griffiths in which the lap record was repeatedly broken. (180)

Lougher always appeared to be in control, but Griffiths – in what was his only ride of the night – took a while to get on the pace and lost the initial tow when he was embroiled in a close tussle with Guy Martin.

The gap stayed fairly constant at between 2.5 and 3.8 seconds, but Lougher never really looked like relinquishing the lead on his yellow-painted Mark Johns Honda Fireblade. Both he and Griffiths (who started off as Ian's mechanic many moons ago) took turns at upping the lap record, but it ultimately ended up in Lougher's possession with a speed of 107.67mph on lap seven.

Lougher's race time of 21 minutes 33.38 seconds (106.47mph) was also a record for the Steam Packet meeting. Guy Martin rounded off an excellent week for himself with a podium finish in third.

Outright Billown lap record holder Ryan Farquhar was never on the pace in the big race, struggling with his aching wrists on the heavier machine. He still managed to finish fourth, but only after Tommy Clucas overstepped his limit exiting Cross Four Ways corner for the final time.

Ryan Farquhar rounded off what was a mixed 2005 TT for him with a double success in the Steam Packet National Road Races at Billown. The Dungannon man opened up the programme with a record-breaking win in the 600cc race and rounded it off with a similar success over Guy Martin in the 1000cc race. Farquhar, riding the same MSS Discovery Kawasaki which brought him success on the Mountain Course three days earlier, soon opened up a three-second lead over the hard-trying Lincolnshire ace in the 600cc race and by lap six was 14 seconds to the good. (181)

Pitching in a new lap record at 104.89mph, Farquhar took the chequered flag some 12.5 seconds in front of Martin at a new race record speed of 103.778mph.

Newcomer to the Steam Packet meeting, but not to the course, Lytham's Kevin Mawdsley did well to get the better of locals Chris Palmer and Paul Hunt for the third spot on the podium. (182)

Farquhar was delighted with his third win in three consecutive road races on the Kawasaki – the North West 200, TT and Steam Packet, having ridden the wheels off the old girl!

The leading 250s of newcomer Chris Barratt and local man Neil Chadwick were right at the rear of the field following the demise of fancied runners Ian Lougher and Yarno Holland – Lougher retiring with a little more than a lap to go when comfortably in the lead.

Lougher did get a good ride in his only other appearance of the meeting, however, battling throughout the combined 125/400cc race with local resident Dave Madsen-Mygdal. (183)

The lead swapped between the two seasoned campaigners several

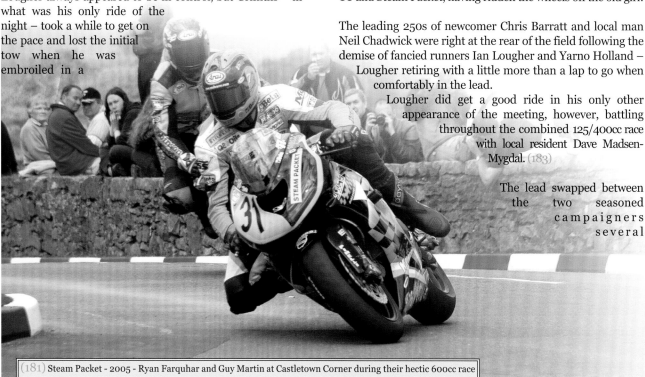

(181) Steam Packet - 2005 - Ryan Farquhar and Guy Martin at Castletown Corner during their hectic 600cc race

'My recollections of the Southern 100 Road Races'

by The Hon J A (Tony) Brown SHK and Member of the House of Keys for Castletown

I am delighted to have been asked to reflect on some of my memories as a child of the early days of the Southern 100 Road Races held on the Billown Road Circuit and in doing so I extend my congratulations to the Club on its wonderful achievement in providing and developing such a great race meeting, a meeting that we are all proud to be associated with and which has become so much part of our community life.

I was 5 years old when the races started and I have to admit that I have no recollection at that age of attending the races, even though I lived in Mill Street and my mum loved to watch motorcycle racing. I am sure she would have taken me along, with my brothers and sister, to watch the racing but I am afraid I cannot recall the races.

Steam Packet - 2005 - Kevin Mawdsley made a debut appearance on the podium (182)

t i m e s
before Madsen-Mygdal just got the drive out of the final corner to take the flag on Billy Woods' 400 Honda.

There was no denying Lougher the 125cc class honours on the Mannin Collections/Lloyds TSB Honda. Dave Corlett rode very well to grab third overall and second

400 in front of Alastair Bayley with Tony Cawte the second of the 125s. Foxdale resident Gail Musson rode her heart out to finish an excellent third 125 in front of best newcomer Phil Harvey.

The 1000cc race proved a carbon copy of the 600 at the sharp end of the pack with Ryan Farquhar leading Guy Martin throughout. But while Farquhar chalked up a new race record of 107.611mph on his big ZX10 Kawasaki, Martin went home with a new lap record of 109.09mph in his back pocket, not too far short of the absolute course best. Guy Martin finished some ten seconds down at the flag, admitting to a big moment at the infamous Black Hole on lap three. (184)

Chris Palmer had a cracking ride on the DSC Racing Dave Hagan-tuned Yamaha to achieve his first ever podium finish on a big bike. He was second to Farquhar on lap one, before Martin squeezed past at Ballawhetstone. Paul Hunt was fourth on the Cringle Suzuki. (185)

Kettering, Northants, newcomer James McBride had a great ride on his Billown debut, having only decided to ride two or three hours before practice commenced and despite a constant misfire with his 1000cc Suzuki, still managed to earn himself a 100mph medal and a fine fifth place.

The Steam Packet National Road Races have brought a different dimension to the races at Billown. What was initially a meeting to keep 'TT fans' occupied whilst waiting for their sailings, is now an eagerly anticipated meeting, when no quarter is given or asked and is enjoyed by riders as they ease themselves back into 'massed start' racing after the rigours of the TT and, likewise, enthusiasts too enjoy the move back to 'racing proper' and all the excitement that goes with racing on the Billown Course.

However, I can recollect from about the age of 7 going to the races and playing on the hay-bales and the grandstand seating at School Hill Corner – the grandstand seating was timber-made and we used to have some great fun playing there. One thing that has stuck with me from those early days was how we were treated by the organisers; they did not chase us away or moan at us for running around and playing on the grandstand and bales, instead they encouraged us all to help them and to take an interest in what they were doing and why. They were very wise people, as they knew that if the future of the races were to be secured then the next generation would have to want to be involved and we were the next generation. They were absolutely right too, many of the present committee were the kids of the 1960s and many like myself grew up to be marshals, officials or supporters of the event.

I well remember, when attending Victoria Road Primary School, the excitement when the Southern 100 races came around, unlike the children at Castle Rushen High School we were not given the Thursday afternoon off school. However, a number of us used to sneak out of school at afternoon break to go and watch the races; of course we were in big trouble the next day – but it was worth it.

Then I had a lucky escape, I unusually had joined the Malew Scouts thanks to the encouragement of Scout Leader Burns; I was deemed too old to join the Castletown Cubs – with only one year left before I was old enough to be enrolled as a Scout, however Skipper Burns (as we called him) got me into the Malew Scouts even though I was really too young. In those days – 1961 – the Castletown and Malew Scouts used to

(183) Steam Packet - 2005 - Dave Madsen-Mygdal got the chequered flag in the combined 125/400cc race

(184) Steam Packet - 2005 - Farquhar and Martin continued their duel in the feature 1000cc race

sell programmes around the Course and as I was a Scout, and all other Scouts involved attended Castle Rushen High School, I was given a special concession to have the afternoon off from Victoria Road Primary School so I could help sell programmes. We used to go around the houses the week before the races selling programmes; my patch on the Course during the practices and races was Church Bends.

When Southern 100 week approached most of the kids used to fix lollypop sticks to our bikes at the rear wheel so that they would catch on the spokes, this made a fantastic noise emulating a motorbike (sort of) and we used to 'race' around the town. The noise was great, we used to have some real fun.

I also well remember the racers and mechanics staying in the homes of many of the townspeople. This meant that the town and its community became an integral part of the Southern 100 Races and importantly this resulted in a fondness for the event, which I believe was unique to such a meeting and that feeling of it being ours still remains today. The town felt, and still does, that the Southern 100 Races belongs to them; it is part of us, part of our community, a part of our year, year in year out.

I especially remember as a young boy spending many hours watching the mechanics, often with the riders, preparing their machines at the back of places like the Duck's Nest Pub (now The Sidings) and at Mr Ennett 's garage which was located in those days at the rear of the Viking Hotel – the single storey building with its tin roof is still there. In those days of course, the bikes were AJSs, BSAs, Nortons and Matchless machines and they were really, really noisy: they had a real deep roar. Then, there was that wonderful addictive smell of 'Castrol R: it was wonderful, I can still remember how that smell filled the air; as kids we were mesmerised by it all, it was so exciting – there was nothing like Southern 100 week to us Castletown kids and there still isn't, even though we are older.

And today, 50 years on, the Southern 100 still generates an atmosphere that we all enjoy; we look forward to the week like no other. The Southern 100 Road Races continue to grow from strength to strength, it is as popular as ever, it is loved by the riders and spectators alike. The Southern 100 is rightly known as 'the friendly race meeting', it has a unique atmosphere all of its own. Over the decades it has seen many of the most famous motorcycle riders in the world competing at the race meeting, names such as Bob McIntire, Phil Read and Joey Dunlop to name but a few and it continues to attract top riders who continue to take part in the event. The continued involvement of such top riders tell a story, after all they do not need to continue to

participate in this race meeting but they do so every year. Why? Because they love the meeting, they love coming to Castletown and being welcomed in such a special way by our community, their friends – it is for them a special annual homecoming.

Most of all they recognise the professionalism of the Southern 100 Committee and their officials in organising and running the races to such a high standard and they know that each and every competitor is important and they care about them and that matters so much to the participants and their families and supporters.

Like the riders, we are all very proud of Phil Taubman (The present Chairman of the Club) and his dedicated committee, officials and helpers, they do us proud, they are a credit to the town and to the Island. Long may we see the Southern 100 Road Races continue into the future, a new generation will gradually take over the reins and I am sure they will secure the Southern 100 Road Races for another 50 years, continuing the tradition started back in 1955 by the originators of the meeting.

Like many others, I have many fond memories of Southern 100 weeks, it is a week we all look forward to, it is now an integral part of Castletown's life. Long may the races continue; this is what a real community is all about, making new friends, welcoming back old ones.

We can all thank those who started this race meeting and who did so against the odds to establish this wonderful annual event; they started something which I am sure they never realised would mean so much to our small community and to so many involved in the world of motorcycle racing.

Well done everyone and especially the Southern 100 Road Racing Club; enjoy this special Anniversary year.

Our thanks go to the Southern 100 Committees past and present, for giving so much to our community and to the world of motorcycling over the past 50 years.

Tony Brown SHK and Member of the House of Keys for Castletown

(185) Steam Packet - 2005 - Chris Palmer achieved his first podium in the 'big' classes

Statistics

Southern 100 winners 1955 - 1967

	250 cc	350 cc	500 cc	125 cc	S/car	S/car
1967	Derek Chatterton	Len Ireland	Bill Smith		John Patrick	P Ogden
1966	Peter Inchley	Brian Davis	Selwyn Griffiths		Charlie Freeman	Ray Weller
1965	Brian Warburton	Billy Nelson	Dave Williams	Fred Curry	Charlie Freeman	
1964	Bill Smith	Dave Williams	Dave Williams	Bill Smith	Charlie Freeman	
1963	Terry Grotefield	Derek Woodman	Chris Conn	Bill Smith	Chris Vincent	
1962	Aurthur Wheeler	Phil Read	Phil Read	Gary Dickenson	Charlie Freeman	
1961	John Hartle	Alan Shepherd & Phil Read	Phil Read	Dan Shorey		
1960	John Patrick	Ron Langston	Ron Langston			
1959	J Murgatroyd	Bob McIntyre	Bill Smith			
1958	Fron Purslow	Bob McIntyre	Terry Shepherd			
1957	Bill Smith	Dave Chadwick	Alastair King			
1956	Bill Smith	Bob McIntyre	Terry Shepherd			
1955	Dave Chadwick	Derek Ennett	Terry Shepherd			

Southern 100 winners 1968 - 1980

	(1A) S/car	(1B) S/car	(2) 250cc	(3) 350cc	(4) 1300cc	(5) 175/1300cc	(6) S/car Consolation	(7) Solo Champ	(8) S/car Champ
1980	Mick Burcombe	Lowry Burton	Joey Dunlop	Joey Dunlop	Steve Cull	Ian Bell	Des Founds	Dave Dean	Lowry Burton
1979	Allen Steele	Lowry Burton	Joey Dunlop	Joey Dunlop	Marty Ames	Joey Dunlop	Dave Saville	George Fogarty	Mick Burcombe
1978	Allen Steele	John Watson	Ray McCullough	Ray McCullough	Joey Dunlop	Joey Dunlop	Jim Norbury	Joey Dunlop	Allen Steele
	(1) S/car					**(5) Prod 1300**	**(6) Prod 500**		
1977	Allen Steele		Joey Dunlop	Bob Jackson	Joey Dunlop	Malcolm Moffatt	Jamie Garrett	Joey Dunlop	Allen Steele
					(4) 750cc				
1976	John Watson		Ray McCullough	Ray McCullough	Bill Smith	David Williams	Roger Sutcliffe	Joey Dunlop	John Watson
						(5) 1000cc			
1975	David Houghton		Neil Tuxworth	Ray McCullough	Bill Smith	Danny Shimmin		Ray McCullough	Bill Hall
1974	David Lawrence		Ray McCullough	Derek Huxley	John Taylor			Steve Tonkin	Steve Rowe
1973	Peter Hardy		Charlie Williams	Charlie Williams	Roger Sutcliffe			Tom Herron	Peter Hardy
1972	John Watson		Charlie Williams	Charlie Williams	Bill Smith			Charlie Williams	John Watson
1971	Peter Williams		Ray McCullough	Selwyn Griffiths	Bill Smith			Bill Smith	David French
1970	Bill Currie		Ray McCullough	Bill Smith	Brian Adams			Billy Guthrie	Bill Currie
					500cc				
1969	Charlie Freeman		Derek Chatterton	Derek Chatterton	Brian Steenson			Brian Steenson	Charlie Freeman
1968			Terry Grotefild	Jim Curry	Selwyn Griffiths			Steve Jolly	Ken Allen

Statistics
Southern 100 winners 1981 - 1989

	(1) Match Race	(2) 1st Classic	(3) 175-1300cc	(4) 250/350cc	(5) 300/1300cc	(6) S/car	(7) Match Race	(8) 2nd Classic	(9) Solo Champ
1989	Dave Leach	Asa Moyce / Alan Dugdale / John Harrison	Dave Leach / Aubrey McCauley (350) / David Johnson (250)	Richard Coates / David Johnson (250)	Dave Leach / Decca Kelly (350)	Geoff Bell	Dave Leach	Asa Moyce / Alan Dugdale (500) / Derek Whalley (350)	Dave Leach
1988	Dave Leach	Bob Hurst / Alan Dugdale (500) / Mike Cain (350)	Dave Leach	Phil McCallen / Chris Dowd (350)	Phil Hogg / Robert Hazleton (350)	Lowry Burton	Dave Leach	Alan Dugdale / Alan Smith (750) / Mike Cain (350)	Abandoned
	(1) Match Race	(2) 175-1300cc	(3) 250/350cc	(4) 300/1300cc	(5) S/car	(6) Match Race	(7) Classic		(8)
1987	Ian Bell	Kenny Harrison / Ian Lougher (350) / Pete Wakefield (250)	Ian Lougher / Kenny Shepherd (250)	Kenny Harrison / Decca Kelly (350)	Lowry Burton	Ian Bell	Bob Hirst / Selwyn Griffiths (500) / Kenny Shepherd (350)		Ian Bell
	(1A) S/Car	(1B) S/Car	(2) 250cc	(3) 350cc	(4) 1300cc	(5) 175-1300cc	(6) S/car Consol		(7)
1986	Mick Burcombe	Dave Molyneux	Richard Coates	Kenny Harrison	Kenny Harrison	Kenny Harrison / Dave Leach (350) / Gavin Lee (250)	Geoff Young		Kenny Harrison
1985	Artie Oates	Lowry Burton	Gene McDonnell	Gene McDonnell	Kenny Harrison	Kenny Harrison / Buddy Yeardsley (350) / Gene McDonnell (250)	Dave Molyneux		Kenny Harrison
1984	John Phillips	Tony Baker	Johnny Rea	Kenny Harrison	Buddy Yeardsley	Trevor Steele	Steve Sinnott		Dave Pither
1983	Tony Baker	Lowry Burton	Neil Tuxworth	Kenny Harrison	Brian Reid	Trevor Steele	Mick Harvey		Brian Reid
1982	Lowry Burton	Steve Webster	Brian Reid	Brian Reid	Ian Bell	Paul Cranston	Mick Burcombe		Con Law
1981	Tom White	Eric Bregazzi	Bob Jackson	Ian Bell	Rob McElnea	Ian Bell	Tony Baker		Dave Ashton

(10) S/car Champ

Rod Bellas

Lowry Burton

(9)

Lowry Burton

(8)

Dave Molyneux

Geoff Young

John Phillips

Lowry Burton

Tony Baker

Lowry Burton

Statistics

Southern 100 winners 1990 - 2005

	(1) S/fnders	(2) Jnr/fnders	(3) Senior	(4) 1st Classic	(9) 2nd Classic	(5) Junior	(6) S/Car	(7) & (8)	
2005	Ian Lougher / Tim Poole (600)	Chris Palmer / Tony Cawte (125)	Ian Lougher	Alan Oversby / Dave M/Mygdal (850) / Ewan Hamilton (350)	Alan Oversby / Dave M/Mygdal (850) / Ewan Hamilton (350)	Chris Palmer / Derran Slous (400)	Nick Crowe	Ian Lougher (600) / Ian Lougher (250)	
2004	Ryan Farquhar / Tim Poole (600)	Ryan Farquhar / Robert Dunlop (125)	Guy Martin	Allan Brew / Ron Soar (750) / Paul Coward (350)	Allan Brew / Ron Soar (750) / Paul Coward (350)	Darran Lindsay / Roy Richardson (400)	Nick Crowe	(600) Guy Martin / (250) Darran Lindsay	
					(8) 2nd Classic			**(7) 250/600 cc**	
2003	Ryan Farquhar / Bob Grant (600)	Ian Lougher / Robert Dunlop (125)	Ryan Farquhar	Dave M/Mygdal / Allan Brew (500) / Barry Wood (350)	Dave M/Mygdal / Allan Brew (500) / Barry Wood (350)	Ian Lougher / Ryan Farquhar (400)	Abandoned	Ian Lougher	
2002	Ian Lougher / Darran Lindsay (600)	Ian Lougher / Robert Dunlop (125)	Ian Lougher	Dave M/Mygdal / Mike Hose (500) / Barry Wood (350)	Dave M/Mygdal / Mike Hose (500) / Chris McGahan (350)	Ian Lougher / Dave M/Mygdal (400)	Dave Molyneux	Jason Griffiths	
2000	Ian Lougher / Adrian McFarland (600)	Ian Lougher / Darran Lyndsay (400)	Blair Degerholm	Dave M/Mygdal / Derek Whalley (500) / Barry Wood (350)	Karl Wilkie / Derek Whalley (500) / Bud Jackson (350)	Ian Lougher / Martin Sharpe (400)	Ian Bell	Blair Degerholm	
1999	Joey Dunlop / Uel Duncan (600)	Ian Lougher / Robert Dunlop (125)	With Race 1	Derek Whalley / Jeff Jones (750) / Barry Wood (350)	Karl Wilkie / Derek Whalley (500) / Dave Thurlow (350)	With Race 2	Dave Molyneux	Jason Griffiths	
1998	Bob Jackson / Paul Dedman (600)	Neil Richardson / Blair Degerholm (400)	James Courtney	Colin Bevan / John Knowles (500) / Bud Jackson (350)	Karl Wilkie / John Knowles (500) / Bud Jackson (350)	Paul Dedman	Ian Bell	Bob Jackson	
1997	Bob Jackson / Paul Dedman (600)	James Courtney / Robert Dunlop (125)	Simon Beck	Derek Whalley / Colin Bevan (750) / Barry Wood (350)	Colin Bevan / Derek Whalley (500) / Barry Wood (350)	Ian Lougher	Greg Lambert	Derek Young	
			(3)	**(4)**	**(2)**	**(10)**			**(8) S/car**
1996	Bob Jackson / Adrian McFarland (600)	Ian Lougher / Neil McCullough (125)	Jason Griffiths	Colin Bevan / John Knowles (500) / Bud Jackson (350)	Karl Bell / John Knowles (500) / Derek Whalley (350)	Jason Griffiths	(A) Geoff Bell / (B) Kenny Howles	Jason Griffiths	Roy Hanks
	(2)	**(1)**	**(5)**	**(3)**		**(4)**			
1995	Bob Jackson / Ian Lougher (600)	Jason Griffiths / Dave Leach (400)	With Race 1	Dave Pither / Vin Duckett (500) / Bud Jackson (350)	Glen English / Vin Duckett (500) / Bud Jackson (350)	With Race 2	(A) Dave Molyneux / (B) Geoff Bell	Dave Leach	Martin Clark
			(5) 300/1000 cc			**250/350 cc**		**600 cc**	
1994	Joey Dunlop / Tim Poole (600)	Joey Dunlop / Bob Jackson (400)	Jason Griffiths	Kenny Harrison / Bob Jackson (500) / Mark Baldwin (350)	Colin Bevan / Danny Shimmin (500) / Derek Whalley (350)	Joey Dunlop	(A) Bill Davie / (B) Dave Molyneux	Tim Poole	Kenny Howles
1993	Jason Griffiths / Tim Poole (600)	Jason Griffiths / Derek Young (400)	Simon Beck	Trevor Reid / Dave Storrey (500) / Bud Jackson (350)	Kenny Harrison / John Knowles (500) / Bud Jackson (350)	Joey Dunlop	(A) Rod Bellas / (B) Dave Molyneux	Joey Dunlop	Dave Molyneux
1992	Derek Young / Johnny Rea (600)	Lee Pullan / Phil McCallen (400)	Phil McCallen	Glen English / Dave Storrey (500) / Barry Wood (350)	Kenny Harrison / Dave Storrey (500) / Barry Wood (350)	Dave Milling / D McCullough (350)	(A) Gordon Shand / (B) Geoff Bell	Phil McCallen	Geoff Bell
1991	Joey Dunlop / Iain Gibson (600)	Joey Dunlop / Bob Heath (125)	Joey Dunlop	Kenny Harrison / Bob Heath (500) / Barry Wood (350)	Kenny Harrison / Selwyn Griffiths (500) / Derek Whalley (350)	Joey Dunlop / D McCullough (350)	(A) Dave Molyneux / (B) Geoff Bell	Iain Gibson / Dave Leach (400) / Joey Dunlop (125)	Geoff Bell
1990	Dave Leach / Derek Young (600)	Ian Lougher / Aubrey McCauley (125)	Dave Leach	Kenny Harrison / Selwyn Griffiths (500) / Derek Whalley (350)	Kenny Harrison / Selwyn Griffiths (500) / Vin Duckett (350)	Ian Lougher / Richard Coates (350)	(A) Jeff Smith / (B) Geoff Bell	Dave Leach / Gavin Lee (400) / Ian Lougher (125)	Alan Warner

Southern 100 winners 1990 - 2005

(10) 125/400 cc	(11) S/car Champ	(12) Solo Champ
Chris Palmer	Nick Crowe	Ian Lougher
Dave M/Mygdal (400)		
Darran Lindsay Dave M/Mygdal (400)	Nick Crowe	Ian Lougher

(9) 125/400 cc	(10) S/car Champ	(11) Solo Champ
Roy Richardson Chris Palmer (125)	Dave Molyneux	Ryan Farquhar
Robert Dunlop Dave M/Mygdal (400)	Dave Molyneux	Ian Lougher
Darran Lindsay Martin Sharpe (400)	Ian Bell	Blair Degerholm
Robert Dunlop William Philp (400)	Ian Bell	Joey Dunlop
Robert Dunlop Mike Cain (400)	Dave Molyneux	Bob Jackson
Robert Dunlop Dave M/Mygdal (400)	Greg Lambert	Jason Griffiths

(9) 125/400 cc	(11) S/car Champ	(12) Solo Champ
Ian Lougher Tommy Diver (400)	Geoff Bell	Jason Griffiths
Dave Leach D McCullough (125)	Bill Davie	Bob Jackson
Derek Young Joey Dunlop (125)	Bill Davie	Jason Griffiths
Bob Jackson Joey Dunlop (125)	Bill Davie	Joey Dunlop
Phil McCallen D McCullough (125)	Dave Molyneux	Phil McCallen
	Dave Molyneux	Joey Dunlop
	Bob Munro	Dave Leach

Statistics

Southern 100 Lap and Race records

Senior Solo Founders			Laps	Time		Speed	Year
Lap	1010	Ian Lougher	1	2 m	18.044 s	110.834	2005
	600	Tim Poole	1	2 m	26.768 s	104.246	2005
Race	1010	Ian Lougher	10	23 m	22.189 s	109.115	2005
	600	Tim Poole	10	24 m	53.388 s	102.452	2005

Junior Solo Founders							
Lap	250	Ian Lougher	1	2 m	29.5 s	102.341	2002
	125	Robert Dunlop	1	2 m	38.7 s	96.408	2002
Race	250	Chris Palmer	10	25 m	18.604 s	100.750	2005
	125	Robert Dunlop	10	27 m	02.5 s	94.298	2002

Senior							
Lap		Ian Lougher	1	2 m	16.750 s	111.883	2005
Race		Ian Lougher	10	23 m	11.125 s	109.983	2005

First Classic Race							
Lap	501-850	Dave M-Mygdal	1	2 m	45.561 s	92.413	2005
	351-500	Alan Oversby	1	2 m	45.552 s	92.418	2005
	350	Paul Coward	1	2 m	52.54 s	88.675	2004
Race	501-850	Dave M-Mygdal	6	16 m	49.780 s	90.911	2005
	351-500	Alan Oversby	6	16 m	49.739 s	90.915	2005
	350	Ewan Hamilton	6	17 m	52.349 s	85.606	2005

Junior							
Lap	250	Ian Lougher	1	2 m	28.2 s	103.238	2002
	400	Roy Richardson	1	2 m	37.8 s	96.958	2003
Race	250	Darran Lindsay	10	25 m	06.83 s	101.537	2004
	400	Roy Richardson	10	26 m	43.21 s	95.433	2004

First Sidecar Race							
Lap		Ian Bell	1	2 m	36.2 s	97.951	2002
Race		Dave Molyneux	6	15 m	49.0 s	96.733	2002

Statistics

250 / 600 Race			Laps	Time		Speed	Year
Lap	600	Ian Lougher	1	2 m	22.075 s	107.690	2005
	250	Ian Lougher	1	2 m	28.0 s	103.378	2002
Race	600	Ian Lougher	8	19 m	19.120 s	105.597	2005
	250	Ian Lougher	10	24 m	59.0 s	102.068	2002

Second Classic Race							
Lap	501-850	Kenny Harrison	1	2 m	43.0 s	93.865	1995
	351-500	Alan Oversby	1	2 m	46.712 s	91.775	2005
	350	Ewan Hamilton	1	2 m	55.593 s	87.133	2005
Race	501-850	Glen English	8	22 m	06.8 s	92.252	1995
	351-500	Alan Oversby	6	16 m	54.557 s	90.483	2005
	350	Ewan Hamilton	6	17 m	45.410 s	86.164	2005

125 / 400 Race							
Lap	125	Robert Dunlop	1	2 m	37.7 s	97.019	2002
	400	Derran Slous	1	2 m	37.139 s	97.366	2005
Race	125	Robert Dunlop	6	16 m	02.4 s	95.386	2002
	400	Dave M-Mygdal	6	16 m	09.727 s	94.666	2005

Sidecar Ch'ship F2						
Lap	Dave Molyneux	1	2 m	35.6 s	98.329	2002
Race	Dave Molyneux	9	23 m	50.5 s	96.260	2002

Solo Championship							
Lap	1010	Ian Lougher	1	2 m	16.989 s	111.688	2005
	600	Tim Poole	1	2 m	25.393 s	105.232	2005
	250	Ian Lougher	1	2 m	30.6 s	101.593	1994
Race	1010	Ian Lougher	10	23 m	11.895 s	109.922	2005
	600	Kevin Mawdsley	10	24 m	53.366 s	102.453	2005
	250	Ian Lougher	12	30 m	27.1 s	100.487	1998

Statistics

Billown Circuit - Fastest average race speeds - Solos

	Rider	Laps	Time		Speed	Year	Race
1	Ian Lougher	10	23 m	11.125 s	109.983	2005	Senior
2	Guy Martin	10	23 m	20.551 s	109.243	2005	Senior
3	Ryan Farquhar	10	23 m	32.053 s	108.353	2005	Championship
4	Jason Griffiths	10	23 m	32.095 s	108.350	2005	Championship
5	Martin Finnegan	10	23 m	44.878 s	107.378	2005	Championship
6	Darran Lindsay	10	23 m	44.978 s	107.370	2005	Championship
7	Paul Hunt	10	24 m	04.999 s	105.882	2005	Championship
8	Chris Palmer	10	24 m	05.388 s	105.854	2005	Championship
9	Blair Degerholm	12	29 m	03.50 s	105.305	2000	Championship
9	Bob Jackson	12	29 m	03.50 s	105.305	1998	Championship
11	Nigel Beattie	10	24 m	13.286 s	105.279	2005	Championship
12	James Courtney	12	29 m	05.60 s	105.178	1998	Championship
13	Joey Dunlop	9	21 m	52.70 s	104.898	1999	Steam Packet 1000cc
14	Adrian McFarland	10	24 m	20.34 s	104.770	2004	Senior
15	Mark Parrett	10	24 m	21.56 s	104.682	2004	Senior
16	Paul Cranston	10	24 m	24.152 s	104.497	2005	Championship
17	Gary Carswell	10	24 m	29.10 s	104.145	2003	Championship
18	Simon Beck	10	24 m	32.10 s	103.933	1997	Senior
19	Davy Morgan	10	24 m	34.662 s	103.753	2005	Senior
20	John Burrows	10	24 m	35.678 s	103.681	2005	Senior
21	Victor Gilmore	10	24 m	36.974 s	103.590	2005	Senior
22	Tim Poole	8	19 m	42.211 s	103.535	2005	600cc
23	Derek Young	9	22 m	13.70 s	103.246	1997	Steam Packet 750cc
24	Dave Leach	12	29 m	50.20 s	102.558	1991	Championship
25	Kevin Mawdsley	9	22 m	23.70 s	102.478	2005	Steam Packet 250/600cc
26	Phil McCallen	9	22 m	26.80 s	102.242	1994	Steam Packet 1000cc
27	John Donnan	12	29 m	56.70 s	102.187	2000	Championship
28	Tommy Clucas	9	22 m	29.95 s	102.003	2004	Steam Packet 250/600cc
29	Derek Brien	10	25 m	05.398 s	101.634	2005	Championship
30	Paul Dedman	12	30 m	12.40 s	101.302	1998	Championship
31	Si Fulton	8	20 m	08.354 s	101.295	2005	600cc
32	Philip Gilder	10	25 m	11.80 s	101.203	2002	Snr Founders
33	Adrian Archibald	12	30 m	20.30 s	100.862	1998	Championship
34	James McBride	9	22 m	45.27 s	100.859	2005	Steam Packet 1000cc
35	Marc Flynn	12	30 m	23.80 s	100.668	1994	Championship
36	Tim Leech	10	25 m	20.30 s	100.638	1996	Senior Race
37	Chris Day	12	30 m	24.60 s	100.624	1994	Championship
38	Gary Radcliffe	12	30 m	25.90 s	100.553	1994	Championship
39	Richard Britton	10	25 m	24.40 s	100.367	1998	250/600cc
40	Ian Armstrong	9	22 m	52.80 s	100.306	2005	Steam Packet 1000cc

Statistics

—— Billown Circuit - Fastest average race speeds - F2 Sidecars ——

		Laps	Time			Speed	Year
1	Dave Molyneux/Craig Hallam	6	15 m	49.0 s		96.733	2002
2	Ian Bell/Neil Carpenter	6	15 m	50.3 s	96.601		2002
3	Nick Crowe/Darran Hope	6	15 m	52.701 s		96.358	2005
4	Roy Hanks/Dave Wells	9	24 m	12.40 s		94.808	2002
5	Geoff Bell/Craig Hallam	9	24 m	26.60 s		93.890	2000
6	Kenny Howles/Doug Jewell	9	24 m	32.50 s		93.514	1998
7	Phillip Dongworth/John Leubke	9	24 m	34.90 s		93.362	2003
8	Greg Lambert/Tony Darby	9	24 m	42.20 s		92.902	1997
9	Andy Brown/John Dowling	9	25 m	10.50 s		91,161	2002
10	Glynn Jones/Ivan Murray	6	16 m	47.861 s		91.084	2005
11	Rod Bellas/Geoff Knight	6	16 m	55.20 s		90.425	2000
12	Mick Harvey/Fiona Baker-Milligan	8	22 m	33.688 s		90.420	2005
13	Alan Langton/Stuart Graham	8	22 m	34.214 s		90.385	2005
14	Mike Ibbotson/Mark Birdsall	9	25 m	26.20 s		90.224	1998
15	Richard Crossley/Karl Ellison	6	17 m	02.70 s		89.762	1996
16	Steven Coombes/Stuart Castles	9	25 m	39.70 s		89.433	2003
17	Keith Walters/Lee Aubrey	9	25 m	42.90 s		89.247	2000
18	Martin Clark/Lee Farrington	8	22 m	55.50 s		88.985	1995
19	Ben Beckworth/Luke Beckworth	8	22 m	56.138 s		88.945	2005
20	Brian Kelly/Neil Kelly	9	25 m	48.70 s		88.913	2000
21	Steve Sinott/Dave Corlett	9	25 m	51.20 s		88.769	1997
22	Roy Tansley/Roy King	9	25 m	58.10 s		88.376	2000
23	Alan Warner/Colin Hardman	6	17 m	21.50 s		88.142	1996
24	Graham Hayne/Michael Craig	6	17 m	21.60 s		88.133	1995

Statistics

Billown Circuit - Ton-up Club

	Name	Time		Speed	Year	Event
1	Ian Lougher	2 m	16.750 s	111.882	2005	Senior
2	Guy Martin	2 m	17.917 s	110.937	2005	Senior
3	Jason Griffiths	2 m	18.739 s	110.279	2005	Championship
4	Ryan Farquhar	2 m	19.283 s	109.848	2005	Championship
5	Darran Lindsay	2 m	20.213 s	109.119	2005	Championship
6	Martin Finnegan	2 m	20.355 s	109.009	2005	Championship
7	Chris Palmer	2 m	22.036 s	107.720	2005	Championship
8	Paul Hunt	2 m	22.515 s	107.357	2005	Senior
9	Blair Degerholm	2 m	22.700 s	107.217	2000	Championship
10	Bob Jackson	2 m	22.900 s	107.067	1998	Championship
11	James Courtney	2 m	23.100 s	106.918	1998	Championship
12	Nigel Beattie	2 m	23.488 s	106.629	2005	Championship
13	Joey Dunlop	2 m	23.500 s	106.620	1999	IOMSPC 1000cc
14	Adrian McFarland	2 m	23.590 s	106.553	2004	Senior
15	Mark Parrett	2 m	23.600 s	106.545	2004	Senior
16	Gary Carswell	2 m	24.500 s	105.882	2003	Championship
17	Tom Clucas	2 m	24.730 s	105.714	2004	IOMSPC 1000cc
18	Paul Cranston	2 m	24.787 s	105.672	2005	Championship
19	Davy Morgan	2 m	25.033 s	105.493	2005	Senior
20	Simon Beck	2 m	25.300 s	105.299	1997	Senior
21	Tim Poole	2 m	25.379 s	105.242	2005	Senior
22	John Burrows	2 m	25.542 s	105.124	2005	Championship
23	Derek Young	2 m	25.600 s	105.082	1997	IOMSPC 750cc
24	Phillip McCallen	2 m	25.700 s	105.010	1994	IOMSPC 1000cc
25	Victor Gilmore	2 m	25.890 s	104.873	2005	Championship
26	Paul Dedman	2 m	25.965 s	104.819	2005	Snr Founders
27	Kevin Mawdsley	2 m	26.449 s	104.473	2005	IOMSPC 250/600cc
28	Dave Leach	2 m	26.600 s	104.365	1991	Championship
29	John Donnan	2 m	26.800 s	104.223	2000	Championship
30	Steve Ellis	2 m	27.100 s	104.010	1998	Championship
31	Alan 'Bud' Jackson	2 m	27.266 s	103.893	2005	Championship
32	Adrian Archibald	2 m	27.300 s	103.869	1998	Championship
33	Philip Gilder	2 m	27.500 s	103.728	2002	Snr Founders
34	Chris Day	2 m	28.600 s	102.960	1994	Championship
35	Si Fulton	2 m	28.630 s	102.940	2005	600cc
36	Mark Flynn	2 m	28.700 s	102.891	1994	Championship
37	Richard Britton	2 m	28.900 s	102.753	1998	250 / 600cc
38	Derek Brien	2 m	29.049 s	102.650	2005	Senior
39	Gary Radcliffe	2 m	29.200 s	102.546	1994	Championship
40	Tim Leech	2 m	29.300 s	102.478	1997	Championship

Statistics

Billown Circuit - Ton-up Club

41	Denis McCullough	2 m	30.000	102.000	1999	IOMSPC 250cc
42	Peter Hounsell	2 m	30.154 s	101.895	2005	Championship
43	Uel Duncan	2 m	30.200 s	101.864	1999	Championship
44	Paul Duckett	2 m	30.200 s	101.864	2002	Snr Founders
45	James McBride	2 m	30.251 s	101.830	2005	IOMSPC 1000cc
46	Ian Armstrong	2 m	30.252 s	101.829	2005	IOMSPC 1000cc
47	Dave Goodley	2 m	30.400 s	101.728	1996	Senior
48	Dave Madsen Mygdal	2 m	30.400 s	101.728	1999	Championship
49	Derran Slous	2 m	30.483 s	101.672	2005	Snr Founders
50	Mike Crellin	2 m	30.600 s	101.593	2003	Senior
51	Gary Dynes	2 m	30.700 s	101.526	2000	250cc/600cc
52	Neil Richardson	2 m	30.735 s	101.502	2005	250cc
53	Yarno Holland	2 m	30.736 s	101.501	2005	250cc
54	Gavin Lee	2 m	31.000 s	101.324	1997	Championship
55	Steve Rathbone	2 m	31.000 s	101.324	2002	Senior
56	Derek Welch	2 m	31.100 s	101.257	2002	Jnr Founders
57	Kenny Harrison	2 m	31.200 s	101.190	1990	Championship
58	Brian Birks	2 m	31.400 s	101.056	2003	Snr Founders
59	Mick Charnock	2 m	31.430 s	101.036	2005	600cc
60	Steve Ward	2 m	31.500 s	100.990	1995	Championship
61	Bob Grant	2 m	31.500 s	100.990	2003	Snr Founders
62	John Crellin	2 m	31.620 s	100.910	2005	Snr Founders
63	Andy Jackson	2 m	31.800 s	100.790	2002	Championship
64	Stuart Jones	2 m	32.000 s	100.657	1992	1000cc Race
65	David Black	2 m	32.000 s	100.657	1994	Championship
66	Richard Coates	2 m	32.000 s	100.657	1997	Junior
67	Steve Hazlett	2 m	32.200 s	100.525	1991	Championship
68	Owen McNally	2 m	32.200 s	100.525	1998	250 / 600cc
69	Stuart Robson	2 m	32.200 s	100.525	2003	Snr Founders
70	Mark McDonald	2 m	32.400 s	100.393	1999	IOMSPC 1000cc
71	Barry Wood	2 m	32.503 s	100.325	2005	600cc
72	Barry Davidson	2 m	32.505 s	100.324	2005	600cc
73	Lee Pullan	2 m	32.600 s	100.262	1992	250cc Race
74	Brian Venables	2 m	32.600 s	100.262	1994	1010cc Race
75	Gavin Feighery	2 m	32.700 s	100.196	2004	Senior
76	Ronnie McAllister	2 m	32.800 s	100.130	1998	Championship
77	Stephen Oates	2 m	32.845 s	100.101	2005	Senior
78	Tim Maher	2 m	32.944 s	100.036	2005	Senior
79	Justin Waring	2 m	32.998 s	100.001	2005	Snr Founders
80	Brian Reid	2 m	33.000 s	100.000	1983	1300cc Race
81	Nigel Barton	2 m	33.000 s	100.000	1991	Championship
82	Dave Milling	2 m	33.000 s	100.000	1993	IOMSPC 250cc

82 members

Statistics

Race winners Pre TT Classic 1988 - 2005

	Single cylinder	Senior	Lightweight	Sidecar	Junior	Unlimited
2005	Bill Swallow *Paul Coward*	Chris Palmer	Roy Richardson	Stuart Digby / Paul Thomas	Mike Hose	Chris Palmer *Decca Kelly*
2004	Bill Swallow *Mervyn Stratford*	Bill Swallow	Mike Hose	Stuart Digby / Paul Thomas	Mike Hose	Paul Coward *John Loder*
2003	Mike Hose *Ted Fenwick*	Steven Elliott	Ewan Hamilton	Geoff Hands / Ruth Hands	Chris McGahan	Bud Jackson *Mike Hose*
2002	Derek Whalley *Dave Smith*	Steven Elliott	Karl Hayes	Geoff Hands / Ruth Hands	Paul Coward	Richard Coates *Karl Wilkie*
2001	No Racing					
2000	Bill Swallow *John Spong*	Mike Hose	Roy Richardson	Geoff Hands / Ruth Hands	Bill Swallow	Brian Kneale *Karl Wilkie*
1999	Bill Swallow *David Smith*	Bill Swallow	Paul Coward	Bernd Tittler / Andre Hohensee	Colin Rodgers	Bill Swallow *Decca Kelly*
1998	Bob Heath *Ted Fenwick*	Bob Heath	Bob Jackson	Geoff Hands / Ruth Hands	Bob Heath	Bob Heath
1997	Bill Swallow *David Smith*	Bob Heath	Bob Jackson	Alistair Lewis / Bill Annandale	Derek Whalley	Bob Heath
1996	Bob Heath *Derek Whalley*	Bob Heath	Bud Jackson	Dave Stone / Owen Dyke	Bob Heath	Bob Heath
1995	Bob Heath *Bob Jackson*	Abandoned	Graham Larkins	John Smith / Andy Smith	Bob Heath	Stuart Jones
	VINTAGE					
1994	Bernard Guerin *Owen Dyke* *Mervyn Stratford*	Bob Heath	Bob Jackson	John Smith / Andy Smith	Stuart Marshall	Kenny Harrison
1993	Bernard Guerin *Geoff Sawyer* *Mervyn Stratford*	Bob Heath	Bob Jackson	Stuart Digby / Nick Cutmore	Mike Hose	Dave Pither
1992	Race Abandoned	Bob Heath	Bob Jackson	Nick Bates / Malcolm Swann	Stuart Marshall	Alex George
1991	Steve Linsdell *Geoff Sawyer* *John Hurlstone*	Bill Swallow	Terry Kermode	Paul Carr / Malcolm Slack	Richard Swallow	Kenny Harrison
1990		Chris McGahan	Mike Cain	Paul Carr / Steve Ellett	Bill Swallow	Dave Pither
1989		Dave Pither		Dave Stone / Owen Dyke	Bill Swallow *Mike Cain*	Dave Pither
1988		Dave Pither		Mark Kay / Richard Battiston	Graham Godward *Mike Cain*	Robert Price

Indicates Class Winner

Statistics

Pre TT Classic Races results

		Race				Fastest Lap			
		Laps	Time		Speed		Time		Speed
Single Cylinder 250cc									
1995	Bob Jackson	8	25	42.6	79.346	B. Jackson	3	03.7	83.287
1996	D.Whalley	6	21	56.8	69.714	D.Whalley	3	35.0	71.162
1997	D.Smith	8	26	27.0	77.126	Bob Jackson	3	03.4	83.424
1998	T.Fenwick (lapped)	7	26	33.4	67.214	D.Whalley	3	28.4	73.416
1999	D.Smith	8	26	31.8	76.894	D. Smith	3	15.1	78.421
2000	J.Spong	8	27	50.0	73.293	J.Spong	3	22.8	75.443
2002	D.Smith	8	26	57.7	75.662	D.Smith	3	17.9	77.311
2003	T.Fenwick (lapped)	7	24	29.1	72.901	P.Coward	3	17.2	77.586
2004	M.Sratford	8	27	04.79	75.332	P.Coward	3	14.8	78.542
2000	J.Spong	8	27	50.0	73.293	J.Spong	3	22.8	75.443
2002	D.Smith	8	26	57.7	75.662	D.Smith	3	17.9	77.311
2003	T.Fenwick (lapped)	7	24	29.1	72.901	P.Coward	3	17.2	77.586
2004	M.Sratford	8	27	04.79	75.332	P.Coward	3	14.8	78.542
2005	P.Coward	6	19	32.148	78.318	P.Coward	3	12.268	79.576
Single Cylinder 350cc									
1995	B.Heath	8	24	17.0	84.008	B. Heath	2	59.1	85.427
1996	B.Heath	6	19	52.3	76.994	B. Heath	3	10.6	80.272
1997	B.Swallow	8	24	40.3	82.685	B. Swallow	2	59.2	85.379
1998	B.Heath	8	26	23.4	77.302	B. Heath	3	10.0	80.526
1999	B.Swallow	8	25	06.3	81.258	B. Swallow	3	05.8	82.346
2000	B.Swallow	8	24	27.9	83.384	B. Swallow	3	00.2	84.905
2002	D.Whalley	8	24	56.8	81.774	T. Stephenson	3	02.6	83.789
2003	M. Hose	8	24	04.6	84.729	M. Hose	2	57.1	86.391
2004	B. Swallow	8	23	43.86	85.963	B. Swallow	2	56.3	86.783
2005	Bill Swallow	6	17	41.267	86.500	Derek Whalley	2	54.689	87.584
Lightweight Class 175 - 250cc									
1988	M.Cain	9	30	53.2	74.303	M.Cain	3	21.2	76.043
1989	M.Cain	9	30	17.8	75.750	M.Cain	3	18.6	77.039
1990	M.Cain	8	28	23.6	71.847	A.Pine	3	27.2	73.841
1991	T.Kermode	9	28	53.8	79.420	R.Swallow	3	07.8	81.469
1992	B.Jackson	9	28	22.4	80.885	B.Jackson	3	04.2	83.061
1993	B.Jackson	6	19	53.2	76.935	B.Jackson	3	13.5	79.069
1994	B.Jackson	9	27	43.4	82.782	B.Jackson	2	57.6	86.148
1995	G.Larkins	9	27	41.1	82.896	J.Lenton	3	01.8	84.158
1996	A.Jackson	6	19	21.2	79.056	A.Jackson	3	09.6	80.696
1997	Bob Jackson	9	26	33.0	86.440	Bob Jackson	2	52.6	88.644
1998	B.Jackson	6	20	35.7	74.289	T.Kermode	3	20.2	76.423
1999	P.Coward	9	27	26.0	83.657	Kelly & Hayes	3	00.2	84.905
2000	R.Richardson	9	27	10.9	84.431	R.Richardson	2	57.3	86.294
2002	K.Hayes	9	27	15.7	84.184	J.Leech	2	58.9	85.522
2003	E. Hamilton	9	27	18.0	84.065	E. Hamilton	3	00.1	84.952
2004	M.Hose	9	27	22.19	83.851	M.Hose	2	59.65	85.165
2005	R.Richardson	9	26	45.700	85.757	R.Richardson	2	56.105	86.880

Indicates Record

Statistics

Pre TT Classic Races results

		Race					Fastest Lap		
		Laps	Time		Speed			Time	Speed
	Junior Class 251 - 350cc								
1988	G.Godward	9	30	33.6	75.098	G.Godward	3	19.6	76.653
1989	B.Swallow	9	28	36.6	80.216	B. Swallow	3	07.4	81.643
1990	B.Swallow	8	26	52.6	75.902	I.Lawton	3	14.8	78.542
1991	B.Swallow	9	27	24.2	83.748	R.Swallow	2	58.2	85.858
1992	S.Marshall	9	28	34.4	80.319	J.Cragg	3	05.8	82.346
1993	M.Hose	9	29	03.3	78.988	D.Whalley	3	09.2	80.866
1994	S.Marshall	9	27	14.8	84.230	S.Marshall	2	57.7	86.100
1995	B.Heath	9	27	03.3	84.827	B. Heath	2	56.8	86.538
1996	B.Heath	6	18	47.6	81.411	B. Heath	3	04.8	82.792
1997	D.Whalley	9	27	15.4	84.199	B. Heath	2	54.4	87.729
1998	B.Heath	6	19	46.9	77.344	B. Heath	3	14.7	78.582
1999	Colin Rodgers	9	26	57.3	85.141	B. Wood	2	55.2	87.328
2000	B.Swallow	9	27	02.9	84.848	B.Swallow	2	58.0	85.955
2002	P.Coward	9	26	55.6	85.231	J.Leech	2	56.3	86.783
2003	C. McGahan	9	26	47.0	85.687	C. McGahan	2	54.5	87.679
2004	Mike Hose	9	26	16.10	87.367	Mike Hose	2	52.40	88.747
2005	Mike Hose	9	26	14.138	87.476	Mike Hose	2	52.160	88.871

		Race					Fastest Lap		
	Senior Class 351 - 500cc								
1988	D.Pither	9	26	59.8	85.010	D.Pither	2	54.8	87.528
1989	D.Pither	9	26	46.8	85.698	R.Swallow	2	54.8	87.528
1990	C.McGahan	8	26	53.6	75.855	R.Swallow	3	09.0	80.952
1991	B.Swallow	9	26	25.6	86.844	B.Swallow	2	51.6	89.160
1992	B.Heath	9	26	11.6	87.617	B. Heath	2	51.2	89.369
1993	B.Heath	9	27	46.4	82.633	B. Heath	3	02.3	83.927
1994	B.Heath	9	25	52.3	88.707	B. Heath	2	50.6	89.683
1995	Abandoned	X		X	X	Abandoned		X	X
1996	B.Heath	6	18	59.2	80.582	B. Heath	3	07.1	81.774
1997	B.Heath	9	25	32.5	89.853	B.Heath/G.English	2	46.3	92.002
1998	B.Heath	9	27	24.8	83.718	B. Heath	2	56.7	86.587
1999	B.Swallow	9	25	51.4	88.758	Jason Griffiths	2	47.9	91.125
2000	M.Hose	9	26	06.0	87.931	M.Hose	2	51.0	89.473
2002	S.Elliott	9	26	21.4	87.074	A.Auinger/S.Elliott	2	52.7	88.592
2003	S. Elliott	9	26	30.8	86.560	S. Elliott	2	54.4	87.729
2004	B.Swallow	9	25	34.25	89.750	B.Swallow	2	47.42	91.386
2005	Chris Palmer	9	25	05.267	91.478	Chris Palmer	2	45.159	92.638

Indicates Record

122

Statistics
Pre TT Classic Races results

		Race				Fastest Lap			
		Laps	Time		Speed		Time		Speed
Unlimited Class up to 1300cc									
1988	R.Price	9	27	58.2	82.052	R.Price	3	00.6	84.717
1989	D.Pither	9	26	16.4	87.350	D.Pither	2	48.4	90.855
1990	D.Pither	8	24	43.4	82.513	K.Harrison	2	58.6	85.666
1991	K.Harrison	9	25	18.8	90.663	K.Harrison	2	46.0	92.168
1992	A.George	9	25	42.6	89.264	A.George	2	48.2	90.963
1993	D.Pither	7	21	50.7	81.712	D.Pither	3	02.5	83.835
1994	K.Harrison	9	25	09.2	91.240	K.Harrison	2	45.2	92.615
1995	S.Jones	9	25	25.2	90.283	S.Jones	2	46.8	91.726
1996	B.Heath	6	18	18.8	83.545	B.Heath	2	59.1	85.427
351 - 750cc Class									
1997	B.Heath	9	25	17.7	90.729	B.Heath	2	46.9	91.671
1998	B.Heath	6	18	53.0	81.023	B.Heath	3	06.1	82.213
1999	B.Swallow	9	25	16.8	90.783	Bill Swallow	2	43.9	93.349
2000	K.Wilkie	9	26	04.3	88.026	B.Swallow	2	50.4	89.788
2002	K.Wilkie	9	26	46.2	85.730	P.Coward	2	49.5	90.265
2003	M. Hose	9	25	45.5	89.097	M. Hose	2	46.2	92.057
2004	J.Loder	9	25	26.91	90.182	D.Madsen Mygdal	2	44.51	93.003
2005	Chris Palmer	9	24	59.701	91.818	A.Oversby	2	44.397	93.067
230 - 1000cc Post Classic Class									
1999	D.Kelly	9	25	17.2	90.759	D.Kelly	2	46.3	92.002
2000	B.Kneale	9	25	28.8	90.070	B.Kneale	2	46.9	91.671
2002	R.Coates	9	25	48.9	88.901	I.Pattinson	2	49.1	90.479
2003	Alan 'Bud' Jackson	9	25	06.1	91.428	Bud' Jackson	2	45.0	92.727
2004	P.Coward	9	25	21.92	90.477	Paul Coward	2	43.49	93.583
2005	D.Kelly	9	25	48.944	88.899	Paul Coward	2	45.489	92.453
Sidecar Class									
1988	M.Kay/R.Battiston	8	27	58.8	72.909	M.Kay/R.Battiston	3	25.8	74.344
1989	D.Stone/O.Dyke	8	28	38.6	71.220	D.Stone/O.Dyke	3	26.0	74.271
1990	P.Carr/S.Ellett	7	27	42.8	64.409	P.Carr/S.Ellett	3	51.2	66.176
1991	P.Carr/M.Slack	8	25	44.6	79.243	P.Carr/M.Slack	3	08.0	81.382
1992	N.Bates/M.Swann	8	25	35.0	79.739	N.Bates/M.Swann	3	03.8	83.242
1993	S.Digby/N.Cutmore	8	28	37.5	71.266	S.Digby/N.Cutmore	3	27.4	73.770
1994	J.Smith/A.Smith	6	19	57.0	76.691	J.Smith/A.Smith	3	12.2	79.604
1995	J.Smith/A.Smith	6	19	45.8	77.416	J.Smith/A.Smith	3	13.9	78.906
1996	D.Stone/O.Dyke	6	23	48.5	64.263	D.Stone/O.Dyke	3	45.8	67.759
1997	A.Lewis/B.Annandale	8	26	41.9	76.409	G.Hands/R.Hands	3	10.9	80.146
1998	G.Hands/R.Hands	8	29	12.6	69.839	G.Hands/R.Hands	3	35.1	71.129
1999	B.Tittler/A.Hohensee	8	27	11.1	75.041	G.Hands/R.Hands	3	04.2	83.061
2000	G.Hands/R.Hands	8	25	15.7	80.754	G.Hands/R.Hands	3	00.4	84.811
2002	G.Hands/A.Smith	8	25	04.3	81.366	G.Hands/A.Smith	3	01.0	84.530
2003	G.Hands/R.Hands	8	26	11.9	77.867	G.Hands and A.Lewis	3	12.2	79.604
2004	S.Digby/P.Thomas	8	25	05.42	81.306	S.Digby/P.Thomas	3	05.69	82.395
2005	S.Digby/P.Thomas	6	18	43.347	81.720	S.Digby/P.Thomas	3	02.067	84.035

Statistics

Steam Packet National Road Races

	Race 1	Race 2	Race 3
	250 / 600cc	**125 / 400cc**	**1000cc**
2005	Ryan Farquhar	Dave Madsen Mygdal	Ryan Farquhar
	Chris Barratt	Ian Lougher	
2004	Ryan Farquhar	Ian Lougher	Ian Lougher
	Ian Lougher	Dave Madsen Mygdal	
2003	Jason Griffiths	Chris Palmer	Ryan Farquhar
	Chris Palmer	Dave Madsen Mygdal	
2002	Ryan Farquhar	Ryan Farquhar	Jason Griffiths
	Richard Coates	Robert Dunlop	
2001		Races Cancelled	
2000		Races Cancelled	
1999	Jason Griffiths	Joey Dunlop	Joey Dunlop
	Denis McCullough	Dave Madsen Mygdal	
1998	Jason Griffiths	Race Cancelled	Jason Griffiths
	Richard Coates		
1997	Derek Young	Glen English	Jason Griffiths
	Richard Coates		
	175 / 400cc		
1996	Joey Dunlop	Gavin Lee	Jason Griffiths
		Derek Young	
1995	Joey Dunlop	Bob Jackson	Race abandoned
		Denis McCullough	
	250 / 350cc		
1994	Joey Dunlop	Joey Dunlop	Joey Dunlop
		Jason Griffiths	
1993	Jason Griffiths	Johnny Rea	Jason Griffiths
		Joey Dunlop	
			750cc
1992	Robert Dunlop	Bob Grant	Joey Dunlop
		Joey Dunlop	
1991	Joey Dunlop	Dave Leach	Dave Leach
		James Courtney	

Indicates Class Winner

250cc/350cc Race

Year	Rider	Class			Time	Speed	Rider		Time	Speed
1991	J.Dunlop		8	23	50.4	85.570	J.Dunlop	2	55.6	87.129
1992	R.Dunlop		10	25	53.8	98.468	P.McCallen	2	32.2	100.525
1993	J.Griffiths		8	20	47.9	98.084	J.Griffiths	2	32.6	100.262

175 - 400cc Race

Year	Rider	Class			Time	Speed	Rider		Time	Speed
1994	J.Dunlop	250	9	23	07.6	99.236	J.Dunlop	2	31.1	101.257
1995	J.Dunlop	250	9	23	11.3	98.972	J.Dunlop	2	32.3	100.459
1996	J.Dunlop	250	9	23	06.6	99.307	J.Dunlop	2	31.1	101.257

250cc / 600cc Race

Year	Rider	Class			Time	Speed	Rider		Time	Speed
1997	R.Coates	200-400	9	23	19.6	98.385	I.Lougher	2	31.9	100.724
	D.Young	401-600	9	22	51.2	100.422	D.Young	2	30.3	101.796
1998	R.Coates	200-400	9	23	58.0	95.757	R.Coates	2	37.0	97.452
	J.Griffiths	401-600	9	22	41.1	101.168	J.Griffiths	2	29.1	102.615
1999	D.McCullough	200-250	9	22	52.5	100.327	D.McCullough	2	30.0	102.000
	J.Griffiths	401-600	9	22	37.0	101.473	B.Degerholm	2	27.6	103.658
2002	R.Coates	200-250	9	23	56.8	95.837	R.Coates	2	38.2	96.713
	R.Farquhar	510-600	9	22	38.8	101.339	R.Farquhar	2	28.4	103.099
2003	C.Palmer	200-250	6	15	44.5	97.194	C.Palmer	2	35.2	98.582
	J.Griffiths	450-600	6	15	13.8	100.459	J.Griffiths	2	30.5	101.661
2004	I. Lougher	200-250	9	22	52.23	100.347	I.Lougher	2	30.91	101.384
	R.Farquhar	450-600	9	22	16.35	103.041	R.Farquhar	2	27.13	103.989
2005	C.Barratt	200-250	8	23	27.396	86.969	I.Lougher	2	33.962	99.375
	R.Farquhar	450-600	9	22	06.877	103.778	R.Farquhar	2	25.865	104.892

125cc / 400cc Supersport

Year	Rider	Class			Time	Speed	Rider		Time	Speed
1991	D.Leach	400	6	18	31.6	82.583	D.Leach	3	00.0	85.000
1992	B.Grant	400	9	25	04.0	91.555	B.Grant	2	43.8	93.406
1993	J.Rea	400	7	19	13.4	92.855	D.Young	2	42.6	94.095
1994	J.Dunlop	125	9	24	45.3	92.708	J.Dunlop	2	41.3	94.854
	J.Griffiths	supermono	9	24	58.5	91.891	J.Griffiths	2	43.6	93.520
1995	D.McCullough	125	9	24	50.3	92.397	D.McCullough	2	43.4	93.635
	B.Jackson	4str >125	9	24	44.6	92.752	B.Jackson	2	42.6	94.095
1996	G.Lee	125	9	24	44.5	92.758	G.Lee	2	42.0	94.444
	D.Young	4str >125	9	24	56.5	92.014	D.Young	2	44.2	93.179
1997	G.English	125only	9	24	44.8	92.739	G.English	2	41.9	94.502
1999	J.Dunlop	125	9	24	09.8	94.979	J.Dunlop	2	37.9	96.896
	D.Madsen-Mygdal	400	9	24	54.5	92.138	D.Madsen-Mygdal	2	43.3	93.692
2002	R.Dunlop	125	9	24	35.7	93.311	R.Dunlop	2	41.6	94.678
	R.Farquhar	400	9	24	35.6	93.317	R.Farquhar & D.Mygdal	2	41.2	94.913
2003	C.Palmer	125	6	16	14.9	94.163	C.Palmer	2	41.4	94.795
	D.Madsen-Mygdal	400	6	16	36.3	92.140	D.Madsen-Mygdal	2	45.0	92.727
2004	I.Lougher	125	9	24	30.46	93.644	C.Palmer	2	41.18	94.924
	D.Madsen-Mygdal	400	9	24	47.29	92.584	D.Madsen-Mygdal	2	43.29	93.698
2005	I.Lougher	125	9	24	40.737	92.994	I.Lougher	2	42.660	94.061
	D.Madsen-Mygdal	400	9	24	40.558	93.005	D.Madsen-Mygdal	2	42.773	93.996

Indicates Class Winner

Statistics
Steam Packet National Road Race results

750cc Race

Year	Rider		Laps	Time	Speed	Rider	Laps	Time	Speed
1991	D.Leach		8	22	44.8	89.683	D.Leach	2	47.4	91.397
1992	J.Dunlop		10	25	01.4	101.904	J.Dunlop	2	26.2	104.651

1000cc Race

Year	Rider		Laps	Time	Speed	Rider	Laps	Time	Speed
1993	J.Griffiths		8	20	10.7	101.098	J.Griffiths	2	28.7	102.891
1994	J.Dunlop		9	22	25.5	102.341	P.McCallen	2	25.7	105.010
1996	J.Griffiths		9	22	32.3	101.826	J.Griffiths	2	27.3	103.869
1997	J.Griffiths		9	22	12.1	103.370	J.Griffiths	2	25.3	105.299
1998	J.Griffiths		9	22	24.0	102.455	J.Griffiths	2	25.6	105.082
1999	J.Dunlop		9	21	52.7	104.898	J.Dunlop	2	23.5	106.620
2002	J.Griffiths		9	21	44.4	105.565	J.Griffiths	2	23.1	106.918
2003	R.Farquhar		6	14	41.1	104.187	R.Farquhar	2	24.8	105.662
2004	I.Lougher		9	21	33.38	106.465	I.Lougher	2	22.10	107.670
2005	R.Farquhar		9	21	19.473	107.622	G.Martin	2	20.245	109.095

1993 reduced laps due to TT overrun

1998 held on SUNDAY 2 events only

2000 meeting cancelled TT Senior held on Saturday

2001 meeting cancelled Foot & Mouth

2003 held on SUNDAY

Indicates Class Winner

Statistics

Close-or-what! Dead heat finishes

The Southern 100 has had plenty of exciting finishes with the dead heat between Phil Read and Alan Shepherd setting the standard. Jason Griffiths has won the Championship twice by less than 0.3 of a second! There are a remarkable 54 races that have been decided by under a second!

Year	Class	First	Second	Laps	Difference
1961	350	Dead Heat Phil Read & Alan Shepherd		18	00 sec
1988	Classic 2	Dead Heat Alan Dugdale & Alan Smith		8	00 sec
2005	Classic 1	Alan Oversby	Dave Madsen-Mygdal	6	0.041 sec
1995	Junior	Jason Griffiths	Denis McCullough	9	0.1 sec
1997	600	Derek Young	Bob Jackson	10	0.1 sec
1999	600	Jason Griffiths	Blair Degerholm	10	0.1 sec
1999	Classic	Derek Whalley	Jeff Jones	8	0.1 sec
1999	125	Robert Dunlop	Ian Lougher	6	0.1 sec
2002	Classic	Dave Madsen-Mygdal	Mike Hose	8	0.1 sec
2003	600	Ian Lougher	Ryan Farquhar	10	0.1 sec
1958	350	Bob McIntyre	Terry Shepherd	12	0.2 sec
1968	500	Selwyn Griffiths	Steve Jolly	12	0.2 sec
1980	250	Joey Dunlop	Conor McGinn	12	0.2 sec
1990	F2 Sidecar Champ	Alan Warner/Cat Jenkins	Artie Oates/Stuart Pitts	8	0.2 sec
1991	600	Iain Gibson	Kenny Harrison	8	0.2 sec
1992	125	Denis McCullough	Ian Lougher	5	0.2 sec
1994	Championship	Jason Griffiths	Joey Dunlop	12	0.2 sec
1995	600 40th Anniv	Dave Leach	Bob Jackson	8	0.2 sec
1996	125	Ian Lougher	Glen English	6	0.2 sec
1998	Junior	Paul Dedman	Ian Lougher	10	0.2 sec
2003	Senior	Ryan Farquhar	Jason Griffiths	10	0.2 sec
2003	125	Chris Palmer	Ian Lougher	6	0.2 sec
2004	Junior Solo F	Ryan Farquhar	Darren Lindsay	6	0.22 sec
2004	Senior Solo F	Ryan Farquhar	Darren Lindsay	6	0.25 sec
1993	600 Regal	Joey Dunlop	Tim Poole	7	0.3 sec
1997	Senior	Simon Beck	Derek Young	10	0.3 sec
1997	Championship	Jason Griffiths	Bob Jackson	12	0.3 sec
2002	125	Robert Dunlop	Ian Lougher	6	0.3 sec
1958	500	Terry Shepherd	Bob McIntyre	24	0.4 sec
1971	Sidecar Champ	Dave French	G Nottingham	12	0.4 sec
1882	Sidecar Champ	Tony Baker	Steve Webster		0.4 sec
1992	Championship	Phillip McCallen	Derek Young	12	0.4 sec
1998	Sidecar Race	Ian Bell/Neil Carpenter	Dave Molyneux/Craig Hallam	6	0.4 sec
2000	Senior Solo F	Ian Lougher	Blair Degerholm	10	0.4 sec
2005	600 50th Anniv	Ian Lougher	Ryan Farquhar	8	0.419 sec
1997	Junior Solo F	James Courtney	Ian Lougher	10	0.5 sec
1955	350	Derek Ennett	Dave Chadwick	12	0.6 sec
1960	350	Ron Langston	Bob McIntyre	18	0.6 sec
1962	350	Phil Read	Fred Stevens	18	0.6 sec
1981	Championship	Dave Ashton	Rob McElnea	12	0.6 sec
1983	Solo Support	Trevor Steele	Neil Tuxworth	10	0.6 sec
1985	Championship	Kenny Harrison	Buddy Yeardsley	12	0.6 sec
1989	Sidecar 1st leg	Geoff Bell/Janet Lowe	Vic Jefford /Pete Hill	9	0.6 sec
1995	Senior	Bob Jackson	Paul Hunt	9	0.6 sec
1997	125	Robert Dunlop	Owen McNally	6	0.6 sec
2000	Championship	Blair Degerholm	Ian Lougher	12	0.6 sec
2004	125	Darren Lindsay	Chris Palmer	6	0.61 sec
1956	350	Bob McIntyre	Dave Chadwick	12	0.8 sec
1964	125	Bill Smith	Gary Dickinson	6	0.8 sec
1988	Solo Founders	Dave Leach	Phillip McCallen	9	0.8 sec
1989	Classic 1	Asa Moyce	Alan Dugdale	8	0.8 sec
1991	Junior Solo F	Joey Dunlop	Ian Lougher	12	0.8 sec
1992	600 Regal	Phillip McCallen	Johnny Rea	9	0.8 sec
2000	Classic	Dave Madsen-Mygdal	Karl Wilkie	8	0.8 sec